Legitimation of Belief

Legitimation of Belief

Ernest Gellner F.B.A.

Professor of Philosophy with special reference to Sociology
London School of Economics

Cambridge University Press

Published by the Syndics of the Cambridge University Press
Bentley House, 200 Euston Road, London NW1 2DB
American Branch: 32 East 57th Street, New York, N.Y.10022

Library of Congress Catalogue Card Number: 74-14337

ISBN: 0 521 20467 4

First published 1974

Printed in Great Britain by
Alden & Mowbray Ltd
at the Alden Press, Oxford

Contents

Acknowledgements

This book was begun in 1968 at the Institute of International Studies at the University of California in Berkeley, to which I am much indebted both for allowing me the time for it and for supplying secretarial assistance. At the LSE, I owe a great deal to the generous secretarial help given by Mrs Thelma O'Brien. I am very grateful to friends and colleagues who have read drafts of the book and much improved it by their criticisms: Eileen Barker, Rhoda and Dennis Duerden, John Hajnal, Ian Jarvie, Jenny Mellor, Jeremy Mynott, and Kenneth Topley. Needless to say, they cannot be held responsible for my views.

London 1973   E.G.

...un homme qui marche seul et dans les ténèbres...

René Descartes

Could men anatomise nature, according to the most probable, or at least the most intelligible philosophy, they would find, that...causes are but the particular fabric and structure of the minute parts of their own bodies and of external objects; and that, by a regular and constant machinery, all the events are produced, about which they are so much concerned.

David Hume

We need only look at the attempts of moralists in this style, and we shall find appeals to human nature...perfection...happiness, here moral sense, there fear of God, a bit of this, a bit of that, an amazing mishmash...

Immanuel Kant

Questions of ultimate ends are not amenable to direct proof...however...considerations may be presented capable of determining the intellect either to give or to withold its assent.

John Stuart Mill

Never as yet has a new prophecy emerged...through the need of some modern intellectuals to furnish their souls with...guaranteed genuine antiques...they produce surrogates...which they peddle in the book market. This is plain humbug or self-deception.

Max Weber

1 One and many

There is a remarkable consensus on one point amongst recent thinkers and schools, even when they are otherwise radically or seemingly opposed to each other: they all reject monism, and warmly espouse pluralism. The world is (or our aims are) many and not one. This appears to be the conventional or folk wisdom of contemporary thinkers. They are indeed very willing to invoke literal folk sayings in support of it: bridges are not to be crossed till they are reached, cases are to be judged on their merits (would anyone have us ignore them?), things are to be taken as they come, and so forth. If we must wag our beards and bandy about wisdom of this kind, I would suggest that individual cases have merits only in the light of general principles or criteria of merit, which cannot ever themselves be elicited from those cases, but are independent of them, and that, by the time you reach a river on an urgent errand, it is somewhat too late to start building bridges. But this kind of talk proves little.

One of the most eloquent and likeable formulations of the anti-monist position is to be found in an early passage of William James' *Pragmatism*.[1] James' rhetoric is attractive just because it contains a good deal of sympathy for, and some understanding of, the monism which he rejects—though he does indeed, with emphasis, reject it. He thinks he has found a middle position between it and its opposite. But there is little snide denigration of monism in his work. Other critics have not been so tolerant or imaginative.

Moreover, James was writing at a time when pluralism was still, in academic thought, a minority opinion. This makes his pugnacious yet sympathetic attack on monism all the more likeable. Our latter-day pluralists speak from the security of near-universal consensus and, despite the confidence which this should give them, they show little generosity to or sympathy for the monist. Their sympathy they can keep, I suppose, but the lack of it deprives *them* of adequate intellectual understanding of that which they wish to oppose.

It is noteworthy that William James considered the dispute between pluralists and monists to be *the* most fundamental intellectual issue:

I wish to turn ... upon the ancient problem of 'the one and the many' ... I myself have come, by long brooding on it, to consider it the most central of all philosophic problems, central because so pregnant. I mean by this that if you

[1] First published 1907. Numerous editions.

know whether a man is a decided monist or a decided pluralist, you perhaps know more about the rest of his opinions than if you give him any other name ending in *ist*. To believe in the one or in the many, that is the classification with the maximum number of consequences.[2]

James of course connected this issue with his famous opposition between the tough-minded and the tender-minded:[3]

The tender-minded	The tough-minded
Rationalistic (going by 'principles')	Empiricist (going by 'facts')
Intellectualistic	Sensationalistic
Idealistic	Materialistic
Optimistic	Pessimistic
Religious	Irreligious
Free-willist	Fatalistic
Monistic	Pluralistic
Dogmatical	Sceptical

His particular way of formulating this big divide is in some ways odd.

Why, for instance, does he suppose that the tender-minded are optimists, and the tough-minded are pessimists? Presumably, he supposes the tender-minded to be optimists because they are monists, and hence can rely on the great all-embracing One to be ever there, in the background, guaranteeing a happy end. By contrast, the tough-minded ones, being pluralists, know full well that human conflicts and endeavours terminate in all kinds of ways, and that many end badly, and that there is no over-arching global guarantor of the final triumph of virtue. The monist is credited with seeing the all-embracing One as a cosmic mother, with universal apron-strings. If you believe in her, the argument runs, you will be an optimist, but if you do not, pessimism is your lot.

This may or may not be good logic, but it is bad psychology. The monist often believes in the One, as the final consolation, precisely because there is so much for which he needs to be consoled. The pluralist, on the other hand, is often a pluralist precisely because he is an optimist, so confident in his own powers or resources or good fortune, so reliant on his star or his own strong right arm, that he spurns the invocation of a guarantor of universal happy ends. Indeed James tells us he took as his paradigms of the tender-minded 'the more studious members of our protestant ministry' who found reinforcement of a modern (by the standards of the time) formulation of their faith in Anglo-Hegelian metaphysics and its idiom, and as paradigms of the tough-minded he took self-reliant, resourceful frontiersmen. But were the frontiersmen, who had no need of such an abstract and abstruse underpinning of their attitude to life and things, *pessimists?* I should have thought not.

Moreover, even as a piece of logic, the connection between tender-

[2] *Ibid.* Lecture Four.   [3] *Ibid.* Lecture One.

2

mindedness (monism) and optimism does not altogether hold. The more sophisticated monists do not personify the One, they think not of one global Mum or Dad, but of some unique principle, idea, criterion or theory. And when the One becomes so abstract, it may still console *cognitively*—for it enables us to hold everything within the compass of one formula—but it no longer guarantees the outcome of specific, concrete crises and adventures. These Anglo-Hegelian abstractions and their Harvard versions, which James had in mind, were primarily the surrogates of a most *refined* God, as James knew full well, rather than of the interfering old Impresario of cosmic conjuring tricks.

But James was not the only one to suppose that the monist was a 'rationalist', addicted to reliance on 'principles', abstract formulations. A contemporary thinker who makes rationalism in this sense the main object of this assault, from a rather pluralist vantage point, is Professor Michael Oakeshott:

The morality of the Rationalist is the self-conscious pursuit of moral ideals, and the appropriate form of moral education is by precept, by the presentation and explanation of moral principles. This is represented as a higher morality (the morality of free men: there is no end to the clap-trap) than that of habit . . .

Here and elsewhere, Oakeshott makes plain his contempt for the morality of ideals, of abstract, unified, codified rules or visions. It is worth quoting his observations on the origins of the attitude of which he disapproves so vigorously:

the politics of Rationalism are the politics of the politically inexperienced . . . the outstanding characteristic of European politics in the last four centuries is that they have suffered the incursion of at least three types of political inexperience—that of the new ruler, of the new ruling class, and of the new political society—to say nothing of the incursion of a new sex . . . How appropriate rationalist politics are to the man who, not brought up or educated to their exercise, finds himself in a position to exert political initiative and authority, requires no emphasis. His need of it is so great that he will have no incentive to be sceptical about the possibility of a magic technique of politics which will remove the handicap of his lack of political education. The offer of such a technique will seem to him the offer of salvation itself; to be told that the necessary knowledge is to be found, complete and self-contained, in a book . . . will seem, like salvation, something almost too good to be true. And yet it was this, or something near enough to be mistaken for it, which he understood Bacon and Descartes to be offering him.[5]

Here the heart of the rationalist/monist is ruthlessly laid bare. He is nervous, cowardly, ill-bred and doctrinaire. These traits are not unconnected, they have an elective affinity. The monist is an upstart, a climber, who aspires to a position for which his background has ill prepared him. Not for him the modest acceptance of an inherited station. Perhaps he

[4] M. Oakeshott, *Rationalism in Politics and Other Essays* (London, 1962), p. 35.

[5] *Ibid.* pp. 23 and 24.

lives in a world in which social change is so rapid that most of the available stations simply cannot be inherited? (Trust the *parvenu* to think of some such excuse.)

He is, at any rate, justifiably ill at ease.

Like a foreigner or a man out of his social class, he is bewildered by a tradition and a habit of behaviour of which he knows only the surface; a butler or an observant house-maid has the advantage of him . . .[6]

One wonders about the very possibility of politics in milieux without either butlers or house-maids. But the rationalist, whom the current shortage of domestic servants has often freed, at least, of the need to feel inferior to observant house-maids, looks around for guidance and reassurance. Perhaps some tutor, or some text, will give him access to the knowledge, poise and mastery which he so sadly lacks? His nervousness degenerates into terror. He no longer seeks, he clutches for the guidebook. When at last he finds one containing a formula he trusts, he clings to it with fanaticism, rigidity and ruthlessness, as if his salvation depended on it, which it does. Do fellow-believers in the same formula interpret it differently? Hunt out the heretics! Has a new situation arisen, unforeseen by the formula? As the formula can never fail, for if it failed, why then everything would have failed, it follows that some unique solution must be deducible from it and applicable to the new solution. Let us find it. Have others deduced a different application? Out with the revisionists! And so on.

The picture is unflattering. But it is accurate. I ought to know. I *am* a monist, or rationalist, and I do find the world unintelligible, and do seek to find a guiding light. In passages such as the ones quoted, I find my inner life, its sources and anxieties, laid bare. It is as well to confess. Whom could I deceive? I shall even attempt a little shamefaced apology for monism, an explanation of why it might make sense to adopt such a position. But first, let us look at some other pluralists.

Not all pluralists diagnose the monist quite so ruthlessly, and their psychological interpretations vary. Some of them have things of interest to say on behalf of pluralism. But the most striking thing is the very widespread nature of the support for pluralism, in all kinds of contexts and idioms, from all kinds of schools and tendencies and styles of thought.

Perhaps I should at this stage warn against one possible misunderstanding: I am in no way decrying one form of political pluralism, the specific view that freedom and social health are best ensured by dispersing power, by avoiding its excessive concentration. This, on the contrary, is a view I warmly endorse. What is at issue here, though no formal definition of monism and pluralism has yet been attempted, is the difference between two styles of conducting *intellectual* life: between the pursuit, and the very high valuation of a single (or failing that, non-

[6] *Ibid.* p. 31.

4

numerous) and explicitly formulated unifying principle or idea, treated with respect and reverence, and on the other hand a derogation of such ideas or principles, and consequently a high valuation of inexplicit and multiform adjustments or devices.

Consider another most important pluralist, Professor Sir Karl Popper. He interprets monism in political philosophy (though not quite in these words) as the *social* variant of the Freudian craving for the safe, warm, cosy womb.[7] For Popper, those who yearn for the Closed Society, for the unified and definite vision, are in thrall, not so much to the wet and dark maternal womb, but its social equivalent—tribal society, blessed, supposedly, with freedom from moral and cognitive ambiguity, from individual responsibility, status uncertainty, and indeed any uncertainty at all. It is this craving which makes people monists or, in his terminology, holists. Popper constitutes an interesting inversion, in political thought, of the conventional fear of anarchy: for him, the greatest menace comes from our excessive craving for order and unity. By contrast, the attitudes which he does commend have a very Jamesian ring. We must learn to love, or at least live with, plurality and uncertainty.

Or take quite another and independent school of enthusiastic pluralists, Wittgensteinian and similar linguistic philosophers. The Wittgensteinian diagnosis of our *Drang* to monism is quite different from Popper's. The famous 'bewitchment by language', from which philosophers in this tradition set out to free us, is really not so much a bewitchment by language as such, as by a mistaken monistic theory of language, a theory mistaken *because* it is monistic. The crucial error, which this school claims to exorcise, is an allegedly mistaken supposition about the nature of language: it is that the general relation between symbols and things can be summed up by some unique, or at worst fairly delimited, principle or principles. It is the supposition that language essentially does but one thing, that 'meaning' is always basically much the same. Liberation from this delusion is said to come with a concrete awareness of the enormous and irreducible variety of uses to which words are really put, and hence of the similarly diversified and complex nature of their relations to things.

Not so very long ago *logic* at least seemed to be a region securely in possession of the monist, as here defined. Within its own sphere, it exemplified the reduction of human knowledge to as small a number of premisses as possible. These premisses were to be secure, and transmitted their own certainty to the rest of the cognitive structure. Such foundations would protect one from the need to retrace one's steps, and Kant, for instance, supposed that logic at least was a science which had reached this blissful condition. And when the dramatic developments in logic came somewhere around the turn of the nineteenth and twentieth centuries, they were still inspired by this ideal, and by the hope of extending its im-

K. Pepper, *The Open Society and its Enemies* (London, 1945) and numerous subsequent editions.

plementation to the whole field of mathematics: if only the whole of logic and mathematics could be deduced from a limited set of safe premisses, the whole edifice would thereby be made trustworthy. Today, what it interesting is not so much that the realisation of the ideal has not been achieved, but rather that the ideal itself has lost its appeal and authority, that many of those who are most respected in these fields, express doubts about the very desirability of pursuing this ideal. One of the most influential among the logicians and philosophers of logic, Professor W. Van Orman Quine, appears willing to have himself characterised as a 'logical pragmatist', and to warn us that even in logic, our premisses cannot insure us against future surprises and the need to retrace steps, that even in logic we as it were haggle and weigh advantages, risks, and convenience, rather than move rectilinearly in marble halls along pathways of clear and indubitable truth. 'Cartesianism' then becomes a pejorative term, a name for the delusive ideal of eternal edifices resting on rock foundations, an ideal whose attraction must be resisted:

Mathematical and logical laws themselves are not immune to revision if it is found that essential simplification of our whole conceptual scheme will ensue ... the laws of mathematics and logic may, despite all "necessity", be abrogated.[8]

Thus nothing is permanent, and the dictates of convenience or simplicity can induce changes in the logician's list of axioms just as they do in a train timetable ... So logic, which seemed to be the last refuge of Cartesianism, of the hope of building up infallible permanent knowledge on infallible bases by a series of infallible steps, no longer provides encouragement for this mirage. It too, evidently, is wont to retrace steps, make opportunist and revocable choices, use anything that happens to be close to hand. It all sounds deplorably like Lévi-Strauss' prehistoric *bricoleur*, that opportunist neolithic handyman who 'makes arrows from any timber that is close to hand'.[9] It is, evidently, intended to sound just like that.

Are things more secure in mathematics? Professor Imre Lakatos has shown that, in the actual life of mathematical ideas, definitions follow rather than precede proofs.[10] Objections to proofs can only be raised and understood after the proof has been formulated; the refinement of the proof in the light of the objection leads to a reformulation of the initial concepts, with a view to weathering the objection or modifying the conclusion. The fully refined and powerful definitions of the initial concepts, and hence the axioms formulated through them, are only the

[8] Willard Van Orman Quine, *Methods of Logic* (New York, 1950) Introduction, p. xiv.

[9] C. Lévi-Strauss, *La Pensée Sauvage* (Paris, 1962). English translation, *The Savage Mind* (London, 1966).

[10] Imre Lakatos, 'Proofs and Refutations', in *The British Journal for the Philosophy of Science* (1963/4). For a far more extreme version of pluralism, see the articles of Paul Feyerabend listed for instance in *Criticism and the Growth of Knowledge* (Cambridge, 1970) ed. I. Lakatos and A. Musgrave.

6

fruits of many, many repetitions of this process. The definition, the official premiss, comes only at the end, not at the beginning—and even this end is only an interim one. The process can never be known to be complete, and indeed is unlikely ever to be terminated. Moreover, the order in which these sequences occur—proof, objection, redefinition—is not something contingent and accidental, something that only happens in the rough work and can be left out on the clean copy; it is, on the contrary, essential to and inherent in the very nature of mathematical discovery. The messy, insecure, step-retracing procedure is of the essence of the subject.

If the Cartesian dream of secure, irreversible progress is not realisable in logic and mathematics, it will come as no surprise to anyone that it should not be viable in sciences whose empirical content is far greater and more obvious. Ever since Hume, at the very latest, this is what one might well expect. In the case of inquiries with a manifestly enormous empirical, substantive content, the reason for the need to retrace steps is only too obvious. Such sciences give, or are, hostages to fortune, to the flow of contingent fact, and every new fact can also be the last one which is still compatible with a given theory. But over and above these general and familiar considerations, there are also further, subtler arguments available. Validity in science is not established in accordance with some simple, orderly criterion, the Natural Law of cognition so to speak; the constitutional law of science is not the logical product of a single mind and one design. It is not like those buildings admired by Descartes, which were designed by one architect, but more like those messy oriental palaces which grow by accretion. It resembles the shreds and patches, the untidy amalgam of a growing, plural, ongoing culture, its law is a customary law which emerges from one contingency and crisis to the next, and not from some supreme constitutional edict issued by Nature.

One author who has argued this case[11] has also put forward a similar position in ethical theory. He has derided the monist view, which he rejects, as the 'citadel theory', the supposition that if only one supreme and all-embracing value or principle could be identified and established, all else would easily follow. Certainly, the strategy of many moral philosophers was one based just on this very assumption. The ancient sage tended to seek the Summum Bonum, seeing himself as a kind of *Which?*, a consumer research service that could identify for us, not so much the best buy, but the *infallible* buy, the moral choice which would remove all risk from the selection of life-styles. The best buy would be incorruptible in all ways and exclude the possibility of deception; and thus the right choice, if only we could identify it, would automatically guarantee itself—for if there were any risk in it, it would no longer be the *perfect* moral buy. Arguments of this kind can be found as late as Spinoza. In more modern times, the Summum Bonum ceases to be the self-guaranteeing foolproof choice of life-style, and becomes instead the one

[11] S. Toulmin, *The Uses of Argument* (Cambridge, 1958), esp. p. 257.

7

over-riding criterion of social policies and institutions.

It is only too easy to deride the unificatory or citadel theory in moral thought. We know only too well how complex life is. And what would we do with the Holy Grail if we found it? Put it on display? It would only prove an embarrassment. In ethics as elsewhere, progress or illumination is piecemeal and retraceable. There is no truth in generality or generality in truth. The point has recently been made, in a forceful manner, by a Wittgensteinian philosopher of the social sciences, Mr A. R. Louch:

And so the only moral recommendations, as the only recommendations for the empirical study of man, come to the same thing—a move here, a move there, zig and zag, after the manner of Aristotle's recommendations with regard to the Mean, everything tentative and subject to change. It is both from overweening generalizations in ethics and the pretensions of general theory in behavioural science that we stand most to fear . . .[12]

For Wittgensteinian linguistic philosophy, such pluralism is of course central. Its outlook has been suggestively transposed to politics and social affairs by Sir Isaiah Berlin in a variety of ways, notably by his re-invocation (as the title of his study of Tolstoy) of the Greek saying about the hedgehog and the fox—the hedgehog knows one big thing, the fox knows many things. There can be little doubt about Sir Isaiah's sympathy for the fox, or of his distrust of the hedgehog, who knows one big thing and, much worse, endeavours to subordinate all else to it. In *Two Concepts of Liberty*,[13] the distinction between the liberal and the totalitarian views of politics is made to hinge, in the end, on the difference between a monistic and a pluralistic conception of the good life:

One of the deepest of human desires is to find a unitary pattern in which the whole of experience is symmetrically ordered.

There is little need to stress the fact that monism, and the faith in a single criterion, has always proved a deep source of satisfaction.

But it leads to

an attempt to preserve absolute categories or ideals at the expense of human lives . . .

whereas, by contrast:

Pluralism . . . seems to me a truer and more humane ideal . . . because it does recognise the fact that human goals are many . . .[14]

The totalitarian or paternalistic vision of liberty as the release and fulfilment of the 'true' or good self, seeking realisation and emerging from the chrysalis of the merely manifest or empirical self, is made by Berlin to depend on the belief in one unique all-embracing moral synthesis, which

[12] A. R. Louch, *Explanation and Human Action* (Berkeley, 1966), p. 208.
[13] Republished in *Four Essays on Liberty* (Oxford, 1969).
[14] *Ibid.* pp. 106, 170, 171.

8

would then be exemplified in that liberated, ideal human self. By contrast, the liberal conception of freedom, as an area reserved for individual and unprejudged choice, is made to depend on a pluralistic awareness that not all goods are one, that there are many and competing values, that no supreme and unique moral solution is available.

Of course, such pluralism in politics and ethics has a long and distinguished ancestry, going back at least to Aristotle's reaction to Plato. Amongst contemporary political thinkers who are quite unconnected with the Wittgensteinian cult, Professor Bernard Crick invokes the Aristotelian precedent in his attempt to define, not merely liberal politics, but politics as such, in terms of pluralism.[15] Politics is in effect defined as the manner in which affairs are conducted in a community whose members refrain from identifying too closely with each other: were they to do so, the unit in which they had submerged themselves would no longer be a *polis*. Politics requires the recognition of a plurality of participants, groupings and aims.

Another independent witness to the charms of pluralism is Professor Bryce Gallie:

Here, in the intelligible but logically unwarranted assumption that morality must have a single, simple basis if it is to be autonomous, we have ... one mistake on which moral philosophies tend to rest. It is a characteristically philosophical mistake: an expression of that passion for intellectual unity and simplicity which is a ... legitimate ... feature of scientific minds. But in philosophy ...[16]

In philosophy it is different.
Or take law or jurisprudence:

It is fatally easy and has become increasingly common to make the transition from the exhilarating discovery that complex words like 'cause' cannot be simply defined and have no 'one true meaning' to the mistaken conclusion that they have no meaning worth bothering about at all, and are used as a mere disguise for arbitrary decision or judicial policy ...[17]

What is interesting in this passage is the almost casual, *en passant,* reference to the allegedly 'exhilarating' nature of the pluralist discovery. Many thinkers in the past found *monism* exhilarating; plurality merely set the problem. The easy dismissal of this rival attitude tells us a fair amount about our intellectual climate. Pluralism was found exhilarating by some of our contemporaries because they embraced, far too uncritically, diverse versions of the view that monism is the source of all error, and that its unmasking is the royal way to truth.

All these testimonials on behalf of pluralism, and the hostile or compassionate psychological diagnoses of monism, were assembled

[15] B. Crick, *In Defence of Politics* (London, 1962).
[16] B. Gallie, *Philosophy and Historical Understanding* (London, 1964), p. 194.
[17] H. L. A. Hart and A. M. Honoré, *Causation and the Law* (Oxford, 1959), Introduction, p. 3.

9

almost at random. Anyone who went about it systematically could collect many more. What makes the consensus so remarkable is that it comes from so many directions and so many fields. Not all the testimonials are quite independent of each other: there is an affinity in the inspiration of Wittgenstein, Toulmin, Hart, Berlin, Louch, and another link between Popper, Lakatos and Feyerabend. But even if we refused to count separately members of intellectual coteries, the consensus would still remain striking.

By contrast, anyone who endeavoured to assemble a similar contemporary chorus on behalf of monism would find his task difficult or impossible. There are perhaps naive monists, so to speak, amongst social scientists—men who assume that a unification of the ideas and approaches in their field is feasible. There is the 'unity of science' movement in the philosophy of science. But on the whole, it is very difficult to find self-confessed and militant monists. In philosophy and politics, the position is so rare as to be virtually eccentric. Perhaps there are secret monists, believers in unique, or at least not numerous principles, who are reluctant to speak up in the face of so high-powered and deafening a pluralist chorus. Who is to oppose so great a consensus, which reached the identical conclusion from so many diverse starting points? It would be rash indeed.

For my own part, I timidly confess to an at least partial monism. Of course it is not courage which makes me defy the chorus. It is rather a case of:

Und ist der Ruf mal ruiniert,
So lebt man weiter ungeniert.

Loosely translated:

If you can't make it by conformity,
Try dissent.

But it does seem to me that those who have recently criticised monism have often missed the point.

GET LOST

The experience of getting lost, say on a long walk in bad weather in uninhabited country, is instructive. When one realises one is lost, the first and appropriate reaction is a sharpening of attention, a heightening of sensitivity. One tries to take in as many signs and clues as possible, in the hope that some of them will lead one back to a familiar landmark.

But now suppose you are badly lost, really lost. On each occasion that a clue is picked up, it turns out in the end to be a false one. It leads one to this or that reading of one's position, but if one acts on that reading and sets out walking in accordance with it, it soons becomes sadly obvious that one is not reaching the points which one ought to be reaching, had the initial clue and the position reading based on it been correct. Confusion grows. The landmarks are no longer there, or if they are, they turn out to be wrong landmarks, refusing to fall into place with the remaining bits of evidence at one's disposal. The jigsaw refuses to allow itself to be assembled: each new piece not merely fails to fit in with the others, but actually undermines such confidence as remains in the arrangement of the previous pieces. Following up one clue merely leads one to lose firm grip on the others. In the end one is no longer sure of directions, distances, time, or anything.

Once this has happened, only one strategy remains open: you must make a fresh start of an entirely different kind.

And now, interestingly, what one must do is the very opposite of what one had done initially, when first realising that one was lost. Then, at the start, the first and instinctive reaction was to prick up one's ears, to try and take in as much as possible, to heighten one's sensitivity, to let nothing pass. By now however, such an attitude would be quite useless. The more you take in now, the greater the confusion. So many clues, good and clear ones it seemed, in fact led nowhere other than the contradiction of other signs and the increase of confusion. They had been worse than useless, leading one away, in all probability, from one's starting point, without at the same time throwing light on where one was or where one was moving. It appears that you actually need not more evidence, but *less*.

So now, you must diminish and restrict your attention and sensitivity. For it has become obvious that some very basic assumption or set of assumptions about one's environment is at fault, and as long as one goes on acting on that as yet unidentified error, or set of errors, things will only get worse. If only one knew just which assumption or set of assumptions was mistaken, one could correct it. But this is precisely what you do *not* know. There are too many possibilities, and generally speaking, one simply does not even think of that one crucial error which is throwing all else out of focus. On two occasions on which I was really badly lost in a mountainous area, it turned out in the end, when the mists lifted, that I was not on the wrong route, but on the wrong mountain. He was on the wrong mountain altogether, you say—what an ass! How right you are. Your own confident reliance on your overall orientation must be envied.

Certain contemporary philosophers tell us that whilst they do not at all deny their own fallibility in matters of detail, the idea of a total, fundamental, pervasive error in their vision of the world they exclude as pathological, 'metaphysical' in a heavily pejorative sense, something which need not be taken seriously, but which they are quite willing to *cure* in others. Yet it seems to me that these pervasive and hidden errors are in fact the important and interesting ones. They cannot be located by finding the appropriate 'fact' which will 'check' them, for they are *diffused* throughout the interpretation of very many facts, and hence individual observations, when made in the conditions of such basic bewilderment, cannot help identify its source. By adding to the general confusion, they merely indicate that there is something to be located.

In his condition, one knows that something, perhaps a lot of things, are radically wrong, but one is not in a position to correct one's vision of the environment and one's place in it, for there is no way of identifying the crucial error. So a new picture must be built up from scratch, in the hope that it will not re-incorporate the pervasive and disturbing error. How is this done?

When lost on a walk, there are various ways of achieving this. Badly lost and confused, there is no point in following up clues in the ordinary way, for somehow one seems to be misreading them all. The simplest device at this point is to start walking rigidly in a straight line, or as close to this as is feasible, systematically disregarding all those little clues and signs to which one had previously been so attentive. One no longer tries to find the *right* direction, for one has learnt that one's assessments of direction seem to be quite haywire. Any direction will do, even one chosen at random, if only you pursue it unswervingly, without tolerating any further temptation to be deflected by apparent indices of what the 'right' direction might be. Now we must stick to a kind of blinkered persistence:

If the fool would persist in his folly he would become wise.
William Blake, *Proverbs of Hell*

What is the point of such a strategy? Systematically disregarding the little signs, in effect one hopes thereby also to neutralise that undentified but pervasive error which enters all one's interpretations and infects them. Moving rigidly in one direction, persisting in folly in the hope of a new wisdom, one refuses to allow those little items of evidence to perpetuate the earlier mistaken picture; indeed one sets aside that entire picture, notwithstanding the lack, as yet, of a viable alternative, in the hope that somehow, new uninterpreted, or rather, partly uninterpreted evidence, will slowly accumulate and at some point, all will 'fall into place' again, a new picture will emerge, and one will once again know where one is.

Normally, this is indeed what does happen in the end. When things have fallen into place again, one may then go back and interpret all the temporarily suspended, insulated evidence. The time of *sursis* is over. Now everything is obvious. Now one knows what had misled one. How obvious—of course, it wasn't a wrong route, it was the wrong *mountain*. But there was no way of hitting on this idea sooner. All the previous attempts at reading the landscape were based, precisely, on this error. The harder one tried to read the signs, the greater the confusion.

The *tabula rasa* method in philosophy, so characteristic of Descartes and the tradition springing from him, is of course not completely analogous to the strategy employed by a person lost in mist in hilly country. A person in such a predicament is not completely confused: he

12

may not know *where* he is, but he knows *who* he is, and he has not lost confidence in his own familiarity with the general properties of landscapes.

A closer analogy is the predicament of a man facing sustained brainwashing. This technique involves not merely inducing maximum confusion concerning spatial and temporal location and sequence, but also a total disorganisation of the wider mental picture, a disruption of all connections and confidence and sense of identity. Above all it is the framework, the criteria of confidence, of moral location, of perspective and plausibility, which are subverted so as to make the victim ready for re-indoctrination. The key ideas which hold all others in place in his mind, which supply the norms, are made as loose and shaky as possible. In the end, nothing can any longer be interpreted with confidence, or only with confidence alternating with powerful distrust. The picture dissolves, nothing is left.

Philosophy is the attempt to cope with this situation.

THE USES OF MONISM

The only possible strategy when facing a situation of total or near-total bewilderment is a monistic one: choose some point, and try to recover a coherent picture by building anew, using it as a base. The choice of base may have to be in some measure arbitrary, and it may even be tentative; it must be arbitrary in as far as the state of hazed confusion precludes the possession of clear, reliable principles which would single out the base in an objective, rational manner. If one had such principles one would not be in that predicament in the first place, and one would not need a new foundation stone. If we had such principles, why then they would *be* the base. But we do not have them, and the new starting-point must somehow be self-sustaining, self-guaranteeing, independent of any further bases or guarantors one step further back. The most famous of all such starting points in philosophy, Descartes' *cogito ergo sum,* was intended to have precisely this self-sustaining quality, to possess a reliability which did not, for once, presuppose something else, for whatever that 'something else' turned out to be would only be part of that tormenting, unreliable confusion which constituted the initial problem.

Of course, it is no use picking on *any* thing, and turning it into the starting point of the recovery of order or orientation. Some single things have a greater inherent plausibility, a greater self-sustaining authority, than others. Such attractive, foundation-worthy starting-points are those around which philosophies of merit are constructed.

In the loss-of-orientation predicament, a monist strategy is really the only possible one. The correct defence of monism does not assert that monism is either valid or feasible. Perhaps it is neither. But for us it is *unavoidable.*

There is one very important objection to monism, which might be called

13

the 'objection from a sense of system'. Loosely formulated, it runs as follows:

The monist hopes to find some reliable and, above all, wholly independent and self-sufficient starting point—an idea, assertation, entity, principle, or whatever it be. But is it really so independent? *Can* it be such? Both for its very existence, and for its perception, recognition and conceptualisation, it requires to be part of some wide system, some framework, some set of alternatives. It does not fill out the world. And things of any kind neither exist, nor are recognised, in isolation. Suppose, for instance, that the privileged base is to be an assertion, a premiss: does it not presuppose at least a part of that conceptual or linguistic framework through which it is articulated?—or the structure of the language in which it is expressed? And do not these systems, in turn, inevitably contain some presuppositions, which are thus covertly and perhaps unwittingly smuggled in with that what was intended to be a pure, solitary, unprejudicial starting-point? Take the historically most celebrated case of the monistic strategy, Descartes: almost immediately after his starting point, he in fact tacitly, but most conspicuously, injects a number of very strong and most dubitable assumptions unwittingly taken from that very world which he intended to scrutinise without *any* preconceptions. The *tabula* was not *rasa,* nor could it ever be such.

All this is entirely correct. But it merely shows that the monistic procedure can never be complete and genuine, that it is ever tainted. It does not show that we can refrain from attempting it—however tainted it be—nor does it imply that the degree of contamination fails to vary from case to case. All cases of such conceptual quarantine, of would-be untainted unprejudicial starts, are far less than altogether pure; but some are far, far purer than others. No *tabulae* are *rasae* but some are more so than others. Moreover, we cannot but try, once we are lost; even if the attempts were entirely spurious, we should have no option but to try. But they are not entirely spurious. They are only very largely spurious. Thus my commitment to monism is not altogether starry-eyed. One does appreciate the weaknesses of the position.

THE DAEMON

There is an important difference between a man who loses his bearings *bei Nacht und Nebel,* and a man facing the characteristically philosophical cognitive predicament. A person hopelessly lost in moorland knows he is lost. But he does not normally need to assume that he is also bewitched, that his confusion is also the consequence of skill and cunning on the part of an unknown but hostile and powerful intelligence. The bewilderment, the loss of orientation, the manner in which all clues and apparent exits turn out to be traps, false clues—all this is taken to be an accident, and not the fruit of design. Nature may be indifferent, but she

14

is not, at least in such cases, an intriguer and schemer. Here we face no wilful opponent.

No such assumption may be made in the theory of knowledge. On the contrary, the assumption of a possibly vicious, but certainly devious, scheming opponent can be made, has been made, ought to be made, and is certainly justified. Descartes did make it.

Admittedly, Descartes in his innocence made the assumption of the malignant daemon, who controlled our thoughts and instilled confidence in false ideas, merely as a kind of heuristic device. He did not believe that such a daemon really did exist, who amused himself by seeing just how much confidence he could inject into our hearts in the most appalling rubbish. Descartes merely used the idea of the daemon as a kind of sorting or testing device: convictions and beliefs which could continue to inspire confidence, even on the assumption of a malignant daemon who fed us our thoughts—such convictions were fit to be the bases of the new edifice. The reconquista of reality could proceed from the redoubt of ideas that had passed this most severe of ordeals, the ordeal by malignant daemon.

The idea which did satisfy this test was the awareness of our own consciousness, thought, exemplified by doubt itself. Doubt as much as you will, doubt itself remains as a specimen of thought. So thought itself is beyond the reach of the devil; however many of our convictions we come to distrust as a result of the daemonic hypothesis, the existence of thought itself remains outside the reach of the all-corrosive anxiety. Doubt is a kind of thought, and thought is the self. So doubt itself establishes the existence of the self. It was thus that the philosophic tradition came into being, which makes our own consciousness into the final arbiter and refuge. We *are* our thought, and thought itself cannot be doubted, for doubt itself is also an instance of thought.

Thus Descartes invoked the daemon half playfully, as a supposition which was to be the acid test, as men are sometimes selected for important tasks by preliminary ordeals which are more taxing and severe than the task itself. But what was in part—not altogether—a mere supposition, almost an intellectual coquetry for Descartes, soon became a reasonable, indeed a compelling suspicion. Even for Descartes it was no joking matter:

Mais ayant appris . . . qu'on me saurait rien imaginer de si étrange et si peu croyable, qu'il n'ait été dit par quelqu'un des philosophes . . . je ne pouvais choisir personne dont les opinions me semblassent devoir être preferées à celles des autres . . .

. . . comme un homme qui marche seul et dans les ténèbres, je me résolus d'aller si lentement . . .[18]

There can be no mistaking the sense of distrust and disorientation. There is no rubbish great enough not to have been asserted by someone. But where Descartes invoked the daemon as a device to help him escape from the condition of uncertainty, we are in the end left with the certainty

[18] R. Descartes, *Discours de la Méthode,* Seconde Partie.

15

of the existence of the daemon. Descartes thinks, therefore the daemon exists. Our thought, the very concepts and schemata we employ in attempts to orient ourselves, are constituted and controlled by mechanisms which we do not properly understand and which, in consequence, we cannot really trust and endorse without reservation. Take a contemporary formulation of this idea:

A person who knows a language has mastered a set of rules and principles ... the characteristic use of this knowledge is free and creative ... in that one can instantaneously interpret an indefinitely large range of utterances, with no feeling of unfamiliarity or strangeness—and, of course, *no possibility of 'introspecting' into the processes by which the interpretation of these utterances ... takes place.*[19]

We speak, therefore the daemon exists. Our power of speech and the recognition of meanings, hence of thought, depends on principles and structures not generally accessible to us. Hence we take them on trust, and are in no position to underwrite the soundness of what and how we think. As Lichtenberg observed, we should say *it thinks* rather than *I think*. But although, for reasons such as these, we know of the existence of the daemon, we know little of his habits. Whether he be malignant or benevolent is perhaps still open. What is certain is that he exists and that the manner of his operation is not easily understood, let alone immediately accessible.

A thinker who has rightly made a great impact and familiarised us with the idea of our enslavement to thought patterns which are unperceived by those who are under their sway, is the late Edward Evans-Pritchard. Speaking of an African ethnic group, he says

In this web of belief every strand depends upon every other strand, and a Zande cannot get out of its meshes because it is the only world he knows. The web is not an external structure in which he is enclosed. It is the texture of his thought and he cannot think that his thought is wrong.[20]

Yet Descartes at least did suppose, forcefully, that his own thought might well be wrong. But in inventing the daemon, in order to highlight this possibility, he spoke far better than he knew. We are now familiarised with the possibility that the very concepts we use are *agents-provocateurs* within us; perhaps the more we endeavour to think ourselves out of this predicament, the more we remain under their sway. Perhaps it is rather like the situation in G. K. Chesterton's *The Man Who was Thursday*, in which the entire central committee of a subversive movement turns out, in the end, to be composed of police spies. Only now it is we who have had our defences penetrated.

Of course, it is fashionable to decry and ironise this anxious view of the

[19] N. Chomsky, John Locke Lectures, published in *The Times Literary Supplement*, 15 May 1969, p. 523. Emphasis mine.

[20] E. Evans-Pritchard, *Witchcraft, Oracles and Magic among the Azande* (Oxford, 1937), pp. 194 and 195.

16

situation. The pluralists suffer from no such anxieties, but it remains to be seen whether their confidence is well-founded.

If they faced the difficulty of the erstwhile Zande confidence in their own beliefs, the pluralists might say something like this: the Azande are savages, and we are not. We are the beneficiaries of Revelation, or of the Enlightenment, according to variant. They might say this, but probably they would not: brazen claims to religious, cultural or ethnic privileged access to truth are not now fashionable, or at least, are not openly asserted. In the main, the pluralists simply have not faced up to the problem arising from the fact that if their own confidence is self-justifying, then so is that of the Azande, though it endorses beliefs which are quite incompatible with their own. If they did face it, they would reach the dilemma that either the Zande circle of ideas is as good as our own (a view impossible to sustain and at variance with the conviction of contemporary Azande themselves), or one must seek a general criterion of trustworthy beliefs or systems, in which case you are covertly returning to a monist strategy and abandoning complacent pluralism. In practice, pluralists avoid this issue.

Since Descartes' unintended discovery of his existence, the daemon—controller of our thought—has been variously identified as mind, history, language, biological history, the unconscious (individual or collective), society, and so forth. The specific mechanisms conceived under the general label of psychological, historicising, etc., daemons introduce further variety; there is more than one kind of historical daemon, and similarly with the others.

In rough historical sequence, the first attempts at identifying the daemon began as efforts to specify the hidden or overt workings of the human *mind,* a tradition which culminated in the work of Kant. If one conjoins the insights of this tradition with an increasing awareness that the scaffolding of concepts, sketched out by thinkers such as Kant, is not necessarily the same in all societies and periods, the way is open for seeing the daemon as working through, or indeed being, history. It was the underlying patterns and mechanics of historical development which had to be discovered, if we were to understand that to which we and our thought are in bondage. With Darwin and the establishment of the continuity between man and nature, it was natural to extend this approach to biological history, especially as Darwinism itself contained the specification of an easily understood mechanism which could be applied to nature and history alike, or so it seemed. So the daemon became biological, his tricks adaptive and survival-oriented, as it was with the pragmatists. Nature being red in tooth and claw, the way was now also open for a fusion of the biologically inspired daemon with the more sombre versions of the historicising daemon, which had been favoured by the romantics, who liked to give themselves *frissons* by envisaged turbulent, dark powers operating behind the scenes of our consciousness.

17

This view was of course an important ancestor of the depth-psychological daemon. A full history of the transformations of the devil has not yet been written, and would in effect constitute a good history of modern philosophy. Recently, of course, theories of the dominance of our thought by language have been prominent.

If one were to plot the structure of modern philosophy since Descartes on a diagram, one axis would indeed tabulate these diverse identifications, from mind to language. But the other axis would correspond to diverse attitudes *towards* the daemon. The principle along which this axis would be constructed can best be conveyed if we consider the two extremes, at either end of the continuum which it expresses: at one end, there are the resisters, and at the other, the collaborators.

The argument underlying the resister attitude is perhaps the most natural reaction to the discovery, or suspicion, that the daemon exists. So some power is systematically interfering with our ideas, making us, in its own interest or for its own amusement, assent to that which is false, and to deny that which is true? So? We must, we *shall* outwit it, learn its tricks, and equip ourselves with some suitable holy water or counter-measures for our protection.

The collaborationist argument leads to the opposite conclusion. The daemon, you say, is powerful and pervasive, perhaps all-powerful and all-pervasive. But if he pervades all our thought, and that of our fellow humans, what sense is there in trying to envisage a contrast to that condition? Not only would we fail in endeavouring to escape his clutches, but no clear meaning, or no meaning at all, can really be attached to such a putative liberation. As an example of this attitude, consider a simplified pragmatism, which asserts that thought is simply an adaptive mechanism like any other, and can only be judged by its adaptive usefulness. If that is all it is and can be, what sense could there be in trying to transcend it? Why not accept that this is what thought and truth *are*?

There is of course no need for a thinker to occupy either of these extreme positions. The continuum between them corresponds to a variety of intermediate, compromise positions. For instance, Kant was both a resister and a collaborator. He thought it of the greatest importance to unmask the daemon—identified, in Kant's case, with the structure of the human mind—if only to proscribe or inhibit certain excessive intellectual pretensions, such as the use of the concepts imposed on us by our minds in spheres inappropriate to them. These concepts must not stray from the fields for which they are designed. Causation, for instance, must neither be applied to realms outside our own experience, nor, on the other hand, be allowed to inhibit our sense of moral responsibility. The unmasking of his particular daemon was, for Kant, at once a means of proscribing the extravagant pretensions of transcendentalism, and of protecting us from a de-humanised, mechanistic vision of man. To this extent, Kant was a resister. Yet in other ways, he collaborated and preached collaboration.

18

There was no point in seeking to know that world as it was independent of our conceptual apparatus; accept our limitations, and ordinary knowledge must satisfy itself within the limits imposed on it.

Numerous other compromise positions exist. It is hardly necessary to pursue them further at this point. The only thing which it is necessary to exclude firmly is the facile suggestion that the problem of the daemon and general doubt is an unreal one.

IN PRAISE OF TRANSCENDENCE

Philosophic thought is primarily an attempt at transcendence. Yet transcendence has of late had almost as bad a press as monism, and for similar reasons. The attempt to transcend in thought the limitations— presumably of this world—is, it is said, a comic, somewhat Victorian weakness. Immanence is *in*, transcendence is *out*. It lacks that fashionable restriction to this world, this language, or to the historically and institutionally specific faiths which are also in vogue. The things which effectively are out of fashion are those allegedly naive nineteenth-century attempts to secure some of the general orientation and comfort once provided by historic faiths, but to do so by rational methods. Faiths are in, but rational appraisals or replacements of faith are out.

It is not in fact my wish to plead for efforts to think ourselves beyond the limits of this world, though such efforts are not quite as misguided as tough-minded immanentists would have it. Surprisingly, our language and concepts do not seem altogether bounded by the world they serve and in which they occur, but on the contrary can single out that world, as one possibility amongst others.

Instead of pleading for transcendence, however, I only wish to consider a certain systematic obfuscation of this issue in recent times. The real question is—transcendence of *what*? Rightly or wrongly, transcendence of *everything*, of the grand totality, the attainment of a stance wholly outside this world and one surveying it from an external, absolute viewpoint—all this can be made to sound comic. Perhaps it is. But it is not the real current issue. What is at issue is not the grand totality of things, but only the transcendence of this, that or the other closed circle of ideas, the presuppositions on which this or that system of concepts is built, the dogmas entrenched in the customs of this or that society. 'Transcendence' of *this* kind is not merely possible, it is—regrettably for some—often inescapable. It is not merely often easy, it is often impossible to evade this kind of liberation. Whether you think of a closed cultural 'form of life' as a prison or as a shelter, either way, it often crumbles and frees you, whether you wish it or not.

One of the main lessons of human history is that these self-maintaining and closed circles of ideas, for all their occasional ingenuity, cunning and viciousness, often disintegrate into chaos. Alternatively, two or more of

19

them coalesce, like clashing galaxies, interpenetrating into an incoherent jumble. But they do not have some inexorable hold over men, and often have difficulties in practising that self-maintenance with which functionalist sociology would too easily credit them.

Karl Popper has dubbed the view that we cannot transcend our circles of ideas—either psychologically, being enslaved to them, or logically, through lacking any external or neutral vantage point—'the Myth of the Framework', and has observed that it 'is, in our time, the central bulwark of irrationalism'.[21]

My aim at this point is merely to draw attention to one very special and important device employed for sustaining this myth: the confusion of the transcendence of everything (comic 'metaphysics', etc.) with the transcendence of specific, rounded-off, self-endorsing, closed visions. The perfectly practicable and often inescapable activity of casting doubt on such a vision, by means of the application to it of some external criterion *which is not itself under its control,* is often systematically confused with quite another activity, which may or may not be feasible, but which, either way, is irrelevant—namely, *total* transcendence. Recent intellectual history has witnessed this remarkable and basically simple confidence trick, the conflation of these two senses. The perpetrators of this confidence trick, who are also its victims, smuggle in, under the superficial cover of a supposedly sceptical abstinence from transcendent claims, something which in fact was the very opposite—a scepticism-abandoning, uncritical endorsement of each and every little local culture and circle of ideas:

What has to be accepted, the given, is—so one could say—*forms of life.*[22]

Forms of life and cultures, are precisely what thought does not and need not automatically accept. Cultures must not be judges in their own case, as the claim that they 'have to be accepted' would have it. They often fail to be viable and collapse through sheer internal incoherence.

But the real point to be noted here is the genuine dogmatism under the apparent scepticism and modesty. The seemingly modest abstention from transcendence, in fact here amounts to the immodest, dogmatic and *carte blanche* endorsement of all and any 'form of life'. This mystification hinges on the two senses of transcendence.

William James, the most charming of the pluralists, did of course class the striving after transcendence with tender-mindedness, as he did monism. Monism and transcendence are indeed intimately connected, monism being the most obvious, and perhaps the only, path to transcendence. Critical assessment must use a limited number of principles or ideas, otherwise it becomes as chaotic, as promiscuous

[21] I. Lakatos and A. Musgrave (eds.), *Criticism and the Growth of Knowledge* (Cambridge, 1970), p. 56.
[22] L. Wittgenstein, *Philosophical Investigations* (Oxford, 1953), p. 226e.

20

conceptually as the intellectual bedlam which it is trying to sort out and evaluate. But neither monism nor transcendence is necessarily or generally tender-minded, in the sense of being inspired by a desire to evade complex reality and find a simple, unified, unproblematic vision. The monism is introduced, in many cases, not for the sake of comfort, but for the sake of orderly and ruthless selection and elimination. It is this point that largely escaped James, and totally escapes most contemporary pluralists.

James' error is best conveyed by a fascinating passage in *Pragmatism* (Lecture One), which might usefully be named the Case of the Candid Student:

I wish that I had saved the first couple of pages of a thesis which a student handed me ... This young man ... began by saying that he had always taken it for granted that when you entered a philosophic classroom you had to open relations with a universe entirely distinct from the one you left behind in the street. The two were supposed ... to have so little to do with each other, that you could not possibly occupy your mind with them at the same time. The world of concrete personal experiences to which the street belongs is multitudinous beyond imagination, tangled, muddy, painful and perplexed. The world to which your philosophy professor introduces you is simple, clean and noble. The contradictions of real life are absent from it. Its architecture is classic. Principles of reason trace its outlines, logical necessities cement its parts. Purity and dignity are what it most expresses. It is a kind of marble temple shining on a hill.

Well, if the candid student were still alive today, he would find the scene changed beyond all recognition. As we have seen in our survey of the pluralist chorus, philosophers of most diverse kinds vie with each in explaining how multiform, irreducible, incommensurate and complex are the things of this world. There seems now to be little relationship between the world of the professors, who rejoice in its irreducible plurality, and the world outside, not perhaps of the street, but of history—a world in which simple unifying ideas and ideals in religion, politics and science, have wrought tremendous, profound social transformations. In the classroom, the professors fall over themselves in their eagerness to assure the student that the world is not amenable to conceptual unification; outside, it is unifying ideas which confer cognitive power and which have dominated the world. The monistic principles of the Reformation, of seventeenth-century science, eighteenth-century Enlightenment, have wrought great havoc, for good or ill. The wheel seems to have gone full circle.

William James comments on the 'classic sanctuary' to which the candid student had drawn attention: it is a 'refuge from the intolerably confused and gothic character which mere facts present. It is no *explanation* (but) ... a substitute ... a remedy, a way of escape.' It exquisitely satisfies 'that craving for a refined object of contemplation which is so powerful an appetite of the mind'.

Here is James' great mistake. No doubt the unifying, pantheistic or quasi-pantheistic vision did satisfy the craving for refined objects of

21

contemplation among the 'more studious members of the protestant ministry' of his time, or among God-inebriated men such as Spinoza. But the monism of the epistemological tradition springing from Descartes, the employment of simple, ruthless, and preferably single principles, has nothing to do with the desire for refined objects of contemplation, or with God-intoxication or the Oceanic feeling, in Freud's term. Quite the contrary.

Corresponding to two types of transcendence, there are in reality two quite distinct kinds of monism. They might be called the oceanic and the critical varieties. Oceanic monism is an unitary vision designed to give the believer a consoling, edifying or exhilarating sense of being merged with, sustained by, dissolved in the great One of which he and all else is a part. Mystics, romantic poets, pantheists, and some philosophers have experienced, conveyed, and sometimes attempted to demonstrate

A presence that disturbs me with the joy
Of elevated thoughts; a sense sublime
Of something far more deeply interfused,
Whose dwelling is the light of setting suns,
And the round ocean and the living air,
And the blue sky, and in the mind of man.

If our contemporary thinkers are to be believed, Wordsworthian sentiments such as these, if not carefully confined to a kind of poets' corner, will lead you into the gravest errors in logical theory, political practice, and the understanding of language, not to mention other fields. William James may well castigate the addicts of this version as tender-minded, and warn them that they will come a cropper when the presence which disturbs them with the joy of elevated thoughts will let them down, good and hard, in the sordid complexities of 'real life'.

What is important to notice is that the merits or otherwise of such pantheistic or Wordsworthian monism are not really relevant. Oceanic monism is not an important or prominent part of our intellectual life. Representatives of this vision can be found: in James' own time, the academically influential movement of Anglo-Hegelians attempted to demonstrate the existence of something far more deeply interfused by means of most abstruse doctrines about the correct interpretation of relational terms—as if the great unity were at the mercy of our grammar. But in our intellectual situation, these are, for better or for worse, relatively marginal rather than central preoccupations.

By contrast, *critical* monism, the attempt to restore intellectual order by the sustained application of simple, delimited, lucid principles, principles designed to isolate and use the marks of genuine knowledge, an attempt which is mandatory in conditions of intellectual chaos such as in fact often obtain—such monism is absolutely essential for our life. It has nothing to do with a bath in a tepid, cosmic fluid. The systematic obfuscation of this distinction, the attempt to foist the motives, spirit and criteria of oceanic monism on to critical monism, is one of the gravest and most conspicuous defects of recent thought.

2   The Copernican Revolution

Roughly speaking, legitimacy is sovereignty recollected in tranquillity. In the classical period of political philosophy, men spoke of sovereignty, wondering who was the rightful ruler, and what made him rightful, in their own society. Today, a good proportion of the discussions concerning the right and proper ordering of society, of the justified occupancy of positions of power, takes place amongst men who live in relatively stable societies, but are concerned with other, less stable ones, which are not at the same time the homes of the theorists themselves. In other words, preoccupation with sovereignty is often vicarious. Those who have most opportunity to theorise about the matter live in societies in which the question is not immediate and urgent, and they ask it about others, for whom it is urgent indeed, but who may be prevented by that very urgency from devoting much time to abstract thought.

Hence a term is required which conveys the fact that such and such a personage, institution or procedure is held to be authoritative, binding or valid in a given society, without at the same time committing the speaker himself to any kind of endorsement of the values in question. The expression ought not convey or hint that he in any way decries or ironises them either. It should be, for the speaker, non-committal. The word legitimacy, as now employed by social scientists, tends to satisfy this requirement, whereas the *sovereignty* of the political philosophers cannot quite be disinfected of the air of endorsement.

To put it another way, most social scientists are members of fairly prosperous and stable societies. Despite the self-advertised revival of 'basic questioning' in the 1960s, the seriousness of which it is easy to exaggerate, sovereignty or legitimacy is not very seriously in dispute in such societies, On the other hand, it is very seriously and endemically in dispute, for familiar reasons, in the poorer, transitional, developing countries. For one thing, it is this area which provides the unstable front line in the conflict between global blocks. Given the nuclear stalemate, the subversion of hostile local governments and their replacement by one's own allies, becomes one of the few devices available for either side. Each side has good cause to worry about the feebleness of the aura of legitimacy surrounding its own allies, and good cause to rejoice over the similarly feeble aura surrounding the rulers aligned with its opponents.

Moreover, in this general region, legitimacy is placed under severe and exceptionally heavy strains. Most of the rulers in the Third World find themselves in a Moses situation, though few of them have the talents of Moses, irrespective of their equipment or taste for it, and irrespective of whether their peoples welcome it. They are obliged, by demographic pressure, poverty, dislocation, and an international demonstration effect, to try and lead their followers across an arid wilderness, to a distant land of milk and honey whose attainment and conquest must often seem sadly problematical. In these long wanderings, their authority is put to severe and repeated tests, by natural calamities or by the machinations of rivals, ever ready to try and achieve power by promising an easier and quicker deliverance.

Comfortable societies may tolerate their rulers from sheer inertia, indifference, fear lest worse befall, or preoccupation with other matters. But Moses-like rulers, who put their subjects under exceptionally heavy strains, need all the ideological help they can secure if they are to stay in the saddle. If only they can anchor their authority in some strong conviction among the populations they rule, this may help them to weather the storm without disaster to themselves.

The observer, fascinated by this political rodeo, intrigued to see how many riders can stay the course and for how long, is often an outsider to the societies in question. Generally speaking, he does not himself share the convictions which help legitimate these precarious rulers. Hence he welcomes a term which describes the relation between a set of ideas and the acceptance of a regime, without at the same time appearing to commit the observer himself to an endorsement of those ideas. Thus legitimacy enables an observer who is himself (say) a pacifist, to note that a given regime has legitimacy for its citizens in virtue of a successful war, or an observer who happens to be an atheist to note the legitimacy of a ruler which is founded in a religious consecration.

Thus the term contains a measure of built-in *Wertfreiheit*, which is required not merely by any general aspiration to neutrality that may be felt in the social sciences, but more specifically and cogently by the concrete circumstances of the contemporary study of politics.

But in addition, the term *legitimacy* has a further and even more important advantage: it applies not merely to the political sphere, but also to any other, for instance the realm of the cognitive. In our world, it is not merely rulers and regimes, but also types of ownership, production, education, association, expression, thought, art, and research which can have, or fail to have, legitimacy in the eyes of beholders and practitioners. This wider range of applicability satisfies an age for which not merely the form of government—let alone merely the identity of the ruler—but equally all other aspects of social life can be questioned, challenged, and placed *sub judice*. 'Legitimacy' is not merely a kind of aseptic neutralisation of 'sovereignty', but also an extension of its range to areas not always scrutinised by classical political philosophy.

Thus it is not merely the identity of rulers or the form of government, but most or all other aspects of life as well, which are placed under scrutiny, face radical alternatives, and require legitimation. Rival parties seek reasons which will make their own claims and favourite options prevail. But disputes in various fields are of course not independent of each other. The solutions or options in diverse fields have natural affinities and incompatibilities with each other, and societies tend to have relatively coherent shopping lists, choosing their options in *roughly* the same style all along the line, or at least along much of the line.

The coherence is far from total, and there are marked exceptions to it. For instance, a society may be egalitarian in politics but elitist in education, and so forth. Sometimes, such incoherences may actually help a society to function, whilst at the same time preventing it from attaining ideological neatness: a society which practises equality in one sphere and not in another, would have some difficulty in blazoning either equality or hierarchy too emphatically and exclusively on its banners. So social coherence is sometimes only obtained, perhaps, at the price of logical incoherence. This is a favourite theme of conservative political philosophers and of functionalist sociologists, who take pleasure in reminding us that a seeming illogicality may, or according to them, *does,* hide a deeper logic. The conservative rejoices in this because it seems to exempt institutions from rational scrutiny, and the functionalist takes pride in his professional expertise, which enables him to discern latent functions under mere manifest absurdity. (Latent function is the new name for what Hegel called the 'cunning of reason'.)

But the nature of things is not endlessly permissive in this sphere, and there are limits to the degree of incoherence which is possible as between one field and another. It is unthinkable that a society should be, say, collectivist–industrial in its mode of production, feudal in politics, *laissez-faire* in culture and education, and tribally local–particularistic in religion. Sociology may not have been as successful as one might wish in eliciting and formulating the limits of possible combinations, the elective affinities and repulsions of social forms; but it has proved beyond doubt the existence of such limits.

The manner in which coherence is or is not present between various 'aspects' of social life, such as politics, economy and education, will itself vary as between diverse kinds of society. Small and simple societies, lacking the scale, the surplus, or the sophistication which would make possible a complex division of labour, cannot go very far in an explicit separation of these aspects of life. On the whole, men can only stress the distinction between production, the maintenance of order, ritual, education, and so forth, when they can assign different personnel to each sphere. In a small roving nomadic band this is hardly possible. Hence different aspects of life are unlikely to possess distinct social charters; whatever legends or beliefs validate current practice are unlikely to distinguish too sharply between the various aspects.

By contrast, complex societies do separate spheres of life, in fact and idea. They do not, of course, necessarily separate them all, or draw the lines at the same points, or always respect the lines they have drawn. But they do recognise that there are lines to be drawn. And once these lines are drawn and stressed, it is possible to treat some activities as more important than others: to value, say, the warrior, or the priest, or the craftsman, or the entrepreneur, more highly than the others. The legitimation invoked for the society as a whole may favour one sphere or another. It may draw its key images, symbols, or premisses, from one favoured region.

To put this another way, the ideological centre of gravity need not always be in the same place. The key premisses, which are at the same time the final courts of appeal in the society in question, may have quite diverse locations.

The present argument contends that in recent centuries, this centre of ideological gravity has shifted in a marked and interesting way in our society. This was not a shift in effective power, but a shift at the doctrinal or ideological level only, a shift in that to which people appeal in the end, as the final court of appeal in cases of intellectual dispute. The best name for this ideological shift is the Copernican Revolution, in Kant's sense of the phrase.

COGNITION AS NORM

The basic idea underlying this shift of vision has long been available. As so often, it is not the mere availability, but the sustained and ruthless application of an idea, which makes a difference. As an example of its early availability, take the following Renaissance specimen:

Saul: And first let me hear why Jove has decided that Truth shall be placed in the highest seat.
Sophia: Easily. Truth is placed above all things ... for if we were to conceive of something that was to be ranked higher, it would also have to be something other than Truth. And if you imagine it to be something other than Truth, you will necessarily see it as not being true, hence, it is false, it is worse than nothing.[23]

Briefly put, anything must be true before it can significantly claim other merits. Without truth, all else is worthless. We must assess the truth of cognitive claims contained in, or presupposed by, anything that lays claims to our respect; and if it fails this first and crucial test, all subsequent ones become irrelevant. No other charms can ever make up, in the very least degree, for the failure to possess this first and pre-eminent virtue.

Thus reformulated, Bruno's point is freed of any mystical neo-Platonist associations it may have had for its author and which are suggested by the

[23] Giordano Bruno, *The Expulsion of the Triumphant Beast,* Second Dialogue, First Part.

reification of 'Truth'. But these associations are irrelevant, and in fact weaken rather than strengthen the case, which can be stated in a hard-headed, down-to-earth manner. In any system of ideas or convictions, truth is the first and pre-eminent consideration, and its absence cancels any other possible virtues.

This point may now seem obvious or even trite. Yet its sustained and ruthless application is anything but innocuous. It is radical, revolutionary, and deeply disturbing. It requires that we look not to things, not to the world, but instead to the validity of what we *know* about things or the world. Before any thing, or indeed any person, can be revered, we must first examine, without any undue and inhibiting reverence, the standing and validity of the putative knowledge concerning that thing or person. Thus, the foundation stone of our conceptual and moral edifice and, quite literally, of our world and our identity, becomes not some specially reliable and reverence-inspiring object or being out there; on the contrary, it is shifted inwards to our cognitive equipment, to our criteria of sound knowledge, of the recognition of truth. First of all, examine how you know things, the criteria you have for assessing the validity, the legitimacy of cognitive claims. If those criteria themselves be sound and legitimate, they will transmit their own validity to the substantive knowledge which has been authenticated by them; but if not, then the whole edifice is worthless. So real intellectual sovereignty lies in the norms of cognition. As Descartes observed, if the first button be wrongly done up, then so will all the other be: and the first button is concerned with *how* we know, how we authenticate truth claims, and not with *what* we know.

This is the Copernican Revolution in philosophy, as conceived and heralded by Kant. Kant rightly held it to be at the centre of his own critical philosophy. He considered his own basic innovation in the *Critique of Pure Reason* to be this: the central features of the world which it is necessary to substantiate for the sake of our peace of mind (such as the regularity of nature) were to be established, no longer by an appeal to the nature of *things,* but on the contrary by an appeal to the inner necessities of *our* cognitive apparatus. The locus of cognitive validation was to be shifted inwards.

Kant perhaps somewhat exaggerated his own originality at this point. The specific execution of this idea found in the three *Critiques* was of course his own. But the transfer of the ultimate locus of legitimacy inwards, to man, to human cognitive powers, characterises not Kant's philosophy alone, but the whole of the epistemological tradition from Descartes to our own day. And it is a key feature of the philosophy of this period that epistemology, the theory of knowledge, is central to it. And the reason why it is so central is the widespread acceptance of the point made in Bruno's dialogue.

This Copernican Revolution does make a tremendous difference to one's vision. What in a way it amounts to is that the world is seen *within*

28

knowledge, and not the other way round. Philosophically unsophisticated vision tends both to see the world in knowledge, i.e. constructed by our cognition and its principles, and at the same time to see knowledge in the world, as one thing or process amongst others within a wider world, to be understood alongside and in the same way as other human activities. If then some features of the world are basic, fundamental, sacred, immovable, they can as it were impose their authority on knowledge, and prescribe for it what may or may not be true. But once the sustained, consistent application of Bruno's point places the world within knowledge and under its authority, this is no longer possible: nothing in the world can any longer be independently sacred and ultimate, but must owe whatever aura of authority it possesses to that sole independent and truly final source of it, which is located in the criteria of truth and knowledge. Thus the Copernican Revolution is a radical one indeed; it is the shift of the ultimate seat of legitimacy to knowledge. The pre-eminence of epistemology in the philosophy of the past three centuries is simply an echo of this shift.

Bertrand Russell rightly commented that Kant's Copernican Revolution was mis-named, that it was really an anti-Copernican counter-Revolution. Quite so. Copernicus' heliocentrism brutally and insultingly removed man from the centre of things and placed him at the periphery. The shift of vision celebrated by Kant places man back at the centre of things, and does not even do so in any kind of underhand or surreptitious manner. The world passes through the lens of our cognition; whatever is *necessary* and hence foundation-worthy in it, owes this status to the lens, not to itself: so philosophy must scrutinise the lens, our selves, our cognitive powers. This anthropocentrism is of course what gives the view much of its appeal. The silence of the infinite spaces out there need no longer frighten us. Their emptiness is irrelevant, if what confers meaning on life and validates our procedures is no longer expected to be out there, but is right here, in our cognitive and other competences. Russell's apt jibe can be accepted, but it does not necessarily constitute a criticism. It is by no means obvious that Russell's own thought, with its preoccupation with the foundations of diverse forms of knowledge, does not itself fall under this very selfsame anti-Copernican counter-Revolution.

A DECODING OPERATION

The argument stresses that the issue of legitimacy is not restricted to political institutions, but arises equally, or even more fundamentally, in other areas, such as the cognitive. Moreover, there tends to be an interdependence between legitimations offered in one sphere and another, and in our time, it is the validation of cognitive practices which is ultimately crucial for the other areas.

Thus, if this argument is correct, the centrality of the theory of knowledge in modern philosophy since Descartes is not an accidental fact, or one explicable by factors internal to formal philosophy, but, on the contrary, reflects something important about intellectual life at large. Knowledge is central, and the norms of knowledge provide a court of appeal for normative issues in other spheres. What ethical, political, economic and other norms are found to be acceptable, depends in the end on what kinds of knowledge are possible, which cognitive norms are held to be compelling. Epistemology is the study of these final norms which serve as a court of appeal for all the others.

To say this is *not* to put forward some absurd theory to the effect that the social history of the past three centuries was but an echo of the ideas then current about the nature and limits of human knowledge. No such grotesque primacy is claimed for epistemology. The whole tangled question of the interplay of intellectual and other factors in history is left aside. What is claimed is that *within* the intellectual or ideological realm, the centre of gravity has shifted in a marked fashion towards ideas concerning knowledge. Ideas about the rightful exercise of power, or the just distribution of rewards, are made to hinge, in a much more systematic way than was ever the case before, on ideas concerning what can be known and how we know it. This is a much weaker claim, which might be compatible with a view that the realm of doctrinal justifications has little or no impact on concrete social life, though of course it does not presuppose any such view either.

Hence the view which is being argued does not constitute some kind of philosophy of history, it offers no secret key to the general developments of the past three centuries. If it offers to decode anything, it is not the general history of this period, but merely the history of philosophy itself.

In his fascinating account of the origin of Marxism,[24] Robert Tucker describes how Marx supposed he was decoding the secret message of Hegelianism:

Marx founded Marxism in an outburst of Hegelising. He considered himself to be engaged in no more than a momentous act of translation of the already discovered truth ... from the language of idealism into that of materialism. He was only restating ... what Hegel had said before him in a confused philosophical form. Hegelianism itself was latently or esoterically an economic interpretation of history.

If Tucker is right and Marx was engaged in a decoding operation, one must conclude, as indeed Tucker himself does, that Marx's translation was unsound. For one thing, he was led by his Rhenish origins to work on an inferior and unsound version of the original message, a garbled account of modern philosophy, in which Hegel played a far greater part than he deserves. Moreover, although there are fascinating parallels between modern epistemology and economic organisation—the individualism, the

[24] R. Tucker, *Philosophy and Myth in Karl Marx* (Cambridge, 1961), p. 123.

subjectivism, the accountant's eye view of the accumulation of either knowledge or of satisfactions—parallels which were not lost on Marx, the fact remains that philosophy is not a coded commentary on economic life, and that the problems of knowledge cannot be solved or dissolved by re-translation into the language of *'practice'*. The contrary view, enshrined in Marx's third thesis on Feuerbach,[25] is indefensible. The disturbing question of the endless regress involved in our attempt to justify our beliefs, cannot be solved by appealing to something called 'practice'. Any given 'practice' may indeed prejudge these questions, it does not answer them.

But Marx's positive solution does not concern us at this point. A decoding of modern philosophy is being offered, one that is parallel and rival to the one which, according to Tucker, Marx was presenting. The present decoding is far less ambitious than the one credited to Marx by Tucker, in that the decoded message is less radically distant from the coded version. Nevertheless, it does differ significantly from the undeciphered message.

What the original and the deciphered versions share is the stress on knowledge. But the original version (i.e. the mainstream of philosophic thought of the past three centuries, with its heavy stress on the theory of knowledge) presents a message written in the indicative mood: it claims to tell us something about what knowledge *is* in fact like. It claims to offer a description or an explanation, or both, of how knowledge actually works. In this, I believe it to be profoundly misleading and in great need of re-statement, of translation. For modern philosophy, and its epistemological stress, gain enormously in plausibility when they are read, not as a descriptive or explanatory accounts of what knowledge 'is really like', but as a formulation of *norms* which are to govern and limit our cognitive behaviour.

The decoding of other people's messages, the unmasking of their true meaning which is hidden from themselves, is always tinged with arrogance. One is saying, in effect, that they spoke wisely, they spoke better than they knew, but they knew not what they said. It takes someone as clear-minded as oneself to make their own wisdom plain to them and to the rest of us. When the men whose messages are thus to be re-interpreted are thinkers of great note, clearly the arrogance is compounded. Hence the claim that the reinterpretation is mandatory, and that one's decoding has succeeded in singling out the one correct translation, had better be well substantiated.

In general, the claim that message A really meant A' can be defended by the following steps:

(1) A, taken literally, is too silly to have been intended, or to have been received with such respect.

(2) A' on the other hand, is important, plausible; it was *needed*.

[25] See below, p. 205.

Someone had to say something like A', for the formulation of A' played an important role, one which so to speak demanded to be fulfilled.

(3) A and A' are sufficiently similar, whether in the words employed for conveying them, or in structure, or suggestiveness, or all of these, for it to be plausible to claim that the manifest transmission of message A really, effectively, latently performed the service of disseminating A'.

Whether Marx's alleged deciphering of Hegel can satisfy such criteria, I know not. But the decoding of the Western epistemological tradition which is being offered here does, I think, satisfy the criteria offered.

DESCRIPTION INTO PRESCRIPTION

One striking feature of theories of knowledge is their extraordinary feebleness, if taken *literally,* as descriptive or, in particular, as explanatory accounts of knowledge. Take for instance the simplest and most celebrated theory of knowledge, empiricism; its picture of how we acquire and retain knowledge is inspired by an image of a kind of cognitive petty accumulation, the hoarding of petty savings which arrive as sensations or 'stimuli'. The idea that the exceedingly complex and at the same time very tightly organised world which we actually inhabit has been 'built up' in our minds by the hoarding of these grains of sensation, that the infinitely varied situations we can recognise are identified through analogy with previous and simpler situations, and that our concepts are but the after-taste of sensations—all this has very little plausibility. For one thing, as Kant and Durkheim stressed so much, this model simply cannot explain the rigid formal organisation of the world, the authority with which certain formal concepts and arrangements impose themselves on our vision and, it would seem, on the things envisaged. Empiricists might reply by suggesting, as Hume tried to do, that this inherent orderliness of the world is but an illusion, or an habituation of the mind which is in no way guaranteed by the nature of things. Perhaps so. The empiricists might also maintain that the apparent inability of their simple model to account for the complex world is deceptive, and arises from a failure to see how much can be achieved by the reiterated use of their one principle—the association of ideas through conjunction, and the reinforcement of that association through repetition. The principle itself, they may say, is simple, and laudably so, but its reiterated application may lead to very complex results.

In fact, the plausibility of such a view hinges largely on the failure to put this programme into practice. It is greatly to the credit of modern behaviourists, who have taken over the empiricist picture and translated it into third-person, experimental language, that they made a noble effort so to implement this programme. They failed. The failure of the model is fundamental, springs from its basic inadequacy for the purpose for which it was intended, and not merely from not allowing sufficiently for the numerous reiteration of the central operation on which it is based.

Perhaps the most celebrated of contemporary attack on this model is Noam Chomsky's review of B. F. Skinner's *Verbal Behaviour*.[26] Chomsky shows, conclusively to my mind, that the empiricist/behaviourist model does not even remotely account for the actual linguistic competence of human beings, and that the seemingly precise terms such as 'stimulus' and 'response' are used by it in a systematically ambiguous way: in experimental situations, they do have a precise meaning—but in this more rigorous application, there is very little real behaviour which is in fact explained. On the other hand, these terms are also used in a looser, analogical, metaphorical sense when they are extended to behaviour at large—but only at the price of then becoming vacuous and circular. Chomsky is eloquent about this:

A typical example of 'stimulus control' for Skinner would be the response to . . . a painting with the response *Dutch*. (Such) responses are asserted to be 'under the control of extremely subtle properties' of the physical object . . . Suppose instead of saying *Dutch* we had said *Clashes with the wallpaper, I thought you liked abstract work, Never saw it before* . . . or whatever else might come into our minds when looking at a picture . . . Skinner could only say that each of these responses is under the control of some other stimulus property of the physical object. If we look at a red chair and say *red*, it is under the control of the stimulus 'redness'; if we say *chair*, it is under the control of the collection of properties . . . 'chairness' . . . , and similarly for any other response. The device is as simple as it is empty. Since properties are free for the asking . . . we can account for a wide class of responses in terms of . . . 'controlling stimuli'. But the word 'stimulus' has lost all objectivity in this usage. Stimuli are no longer part of the outside physical world; they are driven back into the organism. We identify the stimulus when we hear the response.

And he goes on to observe:

It is clear from such examples . . . that the talk of 'stimulus control' simply disguises a complete retreat to mentalistic psychology.

This is indeed the crucial point. As we shall have occasion to observe, the trouble with behaviourism is not its spurious tough-minded shell but its genuine though camouflaged tender-minded core. Its explanations are vacuous and circular: the supposed events or elements which are credited with a crucial role in explaining behaviour, far from being independently observable, can only be identified, as Chomsky shows, through that very thing which is to be explained. Later on in the same article, Chomsky performs the same demolition job on 'reinforcement':

it can be seen that the notion of reinforcement has totally lost whatever objective meaning it may ever have had . . . The phrase 'X is reinforced by Y . . . ' is being used as a cover term for 'X wants Y', 'X likes Y', 'X wishes that Y were the case',

[26] Originally published in *Language* (1959), vol. 35, pp. 26–58, and re-published in various readers and collections.

etc. Invoking the term 'reinforcement' has no explanatory force, and any idea that this paraphrase introduces any new clarity or objectivity . . . is a serious delusion. The only effect is to obscure the important differences between the notions being paraphrased.

For purposes of the present argument, it is important to note that Chomsky's refutation of the applicability of this model to the acquisition of language, can easily be generalised to the acquisition of any complex kind of knowledge.

Nevertheless, it would be wrong to conclude that the behaviourist enterprise achieved nothing. Leaving aside any technical achievements concerning simpler forms of behaviour, where terms such as 'stimulus' were given a meaning genuinely independent of that which was to be explained, there remains another kind of achievement: the behaviourists did at least try, in some measure, to take the model used by associationist psychology and empiricist epistemology, and actually *make it work*. They may have satisfied themselves a little too easily and mistakenly that it did work, but at least they did try, thereby making it possible for others, such as Chomsky, to show that it did *not* work.

Now the differences between empiricist epistemology and many other kinds is that, on the whole, no one has tried systematically to do for other epistemologies what the behaviourists tried to do for empiricism.[27] It is not so much that empiricism is in some way specially vulnerable to the kind of criticism to which Chomsky subjected Skinner; it is rather, that very few thinkers have rendered other theories of knowledge similarly vulnerable, by making a reasonably sustained effort to use them as the base of a genuinely operationalised *explanatory* model. Were this done, it is most unlikely that those other theories of knowledge would fare any better.

By and large, philosophers of knowledge have not made any very determined efforts in this direction. Few have done for their own models of knowledge what, in effect, Skinner did for Hume. Theories of knowledge, when treated as explanatory models, as specifications of the actually operative underlying mechanism, are rather like those wooden toys for very small children, which are 'models' of steam engines, tractors, tanks, and so forth, but only in the most elementary sense: they simulate the most obvious external movements of the objects which they symbolise and resemble. They 'work' only if constantly propelled by the child's hands. The child's imagination generously thinks away the intrusive hands, and 'sees' a steam engine or a tank, just as Skinner tolerantly thinks away the logical gymnastics required to interpret complex behaviour in terms of the ubiquitous 'stimulus' and 'reinforcement'. But it won't do.

Nevertheless, it is very important to remember that empiricism, even as

[27] An interesting exception is what Durkheim did for Kant; this could be seen as a kind of sociologising of Kant's theory of knowledge, which thereby makes it ethnographically testable.

an explanatory model, must not be presumed to be inferior to the other theories of knowledge, simply because some of its followers at least had the seriousness which was required to try and make it work without the intrusion of the child's hands. Other philosophies often live and thrive in an ambience in which any such serious operationalisation would be frowned upon, as unsuitable intellectual occupation for gentlemen. They live in milieux in which nothing is really expected to work anyway, in which the conventions governing toddlers' wooden toys are *de rigueur*. Take that fashionable rival to the empiricist petty-accumulation model, namely the Hegelian view that the growth of knowledge proceeds by a kind in inner self-generated propulsion, through inner conflict and its resolution.

Now no one has done for Hegel what Skinner has endeavoured to do for Hume, to my knowledge.[28] There is no movement, standing in that relationship to absolute idealist epistemology, in which behaviourism stands to classical empiricism. Somehow, this would not be in the Hegelian style. Idealists do not soil their hands by trying to build precise and ambitious models of their own ideas. They are indeed as undemanding as toddlers. When they use their ideas for apparently explanatory purposes, as when the 'dialectic' is said to explain something or other, they easily think away the intrusive hands which really move the wooden toy. They are highly practised at this, and it really does not occur to them that higher standards of explanatory power could be possible or desirable.[29]

[28] The claim has been made that cybernetic models, with their 'feedback', have done it unwittingly.

[29] An interesting contemporary example of this state of mind is the late Mr George Lichtheim. In *Lukacs* (1970), for instance, he offers an interesting and self-exemplifying account of why some continental thinkers should wish to express their political or other anguish in Hegelian terminology. A characteristically obscure purple passage from Hegel's *Phenomenology of Mind* is commended (p. 33) as possessing 'unsurpassed force'. Yet later, when speaking of the Marxist materialist inversion of Hegelianism and of the 'primacy' of matter, he says: 'Such affirmations can be neither proved nor disproved. Their acceptance resolves itself into an act of . . . faith.'

This offhand dismissal of an issue which is central to the quarrel between Marxism and Hegelianism—something which itself is a major intellectual drama in Western history for Lichtheim—is deeply symptomatic. If truth is so arbitrarily chosen, and if you expect so little from explanations, you might as well admire, commend and use the 'Hegelian idea of a self-activating process inherent in the dialectical motion of spirit' (p. 30). Certainly, the type of explanation covered by this mouthful is even less genuinely predictive than the all-purpose, retro-adaptable stimulus-and-response jargon of a facile behaviourist. But those who use the Hegelian variant clearly never expected very much.

Hence authors of this kind have difficulty in understanding why Hegelianism is spurned in some quarters. It is not because some cultures are too 'philistine' (p. 23) to appreciate its profundities. It is because they have not yet quite despaired of possessing genuine explanations and some control over events.

But take a member of the allegedly philistine culture who, contrary to Lichtheim's expectations, admires rather than spurns Hegel—namely, Professor Michael Oakeshott. His doctrine appears to teach that there is an automatic cultural pilot called 'tradition', who communicates with old-established members of the tradition by a private line of

Often, as for instance in the Hegelian view that 'the owl of Minerva only flies at dusk' (i.e. understanding can only come after the event), they actually exclude the very idea of prediction and thus, indirectly, of testing. Where Skinner at least hides the vacuity of his explanations by the sliding-scale variations in the precision of meaning of his key terms (such unwitting hypocrisy being the compliment of cognitive vice to virtue), Hegelianism, brazenly taking pride in the sluggish habits of Minerva's owl, actually glories in it. Marxists do not improve on this aspect of Hegelianism. They merely replace the mystique of contemplation by a mystique of 'practice', the name for a most elusive but conspicuously uncheckable kind of validation of knowledge.

The general point here is that there is no *special* weakness in the operationalisation of the empiricist model of the growth of knowledge. It failed; but it did not fail where others succeeded, it only failed where the others refrained from trying.

Of course, we cannot be certain that the others would fail if they did try. But it seems overwhelmingly likely that they would; the physiological, psychological, social processes involved in our thought are far too complex to be captured by those simple models, those wooden toddlers' toys. Even (or perhaps especially) the human skin, sensibility, that paradigm of the empiricist, needs a most complex structure in order to achieve that amazingly high level of discriminating sensitivity which in fact we enjoy. The wax tablet was a most misleading model. The richness of our actual range of perceptions, our ability to retain, distinguish and so forth, is incomparably greater than, and different in kind from, that which can be assimilated to the imprint left on wax by a hard object.

But the most important point here is this. The failure—if this be granted—of such models as explanations, does not exclude their usefulness or validity as *norms,* as charters of cognitive practices. Perhaps they may constitute sound and cogent norms, well-founded principles governing the limits of cognitive comportment and propriety, even if they fail as specifications of the underlying mechanism of cognition. Something may be a good *touchstone,* even if it is not adequate as a theory of that which it selects. Being a criterion, a principle of selection, is not generally or necessarily the same thing as constituting a good (or any) explanatory model. Theories of knowledge may have been sound and invaluable in performing one of these functions even if they failed in the other, and even if the performance of one function was misread by many theories as the performance of the other.

'intimations', and whose counsels are much superior to those of merely book-trained navigators who either lack or fail to use that private line. Here clearly we have a theory concerning the social role of knowledge, however hazily sketched. But can one imagine any upholder of it trying to put it to the test, as Skinner and co. try to do for empiricism? The very idea sounds blasphemous. The whole tone of the theory excludes the very possibility of its own testing, as deeply incompatible with its dignity.

36

If we take into our hands any volume ... let us ask: Does it contain any abstract reasoning concerning quantity and number? No. Does it contain any experimental reasoning concerning matters of fact and existence? No. Commit it then to the flames: for it can contain nothing but sophistry and illusion.

David Hume

This celebrated passage is normally taken to be a piece of rhetoric. The injunction, the exhortation—these are taken to be but a literary device. Hume, contemporary philosophers like to say, was merely offering 'analyses', whatever they are, as they themselves claim to do.

Such an interpretation is totally mistaken. The declamatory style herê affected by Hume may indeed have been used in part for stylistic effect. But that is quite incidental. The truth of the matter is that in this passage, Hume came closest to an accurate assessment of the status of his own doctrine. Basically, that doctrine consists of a set of well-reasoned cultural injunctions, recommendations for the proper conduct of our intellectual life. These injunctions were not arbitrary ones; they were not lacking in well-argued support.

Hume himself was, of course, often given to supposing that the account of the human mind offered in the *Treatise* was itself a descriptive and an explanatory one, based on introspective observation. But it is not so, though a certain amount of introspection, and, much more significantly, abstract considerations concerning what *could* possibly be there and available for introspection, did help him reach his conclusions.[30] As an *explanatory* account of our capacities of storing, recognising, connecting, etc., items of information about this world, Hume's account suffers from all the defects of the behaviourist model (which is its intellectual descendent, anyway), and is open to the full force of Chomsky's critical comments. But the prescription cited above, and the reasons which underlie it, are not similarly vulnerable.

It is instructive to look at a passage which is often and rightly considered to be one of the modern equivalents of Hume's manifesto:

we are justified in concluding that all metaphysical assertions are nonsensical. The metaphysician ... does not intend to write nonsense. He lapses into it ... ... sentences which simply express moral judgments do not say anything.[31]

[30] For instance: among the most famous of Hume's conclusions are the exclusion of the causal nexus and of objective value. A careful inspection of his reasoning shows that these are not really excluded because—as Hume's own view of his method should lead one to expect—introspection fails to reveal the presence of a corresponding experience. Just suppose a kind of causal glue *were* experienced: what would guarantee its regular conjunction with the items either side of it? Or again, suppose we did introspect something called 'objective value'. Its power to attract or repel would still be a contingent matter of fact. So Hume's conclusions—which hinge on this contingency—would still hold, and are independent of what introspection happens to reveal.

[31] A. J. Ayer, *Language, Truth and Logic* (London, 1936), chapters I and VI.

Here, once again, convention favours a certain interpretation of these passages. It runs as follows: what is at issue here is 'nonsense' in some technical, high-powered, specialist sense. The realms of discourse which are so summarily deprived of any real significance, are only excluded from 'meaning' in a logician's sense. No harm was meant. No moralist or metaphysician need really take offence. Any resemblance between this high-powered technical meaning of 'nonsense', and plain nonsense, is largely accidental. The exuberance or provocativeness of the terminology was only due to the high spirits of the then *enfant terrible*. Ayer himself now appears to favour this interpretation, in as far as he tries to uphold the view that the logical 'analysis' of a kind of discourse, such as for instance of moral judgments, does not affect the standing of the assertions made within that species.[32]

Now this really is nonsense. (In plain English, not in some specialist sense.) For one thing, the amount of genuine technicality behind the reasoning which so castigated metaphysics and ethics was negligible. More important, the abusiveness, the implicit negative injunction, was entirely of the essence of the thing. It was not an accidental choice of phrase, attributable to pugnacious juvenile high spirits.

In the supposed 'technical' sense, the verification principle (of which the quoted passages were simple applications) says only this: assertions not testable in certain approved ways, are not testable in those approved ways. This is not a view one is inclined to contest.

If, however, the injunctive force, the persuasive appeal, are retained, whether in Hume's or in Ayer's version, we get something far from vacuous or trivial. We then have a couple of imperatives: be sensitive to whether or not assertions are testable (in the specified approved manner)! Spurn those which are not! Contrary to superficial appearances, the first of these two imperatives is far more radical, disruptive, and important than the second. Its implementation, even its partial implementation, involves a cultural revolution of staggering proportions. The second, though it sounds drastic, is fairly anodyne. It can only be implemented when the first has already done its work, by which time it makes little difference.

This injunctive interpretation of the verification principle incidentally removes a puzzle which used to haunt logical positivism (the doctrine which upheld the principle). The puzzle or difficulty ran as follows: what is the status of the verification principle itself? It recognises, roughly speaking, two and two only approved ways of testing, which alone can confer 'meaning' on assertions: verification by checking against definitions (or the logical consequences of definitions), and verification by checking against facts. Now is the principle itself a definition (or a consequence of definitions)? Were it so, what would stop us, or others, from choosing

[32] 'On the Analysis of Moral Judgments', pp. 231 *et seq.*, in A. J. Ayer, *Philosophical Essays* (London, 1954).

other, rival definitions? Or is it, on the contrary, factual? Neither Ayer nor any other member of the school was ever observed conducting surveys which established the correlation between 'meaning' and 'verifiability', and it is doubtful whether such surveys could be relevant. (What could be their independent criterion of a meaningful assertion? Anything that people treat as such? But we know that people violate the positivist prescription, so this would unfavourably prejudge the issue. Or would they use some philosophical criterion independent of what people say? This would be a blatantly circular procedure, prejudging the result in favour of whatever theory was built into that criterion.)

Clearly, the principle itself could fit into neither of the two categories which, by its own lights, exhausted the realm of meaning. Ayer tried to convince himself at times that it was itself the corollary of the definition of 'understanding' (what else could 'understanding an assertion' mean?), but this is blatantly circular at one remove, and it is very doubtful whether he carried much conviction even with himself.

By its own lights, the principle ought to have been trivial, simply explicating an obvious definition. But, whatever other defects it may have had, it was not trivial. On the contrary, it owed its own *succès de scandale*, its notorious capacity to produce *épatement*, precisely to the fact that it is anything but trivial. Its consequences are radical.

The solution of the puzzle is simple. Despite the amazing length and complexity of some of its later formulations, its technical content is negligible, its ideas being powerful, important, but very simple, and laudably so. The significant part of its content, however, is precisely its moral or injunctive component. It is this injunctive element which gives it its importance and its meaning, and which alone saves it from being either a trite tautology or a well-falsified generalisation. There is a certain piquancy about this: its correct interpretation consigns it to a category of discourse which, according to its own doctrine, lacks literal meaning. But it is so.

A WORLD 'PAR PROVISION'

Theories of knowledge are basically *normative*. This contention is a crucial step in the present argument. Hence it is important not to misunderstand it.

A certain theory (or cluster of theories) of normativeness is so well-diffused nowadays that there is a considerable danger that it will be automatically projected on to the view that anything is 'normative'. That well-diffused theory has come, I suspect, to be built into the common expression 'value judgment', which has come to imply not merely an evaluation, but an ultimately private and more or less subjective or arbitrary one.

Of the cluster of theories, 'emotivism', the view that moral evaluations or norms express emotions, is the one which is best known to the general public. Within academic philosophy, it is less fashionable. Academic philosophers, however, greatly overrate either the difference between it and the theories which have replaced it, or the importance of that difference. Doctrines such as 'prescriptivism', or the view that moral values express commands, or the existentialist variant to the effect that they express commitments, do not differ very significantly from it.

For the time being, it is important to stress that the 'emotive' theory—or the 'decision' theory, or any similar variant—must not be read into the view argued here that theories of knowledge are essentially normative. They *are* normative. But they are not expressions of feeling, and most certainly they do not record some free-floating emotion of approval which could, fancy free, attach itself to anything (for this is the model which the 'emotive theory' and its variants really insinuate).

The real and relevant objection to the emotive theory—and the reason why its projection on the present argument would completely distort it—is not, as is widely believed, that it is 'subjective', but ironically, quite the reverse; the theory is, in a naive and facile manner, *far* too objectivist.

The point is this: the model in terms of which the emotive or similar theories are articulated (such as 'prescription', to take a recent vogue), and which they presuppose, is that of a *given* world of discrete, isolable, recognisable objects—an environment, people, and their conduct and actions. The same is true of other supposedly 'subjectivist' theories, which similarly contrast something 'subjective' with a supposedly hard, given, objective world. This world is conceived as, so to speak, morally or evaluatively fumigated or colourless—it is roughly like the ordinary *Lebenswelt,* but neutral. The theory then wonders how moral colour can be restored to this world, to give it back its normal evaluative saturation, to overcome the moral anaemia, and it concludes that this reinfusion is achieved by feeling (or decision). Of course, many people find this step hard to bear, for it seems to make morality 'subjective' and relative (which indeed it does). The consequence is that notorious tension between deep moral conviction on one hand, and the emotive theory of ethics, which Russell reports with such candour,[33] and which Ayer mistakenly thinks, that he can overcome.[34] Ayer tries to demonstrate this by invoking the quite mistaken principle that an 'analysis' of a type of discourse does not affect the validity of assertions within that type. In fact, the 'analysis' of morality in terms of emotive expression, in conjunction with the principle that we have no right to treat seriously anything that is based merely on feeling and no reasons (and who is to forbid us to embrace that principle, whatever *its* 'analysis' in turn?), jointly have the most devastating implications for morality, as people quite rightly recognise. Ayer's

[33] 'Reply to Criticism', in *The Philosophy of Bertrand Russell,* ed. P. A. Schilpp (La Salle, 1944), p. 724.
[34] 'On the Analysis of Moral Judgments', in Ayer, *Philosophical Essays,* p. 231.

attempts to evade this conclusion have a deeply paradoxical air.

As indicated, the emotivist position is in one important sense far too objectivist—in that it makes itself a present of a given, objective world, which is *then* to be evaluated (or within which, alternatives are to be evaluated). The picture is of evaluation floating over objects, as the Holy Spirit moved on the waters, ready to settle down where it chooses. These evaluations seem so free ... The puzzle then is—why are moral feelings so very strong, so very firmly welded to their objects, to the point of desperation ... A moral philosopher of this kind can only shrug his shoulders and say that this is a psychological or sociological question which is not his concern. But, in fact, the main reason is not far to seek, and does not require specific psychological or sociological premises. The reason why the idea of moral approval detached in its essence from its objects, sounds so very paradoxical, is precisely this: fundamental moral approval is constitutive of this, that or the other conceptualisation (in effect—construction) of the world, and thus is welded to the objects it has constructed. This is why the idea of very basic (logically pure) approval or disapproval is so very paradoxical—why, in plainer English, moral feelings are so strong, and have such a limpet-like attachment to their objects. The emotive theory is paradoxical not so much because of the emotion it refers to, but because of the implied contrast with the supposedly contingent objects of that emotion. It sees those objects as *already* given and available.

But this is not the level at which serious moral or epistemic crises arise, and this is not the level at which significant moral or epistemological theorising arises. Most certainly, the theory of knowledge, which is our present concern, does not and cannot arise at this level. If you are already in possession of a 'given' world, with isolable, identifiable objects such as people, physical environment, and actions, then quite clearly you have *already* solved, or prejudged, any issue in the theory of knowledge. You already know the world, you possess a world-home and an identity. You must be envied, and congratulated on your lucidity or your complacency; a man with his feet so firmly on the ground, a man with such a secure conception of his own feet and of the ground, should go far. But not in the theory of knowledge, where he has altogether missed the point.

Philosophically interesting moral problems do not concern points of detail. *Within* an accepted way of life, moral issues do not differ so very much from questions of etiquette. They can be resolved by appeal to a shared principle, or by convention as to which principle is to apply in a given new case. (Emotion, if present at all, is present quite contingently. Casuists and lawyers may present their cases with icy calm.) And all this is also true concerning disputes about knowledge, when these occur within a wider, agreed cognitive ethic, so to speak. The merits of specific cognitive strategies need not give rise to very deep or disturbing questions, when they occur only within basic and accepted criteria of truth,

41

intelligibility, or explanation.

But epistemology is precisely about these basic criteria or principles. Hence it cannot make itself a present of a 'given', determinate world. Its questions arise when such worlds have been dissolved around us, or have been placed in a kind of deliberate suspension, *sursis,* when our moral identities have similarly dissolved or found themselves 'bracketed', when we no longer firmly identify with any criteria of validity. The self and the ultimate criteria of validity are correlative; the suspension of one implies the suspension of the other. Of course, we continue to act in terms of the identities, criteria, worlds, which we have inherited from the past, for we must needs act in terms of something—but they all acquire a kind of interim character, for they are themselves *sub judice.* We retain them not because we have confidence in their validity but on sufferance, as an interim measure. Descartes describes this well:

ce n'est pas assez, avant de commencer à rebâtir la logie où on demeure, que de l'abattre ... mais qu'il faut aussi s'être pourvu de quelque autre, où on puisse être logé ... pendant le temps qu'on y travaillera; ainsi, afin que je ne demeurasse point irrésolu en mes actions pendant que la raison m'obligerait de l'être dans mes jugements ... je me formai une morale par provision ...[35]

Some two centuries later, the *morale par provision* was beginning to turn sour. It is plainly envious, bitterly envious, of those who possess unconditional identities:

With people who know how to revenge themselves and to stand up for themselves in general, how is it done? Why, when they are possessed, let us say, by the feeling of revenge, then for the time there is nothing else but that feeling left in their whole being. Such a gentleman simply dashes straight for his object like an infuriated bull ...

Well, such a direct person I regard as the real moral man ... he is stupid ... the antithesis of the normal man ... the man of acute consciousness ... is sometimes so nonplussed in the presence of his antithesis that with all his exaggerated consciousness he genuinely thinks of himself as a mouse and not a man. It may be an acutely conscious mouse, yet it is a mouse ... Now let us look at the mouse in action. Let us suppose, for instance, that it feels insulted, too (and it almost always does feel insulted) ... Apart from the one fundamental nastiness the luckless mouse succeeds in creating round it so many other nastinesses in the form of doubts and questions, adds to the one question so many unsettled questions that there inevitably works up around it ... a stinking mess, made up of its doubts, emotions, and of the contempt spat upon it by the direct men of action who stand solemnly about it as judges ... laughing at it till their healthy sides ache.

Fyodor Dostoevsky, *Notes from Underground*

Living with doubts has its perils, and they could not be insulated as neatly and securely as Descartes hoped. Moreover, he seemed to suppose that the day would come when, once again, we should have a *morale* other than *par provision.* Let that illusion pass, and also the morally corrosive

[35] Descartes, *Discours de la Méthode,* Troisième Partie.

aspect of the matter, which Dostoevsky expresses with such eloquence. What does concern us here is that the suspension, the attribution of a *par provision* status, till the doubts be dissolved, is inherent in this method, not merely for *morale* in the narrower and literal sense, but also, and especially, for the ethic of cognition, for the authority of the procedures we adopt for deciding just which world it is that we happen to inhabit.

In this kind of state of dissolution, with but a *sursis,* suspended kind of identity and world, it makes little sense to say that we choose our values by means of 'feeling' or an act of 'commitment'. Little illumination is obtained by saying that our moral judgments 'prescribe', even if in a sense this is true. It all makes little sense, in as far as these manners of speaking suggest a clear, given identity and world, with a given, understood gamut of feelings (or capacity to prescribe or choose), which then range over a well-defined range of alternatives in the objective world. But all this is precisely what we do not have. Our predicament is not of so simple a kind. The emotivist, and his intellectual brothers-under-the-skin, have set themselves too easy a task, and tacitly assumed that the task is to be performed in too stable, too well-defined, too well-lit a world.

In a sense, subjectivism must go much further than the 'emotive' theory and its variants ever went. The basic choices—call it 'commitment' if you wish—take place in a context in which there is far less to grasp than the emotivist or prescriptivist naively suppose. I do not mean that philosophic thought is carried out in a kind of fever; it is not the emotional state of the thinker which is at issue. What is at issue is the terms of reference he allows himself. These terms require that the thinker allows for the dissolution of his world, and makes only tentative, ironic, interim use of anything drawn from it. Epistemology tries to ex-cogitate convincing norms under such terms of reference. How do we find out which world we are in, presupposing none?

Thus talk of validation by emotion (and its variants) is objectionable not because of its overt stress on the ultimacy and subjectivity of the decisive feeling (or whatever), but because of its covertly uncritical assumption of a hard, well-delineated world within which this moral judgment of Paris is to operate. To which set of values shall we grant the apple? We have only our feelings to consult, they tell us. So personal identity, the conceptual tools for identifying the objects of those supposed emotions, the nature and significance of those emotions themselves—all this is, absurdly, taken as given and read.

But there is no excuse whatever for such an uncritical complacency. If we must in the end accept the ultimate arbitrariness of our norms, in virtue of the argument from regress, then perhaps we must. The problem of the regress of validation possibly has no formal solution. But it must not be confused—as it often is—with a quite different point, the absurd picture inspired by the 'emotive' theory and its later variants and successors, the myth of hard, identifiable objects and options, amongst which our free-floating feelings of approval (a decision, commitments, etc.) flit about, flirtatiously or not, according to taste, and select the objects which are to be honoured by their favour. This is not how we think nor how we conceivably could or should think. Nor are we constrained to think in this way by lack of any alternatives. ('What else?' is the most persuasive argument behind this position.) But, in fact, this is precisely the option we do *not* have.

There is perhaps no escaping the argument from regress. If our foundations are well founded they are not ultimate (and we 'really' have some others), and if they are not well founded they would seem arbitrary. But the force of this argument, which springs from the fact that fundamental norms are *fundamental*, and not at all from the fact that they are *norms*, should not be confused, as so often it is, with the quite mistaken view that norms are inherently matters of emotion. This conclusion (and its variants, to the effect that they are 'only' decisions, prescriptions, and so on) was in any case only reached by a mistaken argument from elimination ('what else could they be?').

In socially and conceptually stable contexts, moral language is in fact descriptive as well as prescriptive—it transmits the positive, identified content which has already been selected for commendation by the society and language in question. (It is not suggested that societies and languages are unambiguous in their commendations.) The idea of a 'pure' approval is a sophisticated one, presupposing a thinker who has already 'suspended' the values and ideas incapsulated in his language or the thinking of his society, who does not automatically endorse them. Modern academic moral philosophy has seized this idea, but its sophistication is very partial and confused. For one thing, it is quite wrong to suppose that this pure notion is in any way an account of the ordinary, daily use of 'moral terms'. (These are in fact saturated with descriptive content.) Secondly, occasion for the use of such pure, detached evaluation only arises when the 'descriptive' world has also been suspended—whereas these moralists talk, as we have stressed, as if this free-floating moral evaluation had been made a present of a clearly identified, delineated world. They were not subjectivist enough—for the most important moral issues are prejudged by the time we identify *objects*.

A real historical situation has imposed a certain task on thought. We do *not* know just which world we inhabit. Diverse faiths and visions claim to tell us. Their confidence, motives and logic are suspect. Others tell us, as unconvincingly, that there is nothing to worry about, that we can continue to feel at home in our ideas. But as we have good reasons for distrusting these various prophets, we must try and determine just which world we really are in, without presupposing any one of them.

It is in this sense that thought was perforce normative. The identification of sound reasoning will tell us what to trust and hence where we are. It is difficult to characterise these terms of reference positively.

J. S. Mill did it in part negatively, in part psychologistically:

It is evident that this cannot be proof in the ordinary or popular meaning of the term. Questions of ultimate ends are not amenable to direct proof . . . We are not, however, to infer that its acceptance or rejection must depend on blind impulse, or arbitrary choice . . . Considerations may be presented capable of determining the intellect either to give or to withhold its assent . . .[36]

It is the central purpose of the present argument to explore just what considerations are available 'capable of determining the intellect to give or to withhold its assent'.

[36] J. S. Mill, *Utilitarianism*, chapter I.

3 All-too-benign judges

Thus the theory of knowledge is concerned with cognitive legitimacy. It is faced with the task of telling us what kinds of cognitive claims are valid and why, *and* of doing this without circularity or an infinite regress. Without prejudice to the question on as to what kind of world we live in, it is to tell us what kinds of knowledge are possible or valid, so that we can *then* find out what kind of world we do live in. The claims it makes must endeavour to be, so to speak, prior to any specific information about the world. They must be made in abstraction from our specific convictions, in a state of artificial suspension of reality.

It is probably impossible to carry out this task rigorously. This is not merely a question of the endless regress of premises. Rigour requires procedures; procedures need to be governed by rules, and the articulation of rules presupposes the concepts and background used for formulating them. But whilst the exercise cannot be performed both rigorously and without circularity, it can be carried out with at least a diminution of the circularity and question-beggingness, and without abandoning rigour altogether. In any case, we cannot but try. There seem to be certain final anchorages, which can terminate the regress, which provide justification for this or that vantage-point, and which possess some inherent claim to our cognitive loyalty. Philosophy, for what it is worth, is the formulation and examination of these anchor points, these ultimate base-lines.

In the philosophy of the past three centuries, there are two main types of such foundation stones. One class consists of what might be called the re-endorsement theories. The other class is that of selector theories. This is the fundamental division, the big divide, within modern philosophy. The great period of selector theories are the seventeenth and eighteenth centuries. The great age of re-endorsement theories is the nineteenth century.

The styles of those two types are quite different. Re-endorsement theories are those which, after profound reflection, reach the conclusion that all is well with existing bank of beliefs, or at least with a substantial part of it, simply in virtue of it *being* the existing bank of beliefs. They act like a commission of inquiry into some suspect establishment, which ends by clearing its name and declaring the suspicions which had caused the inquiry to be in substance unfounded. As their name implies, they re-endorse existing beliefs; they re-endorse the bulk of them, perhaps with a few minor exceptions—but above all, they endorse them *qua* current beliefs, not in virtue of satisfying some unique criterion imposed from outside. They claim to have found some reasons for supposing that current beliefs, simply in virtue of being part of the existing bank of ideas, are sound. No *outside* endorsement is required, they claim.

By contrast, selector theories set up some *criterion,* some touchstone or sifter, which is to sort out the cognitive sheep from the goats. It is of the essence of this approach that the principle of selection claims to be independent of the current and local set of beliefs, to stand outside them and to be endowed with an authority external to that set. Even if it so happens that the operation of a given selector is benign, and re-endorses the majority of current beliefs, they are being re-admitted not *qua* current beliefs, but in virtue of satisfying this independent criterion which thereby, in a way, assumes sovereignty.

The really important difference between the two species is not the nature of the conclusion, but the manner in which it is reached. The conclusions may even on occasion resemble each other. A re-endorsement theory re-endorses in virtue of an argument purporting to show that traditions, social systems, belief systems, are basically healthy; a selector theory re-endorses, if it re-endorses at all, in virtue of the fact that some tradition, some set of beliefs, happens to satisfy an *independent,* external criterion, which is thus cognitively sovereign.

A simple specimen of a re-endorsement philosophy would be, for instance, an argument invoking natural selection. It could run as follows: beliefs only survive if true. Hence the bulk of time-tested beliefs of any society must be correct. Hence it is wrong to be doubtful of the whole bulk of local convictions. All in all, we know that they must be sound.

By contrast, an example of a selector theory would be this: beliefs are sound in so far as they are arrived at by the methods of natural science, which consist of (let us say) accurate observation, and the acceptance of theories only if well-supported by such observation. Then, the philosopher might go on to note that an important proportion of the beliefs of a given society does, or does not, satisfy this criterion. Whether endorsing them or not, the criterion itself remains independent.

WHEN IN ROME

There are three important sub-species *within* re-endorsement philosophy: (a) Relativism, (b) Evolutionism, (c) Negative Re-endorsement.

Relativism is interesting at least in that it takes what others consider to be a problem, and uses it as a solution. The problem: truth is different on the other side of the Pyrenees—so how can it be truth? The relativist turns this upside down: for him it is not so much a problem, but rather a solution. Truth *is* that which is locally believed: it is tied to locality, time, space or culture, as are dress, manners or cookery. There is no 'correct' way of greeting a guest, performing a dance, or preparing a dish—though there are correct ways of doing these things, in given, specified societies. And what is true of greetings, dances or sauces is also true, in the end, of morality, mathematics, theology, or physics ... David Hume commended the Delphic reply to the question as to what rites or worship were most acceptable to the gods: in each city, the rites of that city.

This is the substance of the relativist position. The idea of an unique truth transcending the boundaries of all cities, whether or not it is recognised, waiting to be discovered, and providing a standard for the varieties of error—all this it takes to be an illusion. Relativism may indeed be welcomed as a liberation, as a charter of toleration. It was clearly this aspect of it which appealed to Hume, who contrasted the tolerance of the traditional faiths of classical antiquity with the intolerance of scriptural religion and its exclusive claims.

But the permissiveness of relativism is suspect. Genuine toleration does not say that everything and anything may be true somewhere; it merely says that only arguments, rather than force or pressure of any kind, may be used in persuasion. It distinguishes between social toleration, which is the abstention from the use of a-logical pressures, and logical toleration, which is merely the abandonment of reason. Relativism is tolerant logically, alas. Relativism may also be tolerant socially, but it need not be so, and sometimes fails to be socially tolerant. *Cuius regio, eius veritas* comes naturally to it: if nothing is really, universally true, who are you to defy local custom or the local authorities?

There are of course endless varieties of relativism, differing in the manner in which they reach their conclusion, in the area of life to which they are held to be applicable, in the way they define (if indeed they do define) the 'cities', the units, in terms of which they are articulated, and the manner in which they try to evade the well-known paradox resulting from the application of relativism to itself. (If all truth is relative, is this contention itself valid only in some delimited region?) We are not concerned, of course, with what might be described as mere sociological relativism, the doctrine which says that in fact convictions vary with the milieux in which they occur. What concerns us is normative relativism, which adds or implies that this is rightly so, that truth can be no other thing than that which satisfies some local criteria, and that there are no universal, independent criteria by which a confrontation between local ones could be judged.

We restrict ourselves to this kind of normative relativism not merely because it is interesting and relevant, but also because it is remarkably easy to refute. It is normative: it is a recommendation. It contains or is a recipe for how to overcome our cognitive predicament. The recipe is, roughly—when in Rome, do (and above all, think) as the Romans do.

This recommendation or injunction can be refuted because it can be shown to be void of content. It is a pseudo-injunction: it sounds as if it were enjoining a course of conduct or thought, when in fact it does nothing of the kind. It is strictly comparable to an unhinged roadsign, which is no longer firmly fixed so as to point in some one determinate direction, but which, now quite unattached, points in any and every direction, according to where we choose to push it. No sane man would follow such an unhinged signpost and no sane man should suppose that he can derive guidance from relativism.

The reason for this is simple. In the world as it now is, there simply are no 'Romans' and no 'Rome', whom we could emulate in conduct or in belief. When the Delphic oracle gave the advice which later so aroused David Hume's Augustan admiration, the Hellenic world consisted, for all practical purposes, of reasonably identifiable 'cities'. No doubt a sophist, if he wished, might have found troublesome borderline cases; but in practice, if a Greek was told to observe the custom of his city, he knew what he was being told to do. An inhabitant of our modern world, when given the same advice, quite literally has no idea—no concrete idea—of what is commended. What is 'Rome'? The upper class of the contemporary municipality of that name? Central Italy? The Common Market? Catholic Europe? Countless boundaries, geographic and social, vertical and horizontal, criss-cross each other in a rapidly changing world. Relativism is not so much a doctrine as an affectation. That signpost happens to point nowhere, or everywhere.

To work as a recipe, relativism requires the existence of identifiable 'cities', i.e. units in terms of which the alleged relativity is to work. The extreme case of such possible units would be single individuals, or even moods of individuals, if truth were to be defined as relative to individuals or to moments in their lives. But it is an essential feature of our current situation that there are no such 'cities' inscribed into the nature of things, and even individuals possess no *given* identities. If your problem is, precisely, the location or erection of your city, or the selection of your self or the adoption of a mood, then a recipe which presupposes that these are *already* given, is worthless.

In this sense, the refutation of relativism is conclusive and final. This refutation must not be confused with the widespread view that relativism is emotionally untenable, because we wish our own faith and morals to be absolute. This may or may not be so. We may perhaps learn to live without the absolute. Nor must it be confused with the view that relativism is self-contradictory, because it makes an exception on its own behalf and treats itself as in a non-relative manner. This is indeed so, but ought not to carry too much weight: making an exception on one's own behalf, having difficulty in accounting for oneself, is the professional ailment of philosophies, and is virtually written into the terms of reference under which they work. No: this refutation is simpler, and hinges only on the fact that the recipe is empty. It is like the injunction 'meet me at the town entrance', when the town has countless entrances, or none.

Nevertheless, relativism enjoys a mild revival, and certain formulations of it are quite fashionable in philosophy. How is this possible? Only because those who propound it, content themselves with formulating it in an abstract manner, which refrains from naming, locating, identifying the 'cities' whose customs, lores, faiths we are advised to emulate. 'Forms of life', we are told, carry their own norms of what is real and unreal, and these are sufficient unto them; or 'traditions' carry their own salvations within themselves, and none are to be sought outside them; and so on. But no forms of life are named, and traditions are only hazily indicated. Given that our problem arose precisely from the collisions, total disintegrations, erosions and fissions of these alleged units, the advice to return to them not only quite misses the point of our predicaments but also corresponds to no possible, available course of conduct or of thought. Even if relativism remained unrefuted in some other sense, nonetheless as a recipe it is empty and worthless.

THE GREAT ASCENT

Evolutionism is the other type of solution which attempts to exploit the fact of diversity to attain a reassuring re-endorsement, rather than allowing it to undermine our intellectual confidence. There is indeed diversity, says the evolutionist; but the diversified belief systems fall into a pattern which also points to the solution. The diversity on this view is not without an underlying principle: the various systems do not vary at random or without order. Some of them are more complex, more developed, richer variants of others, and the 'more developed' contain all the features, or at least all the positive features, of the 'less developed' ones, whilst possessing some additional merits of their own. In the end, they all arrange themselves in a grand series, in a kind of order of merit, and jointly point in the direction of perfection and of legitimate belief.

The perceptive critic of this position will quickly note that the arrangement of the various diversified systems in an order of merit is itself, in a covert (and hardly even very covert) way, the smuggling in of an absolute position—whose legitimacy would need to be justified in some manner. To arrange a number of objects, of any kind, in order of merit, is tacitly to enthrone the end-point of that series (which may actually be exemplified by the final member of the series—or it may not, being simply pointed-at by 'the way the series is going'). The evolutionist's defence—or, at any rate, his belief—is that this criterion is not smuggled in from the outside, but that it somehow spontaneously emanates from the diversified objects had been arranged in serial order. Emotionally and genetically, he is quite right; that is certainly how it feels to him (all too obviously), and that is how the terminal ideal, so to speak, has been elicited; we can often hold an ideal, a norm, in a tacit way, remain unaware of it, and only

50

realise that we do hold it at all, and what its features are, if we arrange objects according to their degree of approximation to it. In this sense, the series comes first, and the recognition of the ideal which inspires the ordering of the series comes after. But logically, the evolutionist is quite wrong; it would have been quite possible to arrange the objects in some other order, along a series generated by some other principle, and that other principle—generally, an infinite number of rival principles is available—could equally claim to 'emanate' from the material. We can only single out *one* of the possible principles as *the* evolutionary norm by tacitly smuggling it in as a premiss; and it always really is a premiss, never a conclusion. Paraphrasing a remark which philosophers like to make about values—the conclusions of an argument can only contain such evolutionist contentions as were already contained in the premisses.

Though evolutionism is much richer, more sophisticated and stimulating than mere relativism, it is not at present enjoying any kind of a vogue, at least in formal academic thought. One suspects that it is still very much present in the undergrowth of informally diffused beliefs. But it dominated the nineteenth century. Where relativism appeals to a kind of muddled cultural egalitarianism—all outlooks, all moralities are equal—evolution tends to offend current sensibility by its tendency to rank cultures in order of merit, and it seems tainted by association with racialism, colonialism and imperialism. It was once much given to awarding good conduct marks to societies which were 'more evolved', and thus it helped to ratify their domination over others. Moreover, to its credit, evolutionism cannot quite so easily be upheld in such an abstract manner as would enable it to refrain from identifying the units which it grades and ranks. So it cannot easily be maintained in a way which would allow its difficulties to be ignored or obscured, as is the case with contemporary relativism. But, though not all the reasons for the unpopularity of evolutionism are equally sound, it is as well to have it out of the way. It offers no real solution.

Cyclical theories of history constitute a kind of bastard species, a cross between relativism and evolutionism: cycles as a whole are treated in the manner of the relativist, whilst various positions within the individual cycles are treated somewhat in the manner of the evolutionists—each position being accorded a kind of temporary validity, as long as it makes its contribution to the movement as a whole and allows itself to be displaced by its successor.

It is of course not at all surprising that there is a natural affinity between re-endorsement theories and sociology, and there is perhaps something of a natural antipathy between sociology and selector theories. Selectors are socially blind. Their criterion of cognitive validity is, and is meant to be, formulated quite independently of the specific characteristics of any society, and hence of the particular societies to which it is to be applied. (That, indeed, is its point; it is to judge, select, discriminate, not to

51

re-endorse through some inherent favourable bias.) By contrast, the re-endorsers can be, and are meant to be, sensitive and considerate to the societies to which their ideas are applied. They do not re-endorse everything for all places. They endorse in local terms, the right belief at the right time in the right place, Roman practices in Rome. The right time and place can only be singled out by reference to the social structure with which the belief or practice is placed. Thus a sociological sensitivity is in principle mandatory for re-endorsers (even though contemporary relativists with their stratospheric vantage point manage to have very little of it), and on the whole it is not surprising that re-endorsement philosophies and sociology flourish at the same time. Each is often a reaction to excessively radical reform, whether of our conceptual, or of our political economy—radical reforms often inspired by selector-type idea of a wholly new starting-point, of making a bonfire of old rubbish, of reconstructing everything on sound and independently arrived at principles. Selectors try to sweep clean with a new broom, whereas re-endorsers respect continuity. Thus it is obvious why re-endorsement and sociology, each with a strong sense of the strength of custom and the powerful forces which underpin continuity, should often stand together. The links between sociology and selector procedures are less obvious, but equally important. The sources of radical breaks may on occasion be as deep as those of continuity. Deep discontinuities and extraneous norms may be the most important features of our society.

CARTE BLANCHE

Negative re-endorsement, like the positive variety, confers an unselective blessing on the totality or near-totality of some cultural bank of beliefs. It does not, as selectors do, scrutinise them one by one to see whether they satisfy some independent criterion. It re-endorses them, it blesses them, in virtue of being part of the cultural intellectual tradition; but the argument which gives it licence to do so is a negative one. What defines it is that it invokes, to justify this practice, an argument which claims to show that once some crucial kind of pervasive error has been neutralised, the residue is *ipso facto* sound. It is the elimination of *the* central error which is crucial; error has some single big source. Negative re-endorsement says, or more characteristically implies, that after the ovecoming of the one big error, after the slaying of *the* dragon, there is no problem. The soundness, the self-authenticating quality of the bulk of our beliefs is not so much argued positively, as in the case of positive re-endorsement, but left to stand as a corollary of the doctrine of the single or main source of error.

As an example, take the doctrine that error is the by-product of unconsciously willed self-deception: if then you know yourself, by the one available really effective technique for acquiring self-knowledge, truth will become your birthright; for once you know yourself truly, and know how to overcome the distortions brought into your thought by unconsciously self-imposed distortions, the residue of what you perceive is both unproblematical and true. *This* is the effective epistemology underlying psycho-analytical practice. The theory actually comes to be spelt out when one of the few philosophically sophisticated expositors of this position comes to grapple with the question of whether psycho-analytic ideas are falsifiable and scientific.[37] He tries to show that they *are* falsifiable, but in effect only succeeds in describing, not criteria of testing, but the doctrine that the psycho-analyst is indeed fallible, because he sometimes allows his judgment to be unconsciously misled. But once he sees into his heart, he no longer does so, apparently. Made explicit, this amounts to the characteristic negative re-endorsement doctrine that truth in itself is unproblematical and easily available—the problem is to overcome some interfering distortion. Negative re-endorsement theories then specify what this distortion is and how it is to be overcome.

Or again: error and subjectivity are the by-products of class interests. Once you are free of these, by some self-liberation or thanks to the abolition of classes, truth will be easily available and require no institutional under-pinning.

Or again: philosophic error is the result of the bewitchment by language. Once you are free of this, by realising, for instance, that language is used in a wide variety of ways and that there is no one single underlying pattern in which words are related to things, you are free to see the unproblematical truth.

Or again: error springs from the yearning for *doctrine* and the mistaken supposition that doctrine could be more authoritative than customary, 'practical' behaviour, whereas in reality it is but a simplified and distorted echo of that customary practice. If you but see this and liberate yourself from the one error, you will be heir to as much truth, at any rate, as your rank and residence qualifications within a given 'tradition' allow.

And so forth. What these approaches have in common is that they evade the requirement of a positive specification of truth, and pass the buck, with a more or less elaborate justificatory theory for so doing. They may naively claim that once the scales have fallen off our eyes, truth is there, ready to give herself; or they may be more guarded, and merely promise that no persistent, deep obstacles will then remain; or the buck-passing may be complex, and they may merely say that the positive specification of difficult truths must be left to some other kind of agency, for which they themselves take no responsibility, at least in their professional philosophical role. This, of course, is the crucial step; it is not the feeble and modest-sounding meta-theory, explaining why truth is not their province, which really matters; it is the direction in which the buck is passed that counts. The meta-theory is just so much conjuror's patter.

[37] Cf. R. E. Money-Kyrle, *Man's Picture of His World* (New York, 1961), chapter 1.

Better watch carefully for the direction in which your query is being passed on, in a seemingly disinterested manner. On such buck-passing, it is well worth quoting R. G. Collingwood:[38]

At the moment, I am not concerned with the sophisms underlying this programme, but with its consequences. The pupils, whether or not they expected a philosophy that would give them . . . ideals . . . and principles, did not get it; and were told that no philosopher (except of course a bogus philosopher) would even try to give it. The inference which any pupil could draw for himself was that for guidance . . . since one must not seek it from thinkers or thinking, . . . one must look to people who were not thinkers (but fools), to processes that were not thinking (but passion) . . .

This is no mere rhetoric. Collingwood is right. When a thinker falls all over you and himself in his eagerness to tell you how modest he is, do not pay too much heed to his breathless account of his modesty, his awareness of the limitations of human thought. That is all very well, though he protests too much. But it is important to watch very carefully to see just where and when and how he consigns those questions which he so loudly proclaims to be beyond his and our powers. *That* is the crux. The propaganda of modesty is conjuror's patter. It is generally the rather surreptitious identification of the residuary legatees of the proscribed issues, which is what really matters.

Negative re-endorsement is academically far more fashionable than evolutionism, which has a rather nineteenth-century ring, or relativism, with which however it can be fused, and is indeed fused in the case of at least one very fashionable contemporary style of thought. That particular argument runs: because every language/culture carries its own distinction between that which is real and that which is not, and because no culture may rightly be judged by the norms of another, it follows that each and every culture is quite in order and that we may and must, *qua* philosophers, endorse its beliefs, at least for its members. Philosophers, do not usurp the role of judges of cultures and their faiths. No questions are here asked about the fate and destiny of the culturally *déracinés*, notwithstanding the fact that in our time they may be more typical and numerous than those secure within the norms of some cultural island. This is a specimen of re-endorsement philosophy at its most blatant.

The ideological charms of negative re-endorsement are very considerable and help to account for its popularity. He who has convinced himself that it is permissible, may pose as both modest and liberal: *he* makes no claim, he proudly says, to tell you about either the nature of things or of the good life. He leaves it to you, or to qualified authority, according to variant, and contents himself with eliminating certain obstacles, certain logical or other hindrances to clear vision and the good life, which would otherwise obstruct your vision and restrict your

[38] R. G. Collingwood, *An Autobiography* (Pelican edition, 1939), pp. 36 and 37.

54

freedom. In addition, he has elaborated rules of intellectual decorum which rule out any argument which shows that covertly, by the very way he passes the buck and the direction in which he passes it, he really prejudges everything and is neither modest nor liberal. These rules complete the system and make it quite watertight.

Furthermore, as the negative re-endorsement possesses no overt, visible positive view, this has the great advantage that its substantive views, not being articulated, are not open to criticism. The task it sets itself is thus incomparably easier than that of systems of thought which remain squarely in the open.

Re-endorsers of all these kinds are judges, sitting in judgment on our cognitive inheritance. But they are, on the whole, very benign judges, as their name implies, though often also extremely silly ones. The verdict is, all in all, favourable. But their blessing is cheap, and their comfort shallow. Selectors are not so kind, and deserve separate treatment.

4 Hanging judges

In modern times, three important cognitive selection procedures can be observed:

(1) *Empiricism.* A claim to knowledge is legitimate only if it can be justified in terms of experience.

(2) *Materialism* (alias mechanism, or structuralism, with other possible variant names). A claim to knowledge is legitimate only if it is a specification of a publicly reproducible structure.

(3) *Logical form.* A claim to knowledge is legitimate only if it exemplifies a certain privileged logical form.

Each of the three criteria has here been formulated in a crude and rough manner, with a view to conveying the underlying idea, rather than precise formulation. Hence it might be unwise to base any sustained or meticulous argument on this particular set of definitions.

There is a very important difference between types 1 and 2 on the one hand, and type 3 on the other. Type 3 is a philosopher's philosophy; it is familiar and indeed very important within the world of professional and academic philosophy, and its great importance within that world makes it desirable to give it some consideration. But it is much less important—perhaps not important at all—in the wider intellectual life of the community. Non-specialists, even well-educated ones, are unlikely to be familiar with it: if they know of it at all, they know it as a doctrine or approach which some specialists have adopted, but one which they do not themselves internalise as part of their own intellectual equipment. They do not live with it, or think in terms of it.

By contrast, types 1 and 2 are parts of the common and widely shared intellectual heritage. They are not merely the possession of philosophers, they are the possession of everyone. It is virtually impossible to live in the modern world without encountering and in considerable measure internalising these ideas. (This does not mean that they are necessarily adopted, or if adopted, applied consistently.) Not merely the educated, bookreading public, but virtually everyone, has encountered the ideas—appeal to experience, or appeal to mechanism—which provide these theories with their crucial selection touchstones. People may reject these ideas, or accept them only with qualification, and apply them only selectively—but they are familiar with them, even when they cannot name them, and thus they constitute an extremely important part of the general intellectual climate.

For brevity, it is desirable to give these selector types simple names. The names chosen have certain associations which are, on the whole, suggestive and illuminating.

The empiricist picture can usefully be called the ghost or the bundle theory. The names highlight the following important considerations: empiricism insists on experience, as sufficient and exhaustive. Nothing else exists for it really. This reduces man to the totality of his experience, and the world to the totality of all experience. Substantiality, materials, hard permanence, all evaporate. Matter notoriously becomes the permanent possibility of sensation. Man thus becomes a kind of insubstantial ghost. Non-ghostly materials are treated as conceptual fictions, convenient but without ultimate status.

Experience can also be broken up into parts, generally identified with sensations. Man then becomes, in the famous phrase, a bundle of sensations. Thus *ghost* and *bundle* do convey, in a suggestive, lively and relevant way, the key picture underlying, or generated by, this view of things.

The appropriateness of the term machine, its fitness to be the name of the materialistic–mechanistic criterion of genuine knowledge, is even more obvious. Materialism–mechanism maintains that the world is composed of machines, some too small to be visible, and all of them made up roughly on the same principles, whatever they be, as those which men rely on for the construction and maintenance of sewing machines, typewriters, steam engines and so forth.

Could men anatomise nature, according to the most probable, or at least the most intelligible philosophy, they would find, that... causes are nothing but the particular fabric and structure of the minute parts of their own bodies and of external objects; and that, by a regular and constant machinery, all the events are produced, about which they are so much concerned.

David Hume

This passage sums up the outlook admirably: by a regular and constant *machinery,* all events are produced ...

The terms 'ghost' and 'machine' were of course formally introduced into philosophy by Professor Gilbert Ryle, to ridicule the widely held view that we *are,* in this sense, 'ghosts in machines'.

The name is indeed admirably apt, though the theory so named in no way deserves our contempt. On the contrary, it is in many ways an excellent and admirable theory. But there is no harm in retaining the derisive terms, which do in fact convey a great deal about the inner nature of the thing named. Since Ryle coined the expression, it has also been used by Arthur Koestler as the title of a book highly relevant to the argument.[39]

[39] A. Koestler, *The Ghost in the Machine* (London, 1967).

57

The third theory or principle of cognitive selection—the view that 'logical form' is somehow the arbiter of what is real, of what exists and can be known, of genuine knowledge—this view has not, so far, been given a funny and apposite name by anyone. Happily it is quite easy to invent a name which will pair easily in discussion with either the ghost or the machine: the *skeleton*. Moreover this name, like the others, does convey in a suggestive manner the image underlying the doctrine and the principle based on it.

'Logical form' is not easy to define; the idea is that somehow, under superficial grammatical form, expressions or thoughts have an underlying 'logical form', and that this is mirrored either by the similarly deep structure of the reality which language describes, or indicates the nature of the relationship between language and reality. Thus, for instance, if an assertion has, logically, a subject-and-predicate form, this may be held to indicate that the reality which it seizes has a substance-and-attribute form.

It is thus that, for instance, Professor S. Hampshire sketches Bertrand Russell's devotion to this idea:

the notion that there was a logically clear language to be discovered, and a universal structure of knowledge, beneath the ordinary grammar of natural languages. Russell I don't think ever doubted that it was the proper work of philosophy to look for it . . .[40]

But we do need a name and an image, to sketch in the area within which the argument will take place, and the 'skeleton' serves admirably. On this view, language, or thought, or possibly reality, has or have an underlying firm structure, under the accidental appearance of the softer, more ephemeral, structurally less important flesh. The flesh is easily perishable, the skeleton remains. He who knows the constitution of the skeleton knows the structure of reality. Hence this is the key to truth.

This sketch is all we need, for the time being. No attempt will here be made to define the skeletalist view formally. But the type of thing that is intended will easily emerge from the examples of skeletalist doctrines.

THE GHOST

As stated, the ghost was introduced as a term of trade in Ryle's *The Concept of Mind*. That book argued that a careful examination of the real meaning of the expressions of our language shows that the various problems concerning mind are misconceived: if we really understand the logic of our mental expressions, we shall see that there is no problem about mind–body interaction, determinism, knowledge of other minds, and so forth. More briefly, in the suggestive imagery of the book itself, it is a terrible mistake to suppose that our minds are ghosts, caught in machines, that they need to rely on the machines for gleaning information

[40] Bryan Magee (ed.), *Modern British Philosophy* (London, 1971), p. 27.

about the other world and have to infer the existence of other ghosts similarly encapsulated, and so forth. All this, it claimed, was a mistake. On the contrary, 'minds' are, in a very general way, what we do, the way we act: there is no duality of the mental and the physical which needs to be overcome.

It is very doubtful whether many or any people still believe the contentions of that book, and I do not wish to polemicise with them. In a way it was an admirable book: it spelt out bravely, clearly and without prevarication what other influential thinkers of the time were systematically insinuating, without however asserting it in even moderately clear language. Ryle's candid assertion of the view that the mind–body problem was amenable to 'linguistic analysis' at least made it possible to discuss it openly and to settle it for good.

But whilst I admire it for these reasons—and whilst it is neither necessary, nor at this point relevant, to attack its main theory–I do nevertheless wish to criticise that celebrated book from quite a different viewpoint: for blasphemy and irreverence. These sins, and the manner in which they were committed by *The Concept of Mind,* are very relevant indeed to the present argument.

The book established the habit of referring to a certain theory as the theory of the ghost—the theory being, that we *are* consciousness, consciousness in turn being composed of sensations, and possibly other similar components. It used this name deliberately to help make the theory look silly.

But the mechanics of denigration-by-terminology are interesting, and highly relevant. 'Ghost' is not funny or pejorative because of the sound of the *word.* It is an ordinary English word, and employing it to designate something would not normally either enhance or lower the prestige of the designated object. The word as such, the sound made by speakers of English when they read out the five appropriate letters, does not possess any independent emotive charge, one way or the other. The word can be used to denigrate because it has another, and admittedly related meaning, quite apart from being plausibly applicable to the ghost-of-the-philosophers.

For it also means, quite simply, ghosts. These ordinary ghosts could be distinguished from the ghost-of-the-philosophers as the Ghost-of-the-Society-for-Psychical-Research, or, more simply, spooks.

Personally I am not much interested in spooks, though I am interested in beliefs about spooks and in the social role of such beliefs. But the general characteristics of spooks are well known. They are in the main undesirable, anti-social beings, who take pleasure in frightening people, who behave in a manner contrary to orderly expectations, and who appear to be weightless even in ordinary terrestrial conditions, and who are, above all, insubstantial. You can put your hand through them and feel nothing; they in form can move through a wall or other hard objects without evident difficulty. As many legends illustrate, insubstantiality, or the power to assume diverse substantial forms at will, can be used for the most improper ends.

The ghosts of the philosophers, the bundles of sensations or consciousness, are in many ways markedly different from spooks, but they do indeed share at least one very important characteristic: insubstantiality. This overlap is so important that it does in some small measure justify calling them by the same name. There was indeed some point in extending the term 'ghost' from spooks to the 'bundle of sensations'.

But here the resemblance ends. The most interesting difference between *spooks* and *bundle* is the reason *why* they are insubstantial. It is only too obvious why spooks are insubstantial. This quality serves, only too well, their nefarious purposes. It enables them to frighten poor souls; it enables them to escape pursuers not endowed with a similar insubstantiality. It enables them to by-pass the protection which walls and locks normally provide for property, privacy, propriety and timidity. It has greatly facilitated some quite scandalous amorous escapades. It is really very difficult to put up any convincing defence for the uses to which spooks have put their own insubstantiality, and it is plain that they are insubstantial precisely *in order* to indulge in mischief.

The insubstantiality of the ghost of the philosophers, on the other hand, is required by considerations of a quite different kind: where the one is nefarious, suspect and impure, the other displays an awe-inspiring purity. The ghost of the philosophers is insubstantial out of a severe, unrelenting, uncompromising puritanism—a cognitive puritanism, and extreme conscientiousness concerning claims to knowledge. He has lost his body not in order to escape surveillance or pursuit, not in order to insinuate himself in places where he ought not to be, but simply because he so very conscientiously divested himself of everything which could not be justified by experience—and so in the end found himself with *nothing but* experience, and without body. He lost his body to gain his soul, in order not to betray his cognitive standards. Noting that body is not something which is or can be experienced (it is merely a certain pattern of experiences) he makes do without.

The philosophers' ghost is like a man who supports a boycott of goods which come from some tainted source, and who practises the boycott with such thoroughness, giving little or no benefit of doubt, that in the end his own equipment becomes unrecognizably impoverished. In the end he is reduced to a level which may well be less than the absolute minimum which his needs require. But, being a man of principle and a puritan, and not an opportunist self-indulgent trickster like spooks, he does not relent. He may and does become emaciated but he does not betray his principles.

Let us not make him a figure of fun. The zeal which led him to shed his body may seem extreme. But he is a ghost of great influence. The world

60

and society we live in have been profoundly influenced by him: they would each of them be quite other than they are, had he not exercised this profound, persistent and pervasive influence. It is not an exclusive influence, but it is an important and powerful one.

The ideas of empiricism have long pervaded out intellectual climate. These ideas are above all normative and selective; they have habituated us to applying certain criteria to theories and to assertions and, most significantly perhaps, to concepts. They have sensitized us to whether or not theories or concepts satisfy certain requirements; above all, the requirement of being tied, in some way or other, to the verdict of experience. They have also made us wise to the variety of ways and ploys by which theories avoid or endeavour to pervert that verdict, and they have taught us the cunning of concepts.

All this—the pervasiveness, albeit not the exclusive pervasiveness—of empiricist criteria does not by itself prove the empiricist doctrine or image of the world to be the true one. But it does show it to be an important one, and one may add, it was on the whole a very beneficial one. So the empiricist ghost deserves respectful treatment. He has helped to make our world what it is; and he is, on the whole, responsible for making it better.

Hence it is impertinent, irreverent and also quite mistaken to confuse *this* ghost, the severe empiricist censor who has cleared our world of fictitious entities that were introduced into it by superstition, dogmatism, circular reason, and test-evading contention—to confuse the ghost, who has this enormous achievement to his credit, with the mean, evasive, self-indulgent, vicious *spooks* of superstition.

There is also a further distinction to be made, between diverse philosophic ghosts. There is what may be called the warm ghost, and the cold one. The 'warm' ghost is, in effect, *consciousness,* and consciousness treated as the ultimate arbiter of existence or reality; anything which claims reality must make its impact on our conscious experience, one way or another. This warm ghost functions, as has been pointed out, as a kind of sifter or censor of that which is real as against that which is spurious; that is his most important role in philosophy.

But he also has a role in daily life which is of great interest to philosophy: he is, so to speak, a very plausible candidate for what one can only call our ultimate identity. In states of crisis, when we look with detachment at many of our own traits and aims and assumptions, and are prepared to re-value and possibly reject them, who is that inner self who takes a step back and surveys the scene, including much of the more expendable outworks of the ego, its own past convictions and commitments, and who decides what can be salvaged, what is worth salvaging, and where we shall move next? It is of course very difficult to pinpoint this, and much harder still to *justify* the preferential identity, so to speak, of anything that we do locate; and one may well also refuse to take at face value the feeling, possibly the illusion, that reflexive

61

consciousness, turning upon itself in a moment of re-orientation, really can choose a new course, or has either the independence to make, or the resources to implement, crucial decisions. One may doubt its capacity really to view things with detachment. All this may be so, and I certainly do not wish at this stage to prejudge it. All the same, my consciousness is at least a plausible candidate for my ultimate identity, and reflective people do fall back on it in crisis or when values are re-valued, and there is some connection between this kind of ego—private conscious reflection—and the purified bundle of sensation acting as evaluator of cognitive claims.

So much for the warm ghost, the stream of consciousness or the bolt-hole of identity. The cold one is only found in works of philosophical psychology, and usually old-fashioned ones at that. He is rather para-mechanical, and is invoked to *explain* our various mental capacities. He indulges in activities that usually have names of Latin origin, such as apprehension, conceptualisation, and so forth. I hold no brief whatever for *this* ghost. Explanations in terms of his powers and doings seem to me quite worthless, for various obvious reasons (circularity, absence of direct or indirect observability of the entities invoked in the explanation, sloppy logical connection with the phenomena to be explained). As far as I can see, this ghost has no other role than that of providing (seeming) explanations for human intellectual capacities, and this job he fulfils abominably. He is sometimes identified with the warm ghost, but this identification I repudiate. Ryle's attack on this para-mechanical ghost is fully justified.

The subsidiary charge against Ryle's position arises from his failure to distinguish sharply, or at all, between this admittedly execrable cold ghost of old-fashioned psychologists, and the good warm ghost of the epistemologist. Much of *The Concept of Mind* is concerned with ridiculing, on the whole deservedly, the para-mechanical ghost of philosophical psychology. So far so good. But, explicitly and implicitly, over and over again, the reader is given to understand that the demolition of the para-mechanical, semi-ghostly pulleys and levers, as explanations of intellectual performances, somehow also demolishes the notion of consciousness as a kind of internal theatre. This picture is also very much derided, quite independently. But it deserves no such derision.

The major sin was to conflate the ghost of the philosophers, that splendid empiricist censor of superstitions and (plausibly) the ultimate bearer of our identity, with the absurd spooks of popular credulity. But the conflation of the philosophers' ghost with the para-mechanical cold ghost is just as unwarranted. They perform quite different tasks. The para-mechanical cold ghost performs very badly the task of offering explanations for our ranges of competence (a task for which, admittedly, the warm ghost ought not to be invoked either). Ryle compounds his error by the suggestion that this task need not be performed at all, that our competences are somehow self-explanatory. In fact this task does need to be done, but in a different way.

THE MACHINE

The philosophers' machine, like the philosophers' ghost, is primarily a selector. At least, its greatest importance lies in its role as sifter, as a selector of legitimate or potentially legitimate theories. One important difference between the mechanical, material vision of the world, and the empiricist ghostly one, is of course that mechanism selects among *theories*, explanations, whereas the empiricist scrutiny is directed in the first instance at *information* or data, and thus only indirectly at the theories designed to explain those data. Strictly speaking, pure empiricism is quite unfastidious with regard to types of explanation, and some consistent empiricists have explicitly insisted on this conclusion: *any* kind of explanation, any 'correlation', will do, provided only the data can be deduced from it or summarised by it. The internal structure, intelligibility, the accessibility to imagination of the explanation—all these things do not matter. After all, it is only a fiction, or device, a kind of shorthand. As long as it economically summarises that which is to be explained, its own internal features are of little consequence.

By contrast, mechanism does insist on a certain type of *explanation*; that which is invoked in the explanation must be some kind of machine.

Historically and logically, the ghost and the machine are often in conflict. To some extent, but to some extent only, this conflict can be resolved by highlighting this very point—that one of them is a selector of data, and the other, a selector of explanations. But it would be facile to say that this is the end of the matter.

What is the connection between mechanism and materialism, and between both of them and determinism? At its simplest and intuitively most accessible level, materialism is an ontological prejudice in favour of heavy stuff. Heavy materials are real and genuine, whilst light materials are suspect, and probably have but an illusory reality; and the lighter the material, the more suspect it is.

This ontological prejudice receives some support from the moral similes and metaphors built into ordinary language. To convey that someone is trustworthy, we may say that he is a man of substance. *Solid* is quite a commendation for enterprises or institutions, and *weighty* is a positive characterisation of opinions. A man of substance is a man who deserves some trust. By contrast, airy-fairy, flighty, light, lacking in substance or solidity—characterisations of this kind put us on our guard. In brief, our language seems in some measure to have a bias in favour of materialism, and to insinuate and convey such a bias to its users by its very choice of physical comparisons for desirable and undesirable moral traits.

But is this not just a prejudice? Considering the question abstractly and with detachment, what is so marvellous about weight and substance? Is it not like the aesthetic prejudice of certain tribes in favour of fat women—a valuation which, in the name of tolerance, we must not condemn, but one which, equally, we should refrain from universalising? Do not light and airy substances also play their part, and a valuable one, in our lives, one which may well be distinct from that played by heavy stuff, but one which must be judged on its own terms, and one which deserves our respect and recognition? And does not light cavalry, for instance, sound more dashing than heavy cavalry? Certainly. So let us free ourselves of this somewhat inelegant bias in favour of heavy materials.

Yet the bias did have a certain point. It was not entirely arbitrary. The point is: simpler technology tends to be limited to heavier materials, notably timber, stone, and later some of the more accessible metals and alloys. The basic principle of crude technology is *push*: one object pushes another object, and if some more sophisticated effect is achieved, it is done by, as it were, channelling the movement. All these operations presuppose reasonably rigid and resistant materials. By and large, primitive tools and machines make use mainly of such heavy stuff. It may be, as Lévi-Strauss insists, that the prehistoric *bricoleur* 'makes arrows from any timber that lies close to hand': but on the whole, he must indeed restrict himself to materials such as *timber*. The modern unspecialised handyman, when improvising, is likely to have the same predisposition: the utilisation of chemical and other properties of light, liquid or gaseous materials requires specialised if not theoretical knowledge, whereas the properties of solid stuff, being familiar, stable and fairly universal, lend themselves to improvisation. Those general characteristics of the world which follow from the stable and solid properties of hard, heavy stuff are the ones we can grasp, understand and manipulate more easily than we can any others.

Thus it is no accident that the term *solid* has a favourable emotive charge. The surprising materialist bias of our language is not gratuitous. It has a sound basis. And understanding this basis at the same time explains the connection between materialism and mechanism. Mechanism is a requirement, or predisposition, in favour of explanations in terms of a 'machine'; and a machine is an artefact which can be re-produced at any time, in any place, and in any society, provided the same specified materials are used and put together in a publicly specifiable way. The properties of machines somehow follow, or at least 'flow', from the properties of the materials employed plus the manner of their coming together, even in cases where the constructor does not himself know just *how* they follow; but *that* they follow is evident from the moral and social blindness of machines, the fact that, unlike magic, they work or break down for the just and the unjust alike, which is indeed the most famous characteristic of machines. Their functioning is quite independent, notoriously, of the ritual purity or the moral aims of their constructors or users, or of the moral quality of the ends they serve. The only things that makes any difference, as indicated, are the materials and the way they are put together.

But the more primitive the society or at any rate its technology, the more will the construction of such morally blind machines be restricted to the use of heavy stuff such as stone and timber, and to the operation of *push* and some of its simpler variants. Hence any predisposition in favour of reliable tools and machines at this stage will tend to be, at the same time, a predisposition in favour of heavy materials. When science and technology develop, on the other hand, this association of machinery with heavy materials becomes progressively weaker: machines can be built of all kinds of materials, and some of the constituent parts and forces of modern electronic machinery, for instance, far from being bulky and heavy, can be neither seized by hand nor can even be effectively visualised. So the modern mechanistic predisposition need not be and is not accompanied by any prejudice in favour of weight and tangibility. But the predisposition in favour of mechanism is understandable: it is the predisposition in favour of reproducible, publicly observable and examinable, so to speak culture-free structures. And it is equally understandable why, in more primitive technological conditions, this predisposition should manifest itself as a prejudice in favour of heavy stuff.

The prejudice is kept alive even when technology develops, and when the utilisation of light materials and microscopic, intangible processes confers a kind of respectability on light matter and invisible processes. It is kept alive, above all, by the activities on the other side, by the opponents of mechanistic explanation. If crude technologists must needs prefer heavy materials, in view of their reliability, so those who wish to evade mechanistic, regular, impersonal, culture-free explanation, must fall back on entities that are elusive, which cannot be easily caught in the turning wheels of the machine. In as far as these elusive entities are concretely envisaged (and they often are), the imagery is borrowed from light and airy materials, from breath and the wind and such. The soul is like a breath. So those who oppose the subsumption of all phenomena under regular, morally indifferent rules—in other words, the opponents of the mechanistic world picture—by stressing the existence and status of morally sensitive, culturally specific, 'spiritual' beings or entities, visualised as very ethereal indeed, thereby reinforce the pro-solidity and literally 'stuffy' prejudices of their opponents.

Nevertheless, all this is a confusion. It is the machine which is significant, not the weight of material. Mechanism (and its corollary, determinism) is significant. It is an enormously important selector of theories, and one possible guide towards cognitive legitimacy. But *weight* as such is irrelevant. Moreover, all the important characteristics of the mechanistic model—both the attractive and the terrifying ones—follow from the mechanism as such, not from the choice of material. Weight of material does not aggravate them, and lightness does not mitigate them.

The attractive traits are of course the publicity, reproducibility, and impersonality of the explanation. The fear-inspiring ones are the moral and social blindness, and determinism. The two sets of traits overlap; in some measure, they are the same traits, viewed from different perspectives. They constitute enormously important criteria for what is and what is not real. *Weight*, on the other hand, has no such importance. Weight is no clue to the nature of reality.

THE SKELETON

Both the ghost and the machine deserve a deep reverence; our society, our understanding, have profited immeasurably from the fact that for a very long time now, there has been a sustained and on the whole effective propaganda, requiring the explanations we proffer to satisfy, more or less, the criteria of mechanism, and requiring data we invoke in support of our contentions to satisfy or approximate the requirements of empiricism. A society in which this is not done is morally and intellectually inferior to one in which it is so.

On the other hand, I feel no such reverence, indeed no respect even, for the skeleton. The skeleton, admittedly, is also a selector device, a sifter of truth and falsehood. But he is, to my mind, lacking in merit. Our society would be no worse had he never appeared in its intellectual tradition; rather the reverse. I think I should have known about the ghost and the machine even if I had never read a single book of formal philosophy. They pervade the intellectual atmosphere, and one can easily sense their presence whether or not one can name them or place their ancestry. By contrast, I know of the skeleton *only* from reading books, and indeed I had to encounter him more than once before I could actually bring myself to believe that an idea so unattractive and implausible had a genuine hold on some very intelligent men. As a matter of simple historical fact, quite obviously it did have such a hold, though this is something I find difficult to understand. The reader will no doubt consider the possibility that the fault is mine.

The basic idea in this particular selection principle is that thought (or possibly language) has a 'logical form' and that reality must conform to it. Formulated in this way, the position immediately suggests the question—why should reality be constrained by the limits of the forms of thought? And indeed, what can constrain thought itself within those limits? The first question, at least, can possibly be evaded by treating these forms not, primarily, as the forms of thought, but as the necessary forms of being itself. This then also suggests an answer to the second question: thought must respect these limits if it is to mirror reality faithfully. All this of course merely postpones the question: why *must* reality remain within certain limits, certain forms? I cannot alas answer such questions, and raise them merely to point out that, for purposes of the present exposition, skeletalism embraces not merely doctrines starting out from a notion of logical or linguistic form, but equally those for whom the underlying skeleton is not logical or linguistic, but part of reality itself.

The central idea in skeletalism is that we somehow have access to the basic form of thought or being, and through this can see the general form of our world. For instance, we somehow know, it is supposed, that ultimate reality is substance, defined let us say as that which can exist on its own, and that other features of the world must be attributes of substance or of substances. This alleged insight can naively be treated as self-evident and be taken for granted, or it can be a corollary of a theory of thought or of language; the claim can be that thought or language must have this form, and that reality must be congruent with it if it is to be cognitively accessible to us.

It is probably easier to convey what skeletalism is by examples, rather than by attempted definitions which immediately raise unanswerable problems. Skeletalist doctrines can be classified according to the kind of skeleton in question.

Subject/predicate, substance/attribute skeletalism is probably the most important, most influential sub-species within this genus. Presumably it often just seemed self-evident to skeletalists of this kind that reality had to contain substance and its attributes and nothing else, or that all meaningful assertion had to consist of the attribution of some predicate to some subject.

It should readily be evident how easily and effectively, once such a picture is accepted, it can be used for selection purposes. If the world necessarily has a substance/attribute structure, only two visions of the world appear to be available to us: either only one substance exists, and everything in the world is an aspect or attribute of it; or many substances exist, but each is entirely self-contained, and no one of them can ever communicate with any other. (For if such communication existed, it would be reported in a proposition whose structure was not subject/predicate, but relational: for it would report a relation between *two* substances, whose ontological status is equal. Neither can then be an attribute of the other. Hence the proposition would need *two* subjects, related not only by a predicate but by a relation. But this possibility contradicts the initial hypothesis, namely that all reality is of the substance/attribute form.)

These two alternatives are not merely abstract, logical consequences, ideal types deduced from the premises; they are, in fact, historically occupied positions, well exemplified. Spinoza, and F. H. Bradley in England, provided two celebrated examples of absolute monism, deduced from skeletalist principles. Subject/predicate pluralism, with its consequences of a multiplicity of substances totally separated from each other, is a rarer position, presumably because it is an intuitively repellent one. Nevertheless, it does possess at least one famous and important representative, Leibniz. Moreover, we are fortunate in possessing an important and lucid exposition of Leibniz' thought, Bertrand Russell's, written to illustrate precisely this point—how the picture of the world is a corollary of a view of logical form. This exposition is all the more valuable since Russell himself always had strong skeletalist leanings and hence could interpret Leibniz with sympathy:

I first realised the importance of the question of relations when I was working on Leibniz. I found ... that his metaphysics was explicitly based upon the doctrine that every proposition attributes a predicate to a subject and (what seemed to him almost the same thing) that every fact consists of a substance having a property. I found that the same doctrine underlies the systems of Spinoza, Hegel and Bradley ... [41]

What, according to Russell, was 'almost the same thing' for Leibniz, is indeed the central idea of skeletalism.

Or consider the following passage:

In the belief that propositions must, in the last analysis, have a subject and a predicate, Leibniz does not differ either from his predecessors or his successors. Any philosophy which uses either substance or the Absolute will be found, on inspection, to depend on this belief.[42]

Among monistic skeletalists, it may be useful to take Bradley, since in his case also a useful exposition is available which highlights this origin of his argument.[43] The author of the exposition is not himself a skeletalist, but he has the advantage of training within a philosophic movement which arose as a reaction to skeletalism and is consequently very sensitive to it. Consider the following comments:

Bradley's view of language is ... peculiarly a logician's view.
    It is significant that this same view of language is to be found in the writings of another philosophic logician, one of Bradley's most violent opponents, Bertrand Russell.[44]

And Bradley's conclusion:

It is impossible that the world should consist of a number of discrete facts ...[45]

There is nothing very new about a *partial* use of skeletalist arguments. But an interesting development in this century was the academic revival of skeletalism, for once in a rather extreme and pure form. One factor in this revival, within the English-speaking philosophic tradition, was a reaction against British Hegelianism, against the absolute idealism of thinkers such as Bradley. The 'realists' wanted to deny Bradley's monism, the view that the world was one big thing only, and to say instead that it consisted of very many things, related in a variety of ways. But whilst they wished to

[41] Bertrand Russell, *My Philosophical Development* (London, 1959), p. 61.
[42] Bertrand Russell, *A Critical Exposition of the Philosophy of Leibniz* (1900), p. 15.
[43] Professor Richard Wollheim. *F. H. Bradley* (Harmondsworth, 1959).
[44] *Ibid.*, p. 70.
[45] *Ibid.*, p. 122.

68

deny Bradley's doctrine and conclusion, they did not, as is so often the way, query his operational rule: their pluralism, like his monism, was argued in skeletalist terms. This they took for granted. They just favoured a different skeleton.

And that brings us to the second, and perhaps more important reason for the skeletalist revival: a new and more usable skeleton had just been discovered. This skeleton was the notation of the new mathematical logic. For this notation seemed to be more than merely a way of recording assertions in logic or in the theory of sets: it appeared to capture the very essence both of things and of thought.

One of its philosophically most striking traits was that it allowed *relations*. Mathematics, it seemed, could not manage without relations: one has to be able to say things such that a given number is larger than another one. But before relations had been officially allowed into logic by being given a sign in the notation, logicians were forced to say that an inference hinging on relations (such as: *A* is larger than *C*, if *A* is larger than *B*, and *B* is larger than *C*), is 'formless'. This 'formless' inference looks sound enough, but it is an embarrassment for logic if its notation knows nothing of relations . . .

Mathematics, by apparently having a need of the notational recognition of relations, thereby opened the way to a new kind of skeletalist ontology. Bradley's monism had hinged on the *denial* of the reality of relations, as a step on the way to the denial of a plurality of related things. But now, thanks to the permissibility of relations, that plurality of things could be re-admitted, in a skeletalist style of thought—and this plurality of things no longer had to suffer either the loneliness of Leibnizian monads, or annexation by that most imperialist of concepts, the Absolute. One participant in this movement described it succinctly:

I shall try to set forth . . . a kind of logical doctrine which seems to me to result from the philosophy of mathematics . . . a certain kind of logical doctrine and on the basis of this a certain kind of metaphysics. The logic which I advocate is atomistic, as opposed to the monistic logic of the people who more or less follow Hegel.[46]

Thus a new philosophy emerged early in this century, which had as its starting point logical form, as now revealed or highlighted by the notation of mathematical logic, and which had at its disposal the far more operational, so to speak 'motorised' modern logical theory. Here is an example of how Russell used this version of the skeletalist method:

In every atomic fact there is one component which is naturally expressed by a verb (or, in the case of a quality, it may be expressed by a predicate, by an adjective). This one component is a quality or a dyadic or triadic or tetradic . . . relation.[47]

Just as the theory of the universality of the subject/predicate form of

[46] B. Russell, 'The Philosophy of Logical Atomism', re-printed in *Logic and Knowledge Essays 1901–1950*, ed. R. C. Marsh (London, 1956).
[47] B. Russell, *Logic and Knowledge Essays 1901–1950*, p. 199.

thought generated the metaphysic of the one substance (or of lonely monads), so then the logical notation allowing or highlighting many-stranded *relations*, generated a metaphysic of polymorphous and very numerous things. Moreover, anyone who conjured a metaphysic out of the old Aristotelian logic was to a modern mathematical logician as a man tilling the soil with a hoe is to one using a tractor. The new machinery did not merely allow far more 'things', it was also far more operational.

Machinery which is available must be used. The logical notation generated a picture of the world, mirroring that notation. Despite the modernity of the machine, the resulting picture was in some ways quite old-fashioned. In other ways it lent itself to modernity. It was pluralistic and atomic; the calculus of propositions, the simplest part of modern logic requires that each 'atomic' proposition be quite independent of every other proposition with respect to truth and falsehood: the truth or falsity of any one is totally independent of the truth or falsity of any other. (Though things are allowed to be related, atomic propositions are not.) The shadow cast by this requirement on reality was of course an atomistic one. Looking around for these totally independent and numerous atoms, some philosophers in this movement were naturally tempted by the most likely candidates for such cognitively independent atoms: the sensations of the empiricist tradition.

In other respects, the picture generated was less modern. The substances which were to be clothed by attributes and related by relations, though numerous and no longer lonely and isolated, were nevertheless quite colourless, anonymous bearers of properties. In practice, anyone who thought of them could hardly imagine them otherwise than hard, small, colourless billiard balls, hidden at the bottom of propositions before the colourful attributes were poured in or stuck on. It is a curious fact that at the very time that colourless billiard balls were being abandoned in physics, something remarkably like them was being reintroduced as the ultimate furniture of the world by philosophising logicians.

Within early twentieth-century academic philosophy, this highly motorised neo-Skeletalism—a view of the world born of the projection of logical form, where the specific view of logical form owed much to the notation of mathematical logic—is of very great importance. (Collingwood referred to it as philosophy by typographical jargon.) An exaggerated backlash against it, which however took over its errors rather than its merits, in due course became even more important.

5   The baselines

THE GHOST AGAINST THE MACHINE

In logic and in history, the ghost and the machine are both allies and enemies. Their alliance springs in part from the fact that they are both selectors, sifters, and severe, orderly, systematic ones at that. Hence the worlds which they help to bring about are markedly unlike the locally tied, unsymmetrical, arbitrary, accidentally constructed, time-and-place-bound visions. Those outlooks fuse beliefs, obligations, and a local social landscape into a conflated picture which may serve social needs well enough, but which cannot survive the impartial, locale-indifferent scrutiny of a selector philosophy. As both these principles come into conflict with such faiths and with the theologies elaborated for their protection, and as they both share an universalistic symmetrical character, they tend to be invoked together when battle is joined with such creeds.

Our earlier account of selectors tended to stress their positive or constructive role in helping us to find orientation, to escape from intellectual confusion. This is perhaps their most important role. But they also have the negative, destructive role, being used as battering-rams against the old-established creeds. Old complex structures, with manifold and untidy historical origins, are particularly vulnerable to such attack.

In the seventeenth and eighteenth centuries, that ill-proportioned and ancient city, the traditional European system of beliefs, was indeed under attack. In this assault, the ghost and the machine were, inevitably, allies:

Ainsi ces anciennes cités, qui, n'ayant été au commencement que des bourgades, sont devenues, par succession des temps, de grandes villes, sont ordinairement si mal compassées, au prix de ces places régulières qu'un ingénieur trace à sa fantaisie dans une plaine ... [48]

Both the systematic application of the empiricist criterion, and the systematic application of the mechanistic one, were disastrous to the inherited world-picture, or congeries of overlapping pictures. Partly in virtue of the political principle that those who share an enemy become allies, the ghost and the machine were seen not merely as allies, but were frequently confused or even supposed to be identical. For instance, La Mettrie's *L'Homme Machine* is widely supposed to be, as its name implies, primarily a kind of proto-cybernetic tract. In fact, in the book the empiricist theory of knowledge is at least as prominent a theme as the

---

[48] Descartes, *Discours de la Méthode*, Seconde Partie.

materialistic or mechanistic theory of behaviour. The author supposes that he must establish an empirical theory of knowledge in order to defend a materialist view of man. He supposes that any abandonment of empiricism in epistemology will let in spiritual entities, and he also supposes that the establishment of an empiricist epistemology will guarantee mechanical explanations. Or again, David Hume is (rightly) considered the classical expositor of the ghost position, clarifying its nature and implications with the greatest consistency and profundity. Yet Hume, although he mainly elaborated the ghost, was by no means insensitive to the claims of the machine. On the contrary, in at least one mood, he is tempted by the idea that it has greater claim to our assent than any other:

Could men anatomise nature, according to the most probable, or at least the most intelligible philosophy, they would find, that these causes are nothing but the particular fabric and structure of the minute parts of their own bodies and of external objects; and that, by a regular and constant machinery, all the events are produced, about which they are so much concerned.[49]

Is this alliance of the ghost and the machine simply an opportunist alignment, arising accidentally out of a certain historical situation, when each of them was used by the Enlightenment to batter Christian orthodoxy —or is there, on the contrary, a deeper affinity between the two?

Both the affinity and the conflict between the two great selectors would seem to be rooted in the nature of things rather than in an accident of history.

Consider first the affinities and compatibilities:

(1) Each is a selector, and as such, cannot easily be in harmony with systems of ideas that are mere uncritical conglomerates, historic accumulations, social conveniences serving many ends other than cognition.

(2) Each has a strong bias towards public testing. This will turn out to be crucial.

(3) One of them is concerned with data and their source, the other with explanation and its structure. This is not an affinity, but a reason why their conflict may be less than total: they do not clash all along the line, and they do not clash directly at the points which concerns each of them most.

The points of conflict are quite other:

(1) The ultimate world pictures generated by each of them are quite distinct and seem immediately incompatible. The world of the ghost dissolves into sheer experience, warm, qualitative and structureless. Structures, hardness, continuity—these must needs become fictions, conceptual devices, artefacts, possibly convenient as guidelines or mnemonic devices, but without ultimate reality. For the mechanical world-picture, the very reverse is true. Persistent structures, not qualities, are

[49] Hume, *The Natural History of Religion,* section III.

the ultimate reality.

(2) Consequently, the ghost finds it relatively easy to cope with determinism: causation being like matter a fiction or convenience, the problem barely arises. By contrast, the problem is acute for the mechanical picture. Even if the old structures, constituted of hard, permanent matter, governed by strict laws, are replaced by modern structures whose basic components are more ephemeral, and which are governed by statistical rather than rigid laws, this does not really help. They remain orderly, subject to impersonal generalisations which are hard to reconcile with free choice.

We would misunderstand our intellectual situation if we were to ignore or in any way underrate either the congruence, or the strain, between the two outlooks.

THE PROBLEM OF REALISM AND THE CONCEPT OF EXPERIENCE

One issue which brings the ghost and the machine into conflict is the question of the reality of the external world. The mechanical picture, materialism, naturally leads to the assumption of a permanent, continuous reality, quite independent of consciousness; the reality of those elements, or of that stuff, which is employed for the construction of the machines— the stuff whose properties determine those of the machines, and which thus provides the major premiss for any scientific explanation.

By contrast, the ghost leads to subjectivism and the vision of a discontinuous, fragmentary world, of 'bundles', 'sensations' and so forth. The data are private, discontinuous and fragmentary; stability, continuity, permanence, hardness—these are only conceptual devices, fictions of a kind, introduced by us with a view to ordering the material, giving it an appearance of stability. Permanent substantiality is merely the name given to the re-appearance of certain patterns. It cannot conceivably be derived from the material itself which is ever fragmentary; hence its authority can only be derived from our mental custom, convenience, conceptual or compulsion, individual or collective. (The details vary with individual theories.)

We have here a very radical conflict, and one without any facile solution—perhaps ultimately without any solution at all. The considerations on either side deserve some scrutiny.

The considerations on the ghostly side are the most obvious. The key premiss is a tautology: we only experience what we experience. What we do not experience, we do *not* experience. But, tautological though the premiss may seem, it also appears to be pregnant with the most important consequences. It is not really all that puzzling that this should be so: the tautology can be so pregnant, because it is in conflict with all the doctrines and concepts which violate the view that what we do not experience, we do *not* experience. Those doctrines manage to violate it by postulating, or using, elements which are, in one context, admitted to be outside the range of experience, and in another, treated as if they were accessible to us after all. This shifty, double-faced, logical ambivalence is at the very heart of most belief systems. The importance of the tautology lies in the implicitly stressed injunction that we should be consistent in noting what is or is not observable, what is or is not experiential. A concept cannot be experiential on weekdays and transcendent at the weekend. Most cultural systems of ideas depend on inconsistency at this point, and indeed on cultivating a low sensitivity to this distinction in their devotees.

By considering carefully, as Hume did, what we do and do not experience, we note that we do not—and could not—experience either the permanent, persistent substantiality credited to material objects by common sense, or the causal links which bind events, and which make the world predictable and manipulable, to a degree at least sufficient for a tolerable human habitat. The 'naive realist' attitude towards both objects and towards the connections between events, an attitude which had full confidence in their inherent reality, is possible only thanks to a kind of confused double-think, which conceives the gaps in the series of data as, all at once, *not* being gaps after all, but being permanently filled. But what is the point of saying that objects are 'really there' even when no one is looking at them? How could you establish this? You cannot look without looking. The very terms of reference preclude an answer.

Epistemological realism is a terrible muddle: it consists of saying that we can peep at what we cannot look at. Psychologically, philosophical realists tend to be people so imbued with the conviction that the way in which they think of things, things must also 'really be', that they cannot stomach a doctrine to the contrary. Their epistemic dignity is outraged. *They* be the subjects of illusion? They compare their own ideas with their own ideas and find, much to their satisfaction, that they match—perfectly. The results of this interesting *Gedanken-experiment* show that reality and our ideas are congruent. This is known as epistemological realism.

Those who are more sensitive to the subjectivist argument, which underlies the ghost picture of knowledge, of the world and of ourselves, endeavour to be more consistent and not to pretend to peep at what they cannot see. If we cannot peep at what is behind phenomena—for anything we can see is, by definition, just another peep, and hence one further phenomenon—and if we cannot see whether or not there is continuity in the gaps—for if we could see, it would not be a gap—well then, we must reinterpret those attributions of substantiality, causality and so forth which do not correspond to anything we actually experience; we must reinterpret them as performing some direct role in arranging the material which is actually experienced. And if so, then just how are these entities, and relations, to be reinterpreted? They are to be seen as important, useful *fictions*. There is no causality 'really', but there are regular patterns of succession, and the best way to visualise these repetitions is to think of

74

them as linked by a kind of nexus—which, perhaps under the influence of a kind of animist hangover, we see as 'compelling' and thus tend to 'reify'. There are no substances 'really', but we can think and behave 'as if' there were, for this is the most useful, economical, mnemonically and otherwise suggestive way of thinking of those bundles of sensations which, providentially, cohere and re-appear with each other in orderly fashion and make our environment manageable.

This is of course an extremely familiar theory. It is *the* classical empiricist solution. It is not particularly fashionable at present amongst professional philosophers, for reasons which however are not very good ones. False it may be, but hardly for the reasons recently offered (in substance, that it offends common sense). Such unpopularity as it also encounters among non-specialists (and to some degree among specialists too) is largely due to a certain paradoxicality which seems to attach to it, and which is well brought out by the name *ghost*. What is seems to say is that there is no body: the world is made up of consciousness. This aspect of the theory of course greatly pleased one of the great proponents of this viewpoint, Bishop Berkeley: and for people of such a frame of mind, the fact that the theory excludes both matter and the machine, is a positive attraction. This is different from those other empiricists, who liked the ghost not so much because of any exclusion of stuff, but because he excluded *dogma*.

But the apparent paradoxicality of the ghost, which is a stumbling block to many, is in part a consequence of a misunderstanding. In daily life, we *live* largely in the world of touch, but we *know* mainly through the world of sight. Day to day survival and the avoidance of pain is largely a matter of not coming into violent contact with hard objects, and of the adequate intake of appropriate foods. What really matters, at any rate for the physical well-being which is the precondition of most other kinds, is events experienced through touch and contact. At the same time, our tactile and similar experiences are very low-powered as sources of precise information and as bases of prediction. By contrast, nothing that happens to us visually matters very much in itself—leaving aside people whose aesthetic sensibility is very highly developed—but sight is enormously important as a source of advance information about what can hurt us and what we can consume. In brief, pleasure and pain take place largely in the sphere of touch, but valuable information about attaining these reaches us through sight.

The 'phenomenalist' doctrine of the empiricists, which restricts reality to experience, and 'reduces' all other entities to fictions which refer to experiences indirectly, sounds paradoxical largely because it *seems* to be saying that the world of sight is real in some ultimate sense, whereas the world of touch, of pressure-resisting three-dimensional objects occupying space, is but a logical fiction. It seems to be denying the reality of hard pebbles held in the mouth or in a clenched hand, or of one's sense of one's own extended body. For it is an interesting thing about our conceptual equipment that certain ideas ('pebble') are theoretical and explanatory at the level of sight (the 'pebble' as it were unites the various visual aspects of a pebble, without in a way being very close to them), *and* also concrete, specific, descriptive, 'phenomenological', at the kinaesthetic level or that of touch. (It is natural to say that my clenched hand holds the pebble itself, not aspects or manifestations of it.) Through this ambiguity in the status of some of our concepts, a doctrine which, in a relatively inoffensive way, denies ultimate status to ideas which merely serve to bind together diverse experiences under one label, becomes violently offensive by also seeming to deny a concrete part of our experience. All the more so, in as far as what really matters in life, pain, pleasure, danger, death, is generally constituted by or caused by events occurring in the medium of touch.

In fact there is nothing in the inherent logic of the theory to make it say anything of the kind; it does not attribute more reality to 'views' such as those taken on postcards, than to plum-stones felt three-dimensionally, 'extended', in the mouth. It does not favour one kind of experience as against another. It does not favour sight against touch. It is, I suppose, a contingent accident that pleasure and pain are concentrated in tactile experiences, that it is in the tactile world that we 'live' in as far as it is mainly events located in it that can please, hurt or kill us. By contrast, the potential of sight for pleasure and pain is very limited, whilst its predictive potential is very great. It is hard, though not impossible, to torture someone through sight or hearing, without using touch or heat, though admittedly really sensitive souls do claim to suffer acutely through bad visual 'taste'. It is, perhaps, not quite so accidental and contingent that sight is powerfully predictive and touch is not: were it the other way round, would we talk of 'sight' and touch' in the sense which we now employ? A powerfully predictive 'touch' would become a kind of sight: non-predictive sight would degenerate into a kind of touch.

Be that as it may, it is these confusedly perceived considerations which make the ghost doctrine appear paradoxical and prevent common sense from finding it acceptable (though of course it was also these very consequences which gave the doctrine its appeal for Bishop Berkeley and those like-minded). The doctrine *seems* to eliminate hard, heavy, crude stuff from the grand inventory of what exists in the universe. But this is largely a misunderstanding. The ghostly 'bundles' ought not to be seen as disembodied *specifically visual* experience, such as is the fate of a cinema-goer who shares (roughly) some of the visual experiences of the characters in the film, without sharing their tactile ones—though this is just how radical phenomenalist empiricism *is* seen. The bundles should, rather, be seen as including those experiences which we should normally describe as, for instance, the clasping a small hard ball in the palm of the hand—a very tactile, 'hard' and three-dimensional 'experience'. There is nothing in phenomenalism as such to exclude such an experience, and to force us to

76

make it derivative from a two-dimensional, visual perception of a squash-ball. Of course, reality *does* remain 'full of holes', discontinuity is maintained, continuity is a 'fiction'; but the real experiences surrounding the holes are not necessarily visual, and the 'fictions' which convey continuity need not borrow the language of touch.

Thus the objection which is, more than any other, responsible for the popular inacceptability of radical empiricism as a formal doctrine, is probably based on a misunderstanding. This is perhaps not a point of very great importance, as the real social significance of empiricism is not as a formal coherent doctrine but as a semi-tacit, unformalised though pervasive attitude in the scrutiny of concepts.

I shall nevertheless borrow the imagery underlying this probably misguided objection and distinguish between the 3-D real world, and the 2-D world of the empiricist epistemologist. But the distinction I have in mind is not the one between the world of touch and the world of sight (which is what the objectors generally have in mind), but something a little more sophisticated: the 3-D world is the full rich world of manifold things, the world of 'common sense', our *Lebenswelt*, whereas the 2-D world is the deliberately impoverished world of 'experience alone' (sight, touch, and all), artificially invented by the theory of knowledge for purposes of scrutiny of the world of common sense, or of any other. The distinction is introduced tentatively for purposes of exposition and is not meant to prejudge whether or not such a selective *ante*-world, i.e. the raw material of reality as it is before we add our 'fictions', is possible at all.

The important thing to realise is just how *very* powerful the ghost, radical-empiricist, subjectivist argument is. This is important in itself, and particularly important at present, when, largely for quite inadequate and confused reasons, that argument is supposed to be *dépassé*. It is not. We misconstrue our cognitive predicament—as important as our moral predicament, and perhaps more so—if we suppose either that the empiricist argument can never be 'refuted' on its own premises, or that those premises are anything less than powerful, sensible and persuasive.

How very elegant is the solution of the ghost! The simplicity, elegance and—very nearly—the adequacy of its theory of the world compel admiration. There is a set of hard data—what we sense—isolable, and with discrete characteristics. *That is all.* The apparent complexity, continuity, indefinite extension of the world are but a set of conceptual, or notational, devices for ordering those data. In effect, the world is seen as a kind of mosaic, and a rather fragmentary one at that, like one of those dug up in ancient Mediterranean sites and damaged by time and wear. Each place is there, available for its stone, though only some are filled. The empirical specificity of the world is determined by the fact that this stone is green, that one turquoise, and so forth. The formal nature of the world —the 'logical structure of the world', to use the phrase of one modern theorist—is exhausted if one says that there are places for stones, of diverse colours and textures. That is all.

One very great philosophic merit of this picture is that it answers, with great lucidity and, on its own terms, with absolute finality, the crucial questions about the status and legitimacy of knowledge. Cognitive sovereignty and cognitive dependence are clearly located; here everyone knows his place, there is no haziness. The data, the stones on the mosaic, are sovereign and ultimate. Nothing can really explain them or go beyond them. Mystery is excluded, at the level of data, by being absolute; there is no room even for a question. The brutality of the 'given' is unmitigated. By contrast, all else is intelligible and man-made. The groupings, the summaries of data, in as far as they do not violate what is given, are man-made and rooted in convention. The bases of the world are beyond all understanding because, like Mount Everest, they are there; all else is intelligible because *we* make it. On this picture, we certainly know just where we stand. That which is given with impenetrable brutality, and that which is transparent because it is man-made, between them exhaust our world. There are hard immutable external facts, and there are our conventions, and we can understand the status of each.

An important implication of this theory is that the 2-D world of the 'given' mosaic is sovereign, and holds the 3-D *Lebenswelt*, which we normally live in, in thrall. The elaborations and conceptualisations and classifications we indulge in when constructing that world are our own affair, and we can please ourselves in the light of our various interests as to which of various alternatives we adopt – *provided* they are in harmony with the independently given ante-world of the mosaic.

There are, of course, various powerful arguments, and some not so powerful, employed against the empiricist picture. The powerful ones show that the ante-world of pure data is not in fact independent and self-sufficient, but is in turn and in circular fashion in thrall to the other, 'real' (in daily terms), 3-D world. One formulation can be found in Bertrand Russell:

We all start from 'Naive realism', i.e. the doctrine that things are as they seem . . . But physics assures us that the greenness of grass, the hardness of stones, and the coldness of snow are not the greenness, hardness and coldness that we know on our own experience, but something very different. The observer . . . is really . . . observing the effect of the stone on himself . . . Naive realism leads to physics, and physics, if true, shows that naive realism is false. Therefore naive realism, if true, is false; therefore it is false.[50]

Whereas empiricism shows that the real world or *Lebenswelt* is a set of fictions only deriving such validity as they possess from their relationship to the basic data, this argument, just as powerful, shows that the alleged pure base is but a small and rather insignificant, epiphenomenal set of events in the wider world consisting of those alleged fictions. It is very

[50] B. Russell, *An Inquiry into Meaning and Truth* (London, 1940) pp. 14 and 15.

hard to doubt that, in some sense, this is so; the supposed sovereign is but a very minor and unimportant citizen in the wider realm of the 'real world'. Yet, as the Russell quotation shows admirably, each holds the other in thrall.

There is an alternative and more fashionable argument which insists that there is no isolable and characterisable ante-world of pure data; the basic-mosaic analogy is inapplicable. The colours or other attributes could never be credited to those pure, initial stones of the 2-D mosaic; any attributes we can operate with, and any objects we can isolate and characterise, already belong to the 'real' 3-D world. This argument has often been formulated. A version of it can be found in Professor Kuhn's *The Structure of Scientific Revolutions*:

But is sensory experience fixed and neutral? Are theories simply man-made interpretations of given data? The epistemological viewpoint that has most often guided Western philosophy for three centuries dictates an ... Yes! In the absence of a developed alternative, I find it impossible to relinquish entirely that viewpoint. Yet it no longer functions effectively, and the attempts to make it do so through the introduction of a neutral language of observation now seem to me hopeless.[51]

Kuhn then proceeds to quote, convincingly, the testimony both of psychology and of the history of science, which shows how expectations and concepts determine 'what one sees'. Certainly, the evidence does support Kuhn's contention: there are no 'pure' data. Total epistemic decontamination of experience from concepts has never been achieved; moreover, it seems in principle impossible. But if the 2-D ante-world is not pure, how can it sit in sovereign judgment on the *Lebenswelt*, or arbitrate between rival and conflicting *Lebenswelten* ? The supposed judge appears not to be independent of the litigants. Being suborned by them, how can he presume to sit in judgment on them?

The general trouble with empiricism could be summed up by saying that the pure data turn out to be neither pure nor entirely data, and similarly that the alleged conceptual fictions turn out not to be fictions. The data can only be located and identified with the help of those putative fictions, which seem to have a life of their own, and not to be mere notational devices. They are not inert fictions. We live in terms of them, the world is permeated by them, and they affect the 'data' found. In so far as the claim for the authority of the data hinges on their purity, the claim lapses, for they are not pure.

Yet at the same time, it simply will not do to say that because the attempts at 'reducing' the 3-D world to a 2-D one has failed, therefore the 3-D world, the *Lebenswelt*, must be taken as given. This is a dreadful fallacy. The question of 'how it comes to be known' continues to be insistent, above all because there is not one but many rival 'lived' worlds. Some recent philosophies have tried to evade the question, and developed rather

[51] Thomas S. Kuhn, *The Structure of Scientific Revolutions* (Chicago, 1962), pp. 125 *et seq.*

shifty and entirely question-begging devices for inhibiting the very asking of it. The world is taken for granted, and within it those who ask the question are to be 'cured' of the desire to ask it.

As there is more than one 'real world', as they vary with faith and culture, and as they are often in conflict, this kind of facile world-acceptance is useless. Our world is not self-justifying, nor can it be corrected in a merely piece-meal way. Individual pieces are sustained by the rest and pervaded by doubtful assumptions. It is the pervasive assumptions which need to be queried.

THE PROBLEM OF IDEALISM AND THE CONCEPT OF STRUCTURE

Philosophically, the ghost ends in an impasse. He can and does in some good measure perform the job he is required to do—select and sift the acceptable ideas, concepts and theories from the frauds—but he does stand convicted of impurity. This is a serious matter, for his claim to authority seemed to be based precisely on his pretension to purity; without it, how can he claim to arbitrate between the rival constructed worlds? If he is tainted, as they are, by interpretation, who is he to stand in judgment on them?

The empiricist is unlike the virgin in that for him it is experience, and not its absence, which aspires to purity. Unsullied experience, and it alone, could judge the conceptual and doctrinal structures which are erected by us, precisely because it claims to be prior to them all, independent of them all, and hence a fair, neutral judge. But if it is not so independent, if it has no such priority, if indeed it is part and parcel of more general and complex visions (merely an abstract derivative of them, its enemies say), then the whole programme of decontamination from error and preconception, which was to be executed through it, would seem misguided. How could experience judge those total, pervasive cultural visions, when it is inescapably part of them?

Let us leave it in that impasse for the time being, and consider the parallel impasse faced by its rival, the machine. The two predicaments are by no means exact images of each other, but they nevertheless offer an important contrast.

The sustained and consistent application of the empiricist criterion empties the world of all solid substance, and indeed of selves, and leaves us with free-floating sensations, combining with vertiginous arbitrarinesss into happily rather stable bundles of things and people. The world generated by the sustained application of the materialist–mechanistic criterion is quite other. It does not lack for stability. It is full of permanent, orderly structures, made (at least in the older versions of this kind of world) of comfortably solid, inpenetrable stuff, each firmly in occupancy of its particular part of space. Elusiveness, intangibility, precariousness, subjectivity, are not the problems of this world. Its problem is the very opposite. It deprives the world of subjectivity, of the warm, private, sensuous centres of awareness which we also know ourselves to be. If only structures are real, the barely structured bundles or centres of consciousness become suspect, illusory, epiphenomenal or irrelevant. Just as some of the extreme empiricists delight in the elimination of matter, so the extreme materialists (behaviourists) actually delight in the elimination of mind. But for most of us, this remains a problem, an embarrassment or a source of regret. Note that the elimination is difficult, perhaps impossible to avoid. If your cognitive selector applies the principle that nothing is to count as knowledge unless it has the form of an explanation in terms of a publicly available structure, or one that can be erected, it follows that the warm private stream of consciousness will never acquire the important status of that which explains. If it survives at all, it will survive in the dependent, client status, as that which *is explained*. It becomes, at best, epiphenomenal.

Though this may be attractive, even *frisson*-engendering for some, for most people such vision is repellent. As the tidal wave of science advances, and as its explanations generally seem to have this form, this provokes a fear, indeed a terror, of the de-humanisation of the world and of man by scientific explanation. Defensive reactions are numerous, and varied in kind. Romanticism was the best known reaction, and it tended to make use of various idealist counter-arguments, all purporting to show that the items which satisfied the mechanistic–materialist criterion could not suffice to fill the world, and that the world also contained, or even contained exclusively, much more congenial inhabitants, and that the stuff of the world was human.

The defensive arguments vary in kind. Many are borrowed from the ghost—notably, the argument that as experience is primary, that it alone is the stuff of reality. Or: the explanations whose mechanical inhumanity we fear are mere conceptual devices, fictions, conveniences, that *we* have made and which consequently we need not fear. Like hired servants, we can dismiss them when they inconvenience us. Some of the arguments are not borrowed from the ghost—notably the absolute idealist view that the totality comes prior to all its parts, that as a totality it is rounded, embracing, kind and maternal, and that the angular machines are but fictions, not so much because we made them, but because they are arbitrary abstractions from the whole. There is also the fallacious argument that as the social and human world is *made* by the concepts of the participants, it consequently cannot be alien to them, and that nothing can possibly show the participants' concepts to be illusions. We are what and as we think. This might be called the delusion of the *Almacht des Begriffes*.

Thus there is a fair amount of parallelism between the predicaments of the ghost and of the machine, as extremes may mirror each other. Both are introduced as selectors. Each does its job well, but each runs into a major difficulty: one generates a world rather more unstable, elusive and private than we can bear, and the other, a world more cold, inhuman and rule-bound that we can easily tolerate, or than is compatible with our favoured, normal assumption of our free participation in the world.

There are some interesting contrasts between the two visions. Philosophically, the ghost seems more formidable than the machine. Any philosophy faces the problems of the regress—the question of how it justifies its own starting point without at the same time using some *other* starting point, and perhaps no philosophy can surmount this. It must always face the dilemma between question-begging prejudgment (i.e. using some other, independent premiss) and total arbitrariness (i.e. not using it). But empiricism seems to come closer to escaping this dilemma than most: by allowing only that which is inescapably *given*, and judging all else in terms of it, it would seem to have found as self-sustaining a basis as any. Bishop Berkeley dwelt on this given, ineluctable quality of sensation:

But, whatever power I have over my own thoughts, I find that the ideas actually perceived by the Sense have not a like dependence on my will. When in broad daylight I open my eyes, it is not in my power to choose whether I shall see or no, or to determine what particular objects shall present themselves to my view . . .[52]

Note how it is this proud and total independence of sensations from our will (and, Berkeley might have added, more contentiously, from our concepts and hence our cultures), which make them so attractive as cognitive arbitrators. Corrupt, dependent arbitrators are worthless, but the empiricists at least make out a case for having found a fairly uncorrupted one.

By contrast, the premiss of the machine has no such intrinsic plausibility. The idea that only structures are real may be attractive or repulsive, and clearly it is both, sometimes even to one and the same person, but it does not carry any kind of luminous air of self-evidence, of logical self-sufficiency. It is certainly an idea which is important, influential, and pregnant with consequences; its historical role or its logical fecundity cannot be gainsaid. But it is not immediately appealing simply as a self-sustaining premiss, as a regress-terminator.

This perhaps helps to explain a striking historical fact, namely that the ghost is far better represented among, as it were, the top eleven of the world's philosophers, than is the machine. The ghost is extremely well-served by its actual champions, its case is presented by the best counsel. By contrast, for a presentation of the materialistic–mechanistic vision, we must go either to the second rank, or to thinkers whose centre of gravity is not their materialism, but elsewhere (for instance, in political theory). This could be just an historical accident, but I suspect it is more than that.

The source of conflict *between* the two visions is obvious: each eliminates, when rigorously applied, the very foundation of the other. This

[52] G. Berkeley, *The Principles of Human Knowledge*, 29.

82

gives rise to what might be called the Berkeley/Lenin debate: is the world made of experience, with material stuff being but the patterns of experience, or a set of fictions added on so as to name and organise those patterns—or is it made of hard impenetrable stuff, with experience but an echo of it, an echo which selects and amplifies in accordance with the mechanism of one further structure, namely our own cognitive apparatus? There would seem to be no compromise possible between these two visions.

At the same time, the two visions do on occasion converge. There is, as stated, the opportunist/political consideration—neither is compatible with religious orthodoxy, and the enemy of my enemy is my friend. Also, empiricism is concerned with selecting *information*, whereas mechanism selects patterns of *explanation*. This might at least avoid or minimise the collision, by making the two doctrines live at different planes. We shall see whether the compatibility might, in some circumstances at least, be even closer than this.

THE INCOMPETENT GHOST

The area of ultimate validation, of the selection of permissible evidence for our picture of the world, is not the only area in which the ghost and the machine come into conflict. They also clash, very significantly, in the field of what may be called explanation of competence or intelligence. How does one explain behaviour? And, in particular, intelligent human behaviour? How does one explain competence, the ability to recognise and satisfy certain standards, over a large, indefinite or infinite range of situations, or even the capacity to innovate, and to innovate radically?

Both the ghost and the machine have been invoked as the basis of explanatory models intended to answer this question, or at least to indicate the direction in which the answer to it is to be found. We thus have both a materialist or structuralist explanatory theory on the one hand, and an empiricist explanatory theory on the other.

But in this field, the merits and demerits of the two theories are by no means evenly balanced. An empiricist explanatory theory, an attempt to use the ghost to account for human competence, does exist; it has been put forward by thinkers, even by thinkers of genius, and in modern times systematic efforts have been made to 'operationalise' it. But it is a theory of little value. It is interesting mainly for historical reasons, or for purposes of contrast, for highlighting viable alternatives through the stressing of an unviable one.

It is however extremely important to remember that the feebleness of the empiricist explanatory model of behaviour does *not* prove much, one way or the other, about its merit as a selector of permissible evidence. On the contrary—it highlights the independence of these two aspects. It is a common and disastrous mistake to suppose that the two aspects stand and fall together. This supposition often springs from a prior failure to see that there are indeed two separate questions.

In the work of the greatest empiricist, David Hume, and in the minds of many other people, the two aspects of empiricism are conflated and confused. Hume's *Treatise* was conceived by him both as a work delimiting what we could know, what kind of things could be true (as a selector doctrine, in our terms), *and* as a psychological explanation of how our minds actually work. One suspects that Hume would indeed have stressed the latter aspect, though modern opinion (rightly, in my view) considers his contribution to be far more important in the former sphere. He was a great thinker, but he was probably mistaken about the area in which his greatness lay.

The modern stress on the selector aspect of empiricism has led some philosophers to forget that empiricism did also offer such psychological, explanatory theories of human conduct—that the ghost also tried to *be* its own machine. Philosophers have on the whole recently refrained from trying to make that machine work in any real sense, but they have, sometimes unwittingly, encouraged many others to try—notably behaviouristically inclined psychologists, linguists and so on. So, the ghost *as* (not *in*) a machine is quite frequently encountered. The name for this programme is behaviourism, which is a bastard doctrine, a fruit of miscegenation between empiricism and mechanism—for it takes over from the machine the structural, external, objective, 3-D ideal of explanation, and from the (selector) ghost the restrictive principle concerning what may or may not be employed, namely the principle that only that which is experienced may be used. The resulting programme is a difficult one indeed; the behaviourist tries to erect a model to explain our conduct, but the model may only contain familiar, so to speak well-experienced elements—such as the 'association of ideas', rechristened (in the interest of a scientifically decent third-person language) 'stimulus and response'. Variants of this programme account for a fair amount of 'scientific psychology' and related subjects.

It is interesting to find Professor W. V. Quine offering precisely this account of the origin of behaviourism, except that, oddly enough, he actually favours this transformation, and considers it to be an improvement:

Empiricism of the modern sort, or behaviourism broadly so called, comes of the old empiricism by a drastic externalisation. The old empiricist looked inward upon his ideas; the new empiricist looks outward ... When empiricism is externalised ... the idea itself passes under a cloud; talk of ideas comes to count as unsatisfactory except in so far as it can be paraphrased into terms of dispositions to observable behaviour.[53]

This account of the genesis of behaviourism cannot be faulted. What is

[53] W. V. Quine, in *Language and Philosophy*, ed. Sidney Hook (New york, 1969), pp. 97 and 98.

odd is that Quine should consider this metamorphosis to be a change for the better. Empiricism in fact has no business whatever translating itself into a third-person language, and it turns itself into an absurdity when it does so. The error springs precisely from a failure to see that two quite separate questions are under consideration:

(1) What kind of evidence can, in the end, settle issues about the nature of this world?—and

(2) What type of model will best explain human and other intelligent behaviour?

Empiricism supplies an enormously important and persuasive answer to the first question – and for the purpose of answering this question it might just as well—indeed it would better—stay in the 'internal' language of ideas, in that 'language of Hobbes, Gassendi and Locke' which Quine thinks is out-of-date. This is in fact a very good language, for it highlights the important fact that in a liberal individualist society, it is, in the end, individuals who make up their minds, in the light of *their* experience, whether or not theories are acceptable, and that when an individual privately considers such an issue he does, in the end, translate the evidence into first-person language.

But empiricism can also be used to provide a very feeble answer to the second question, an answer which consists of a restrictive injunction, limiting the levers and pulleys and mechanisms used in the explanatory model of behaviour, to the crudest elements allegedly found in experience. Not surprisingly, a machine produced in so restrictive a workshop does not amount to much. But the feebleness of this answer is in no way redeemed or mitigated by its articulation in 'external', third-person language. All it achieves thereby is to obscure the underlying idea, which could be summed up, paraphrasing Durkheim, as a curious determination to explain the conscious by the conscious. Whatever merit there might be in this, is obscured by translating the first-person language of ideas into the third-person language of stimulus and response. It then consists of a methodological restriction on explanations that is both arbitrary and unworkable.

Thanks largely to its own sustained propaganda, behaviourism is widely credited with being tough-minded. Its protagonists do of course believe this in all sincerity, and have succeeded in convincing their opponents on this point, so that there tends to be an element of admiration mixed with the fear and hostility with which behaviourism is viewed. The behaviourists themselves are not unaware of this, and proudly take this ambivalent admiration as something which is their due: are they not men strong and brave enough to forego the comforts of illusion, of the mentalistic vision of man, in the interests of lucidity and the advancement of learning?

Alas, just this is their error. What makes the behaviourist recipe for model-construction so feeble is not its quite spurious tough-minded husk, but its genuinely soft, mushy, mentalistic centre. Its restrictions on elements which may be employed in models are inspired, precisely, by the 'inward', mentalistic distinction between what is and is not very familiar to us in daily experience. ('Association' is very familiar and hence permissible.) No amount of translation of this tender-minded restriction into tough-sounding third-person language, loosely (very loosely, as Chomsky has shown) attached to laboratory procedures, can make this any less tender-minded.

Chomsky's celebrated attack on the behaviourist programme[54] unfortunately also contributes to the confusion, for Chomsky, like Hume and like his opponents, does not distinguish clearly or consistently enough between empiricism as a selector doctrine, and as a recipe for explanatory model construction. It is the latter which he really attacks. Empiricism self-consciously transformed into a scheme for all explanatory models of conduct, *is* behaviourism. Confusion is increased by Chomsky's tendency to speak as if empiricism *as such* were the object of attack, rather than the behaviourist endeavour to extract an explanatory model of conduct from it. However, in following his argument we may on occasion need to adopt his language and speak as if he were attacking 'empiricism'.

Chomsky's particular failure to distinguish between the two aspects seems to spring from a curious failure of historical imagination: he takes empiricism as a selector, as an arbiter of theories, so completely for granted that it need not be asserted, defined or defended:

All conjectures . . . must 'eventually be made sense of in terms of external observation'. This is, to sure, a sense of 'behaviourism' which would cover all reasonable men.[55]

'Reasonable men' appear to be defined in terms of automatic acceptance of selector-empiricism . . . ! But time was when empiricism was not held to be quite so self-evident (even assuming that it has achieved such a status today). Time was when men believed in 'innate ideas' as an explanation of *why some ideas were valid*, in other words as a *legitimation of beliefs*. If Chomsky remembered this, he might be less inclined to take it as read and as too obvious to need saying. But in fact he is content to call the doctrine he attacks 'empiricism', though what he is really attacking is the bastard empiricism of the behaviourists, the conjunction of the machine ideal of explanation, with restrictions on the elements from which the machine may be built, restrictions borrowed from empiricism, as an insistence on the exclusive use of 'experiential' elements. But a restriction which makes a fair amount of sense and works

[54] Review by N. Chomsky of *Verbal Behaviour* by B. F. Skinner, (New York, 1957). The review itself is reprinted in J. Fodor and J. D. Katz, eds., *Structure of Language* (Englewood Cliffs, 1964) and L. Jacobovitz and M. S. Miron, eds., *Readings in Psycholinguistics* (Englewood Cliffs, 1967).

[55] N. Chomsky, John Locke lectures, reproduced in part in *The Times Literary Supplement*, 15 May 1969, p. 523

tolerably well for delimiting the permissible range of evidence, in the final court of appeal in which claims about the nature of our world are to be heard, does not either make sense or work when applied to a completely different task—namely, how to construct a model accounting for a given range of competence. It is then neither required nor feasible. Only the confusion cited makes it *seem* required.

Chomsky's convincing attack on the behaviourist programme contains several arguments. In particular, he shows how the 'stimulus–response' account fails utterly when it is applied to the enormously rich range of actual human verbal competence. Far from it being the case that the allegedly independent 'stimuli' somehow produce our ability to use and understand all the descriptive and nominal terms in our language, by the process of association and reinforcement, on the contrary, the alleged 'stimuli' themselves can only be identified retro-actively, as those aspects of situations which (to save the theory) are said to 'control' the use of the descriptive term in question. Our incredibly rich and complex power to generate and recognise sentences simply cannot be explained as consequences of like responses to like stimuli.

Chomsky shows that if the tough-minded, operationalised, experimental language is used strictly and literally, it does not get anywhere near explaining actual human conduct; if, on the other hand, it is applied to the complexities of actual behaviour, the seemingly tough-minded terms are only used in an unbelievably extended, analogical and loose manner.

All this is rather obvious, at any rate after and thanks to Chomsky. The ghost is incompetent, and simply cannot be used to account for the types of competence which in fact we do possess. But if it is so obvious and undeniable, why is it that highly intelligent men find the alleged insights and the programme of behaviourism so compulsive?

The answer seems to be that, like Chomsky himself, they tend to conflate and confuse empiricism as a censor doctrine, as a criterion of permissible evidence, with empiricism as a (quite illegitimate) limit on the elements employable in explanatory model-construction. Once this confusion is perpetrated, behaviourism is automatically treated as the last or only bulwark against supernaturalism and apriorism: if our minds were allowed to work in any way other than the 'ghostly' one, if they were more than receptacles for incoming sensations, more than 'bundles', why then the door would be open to *a priori* claims to knowledge. If it were admitted that the mind works in some more complex way, this would—so runs the fallacious inference—be a warrant for cognitive claims which would place themselves beyond the reach of factual checks.

The obverse of this fallacious inference is of course the belief that if behaviourism is destroyed by arguments such as Chomsky's then this justifies some kind of 'spiritualist' vision of man. This inference is equally misguided.

The obverse of the incompetent ghost, the self-collecting bundle which spins the world from its own sensations, is the all-knowing, or at any rate extremely well-clued-up or well-programmed baby, in possession, at least potentially, of all the ideas required to grasp the world. The conflict between these two is an old, deep and important one. What is interesting is the manner in which this profound issue has been revived recently in connection with the work of Noam Chomsky in linguistics.

Let it be said and stressed once again that the fascinating and important recent debate[56] derives much of its complexity from the unnecessary confusion of three separable questions:

(1) whether the capacities displayed by human minds in acquiring language, knowledge, etc., can be explained as manifestations of a simple mechanism (such as one working on the principles of stimulus and response), of whether, on the contrary, they can only be explained as manifestations of some *far more complex structure*;

(2) whether these human capacities can be explained by *any* mechanism, or whether, on the contrary, they can only be explained in a 'mentalistic' manner, whatever that may mean. In practice, it tends to mean either giving a kind of explanatory *carte blanche* to notions such as 'spontaneous creativity', 'thinking substance', or whatnot, or alternatively insisting that human minds can only be understood 'from the inside', in terms of the concepts they themselves employ in daily life, and not in terms of some constructed mechanism;

(3) whether or not empiricism gives a correct account of how claims to knowledge are in the end validated or, in other words, whether all cognitive claims must in the end submit to the verdict of experience.

Chomsky's revival of the doctrine of innate ideas had, in academic philosophy, a kind of *succes de scandale*. The notion that we possess ideas prior to experience had supposedly been exorcised at least from English-speaking philosophy for so long that its revival struck many as similar to, say, the revival of a belief in witchcraft. To find a reputable, nay a brilliant thinker espousing so outrageous a notion was a shock indeed.

Much of the outrage is in fact unnecessary and springs from misunderstanding, from the unwarranted conflation of the three distinct issues – though this is a confusion to which Chomsky himself, it must be admitted, has made his contribution. The philosophical overtones and implications of his work, over and above the question of innate ideas, have also often been misunderstood in consequence of the same confusions.

The centre of gravity of Chomsky's work in linguistics is relevant above all to question (1). He shows that the extraordinary power we possess of

[56] Contributions by N. Chomsky, H. Putman, and N. Goodman in *Synthese*, vol. 17, no. 1, March 1967, and by N. Chomsky, W. V. Quine, R. Wells and others in *Language and Philosophy*, ed. S. Hook (New York, 1969).

producing and recognising countless quite novel sentences, cannot be explained by the 'echo' or 'petty accumulation' of stimulus–response models deriving from classical empiricism and elaborated by behaviourist psychology. Over and above this, he endeavours to specify the kind of structure which could or does account for our competence in these matters. Irrespective of whether these positive endeavours are successful, his negative, demolition work seems to be entirely conclusive.

'Generative' power, with which Chomsky is concerned, is a rather special kind of causation. This can be made clear with the help of a simple example. If we look at a typescript, we can specify the minimal richness or 'powers' of a typewriter which would be capable of generating the patterns of a given range or variety. The specification of the kind of structure the typewriter would need in order to generate all the patterns within that range would be a kind of minimal explanation of its powers. This specification is in its way quite independent of the question as to whether the choice of patterns typed, the behaviour of the fingers pressing the keys, was or was not 'causally controlled' or how it was controlled. There is nothing even to indicate that within the general Chomskian strategy, there is anything to lead one to tackle this issue. What the approach and its findings *do* exclude is merely the contention that the powers or mechanism of the typewriter could ever be explained on the 'echo' model, with 'bits of experience' as the sound echoed, and sentences as the echo. Chomsky clearly and conclusively showed that this is a pseudo-machine or a pseudo-explanation.

But his work is really concerned with problems of the range of sentences that the typewriter can record, and not at all with what it is that determines the sequence of actually typed sentences. No doubt, if one were to turn to this latter problem, one should rightly also be constrained by his conviction that mentalism is vacuous and explains nothing, that one must seek some 'structure'. And note that the really distinguishing feature of mentalism is the treatment of mental powers as self-explanatory. This dreadful error is found not merely in overt mentalists who speak of 'mental substance', the 'creative human spirit' or whatever, but equally, and more surreptitiously and hence harmfully, in those would-be practitioners of tough-mindedness, who treat either the echo-phenomenon ('stimulus and response'), or our intellectual powers as characterised in pithy Anglo-saxon words ('analytical behaviourism'), as somehow *self-explanatory*. They are nothing of the kind.

It is at this point that philosophic misapprehensions creep in. The first one is not yet epistemological, but concerns the status of the human spirit. Chomsky shows the behaviourists to be mistaken. The behaviourists are supposed to be tough-minded, especially by those who fear and dislike tough-mindedness in the interpretation of man. So, if Chomsky is right and they are wrong, is this not a rebuttal of reductionism, and hence the long-sought affirmation and vindication of the free, creative, spontaneous, irreducible human spirit?[57]

No. Chomsky's work is relevant to the question concerning whether our minds are simple or complex mechanisms. (He makes it obvious that they are complex ones.) It is not really all that relevant to the question whether they are mechanisms at all, a question on the whole he prejudges, in favour of the commendable assumption that they must be mechanisms— for what else could ever explain *anything*? The idea or assumption that only structures can explain anything, and that mentalism—in the sense of invoking 'mind' as an *explanation*—is vacuous and explains nothing, pervades Chomsky's thought so much that he does not bother to stress it.[58] This is one reason why some people are misled concerning the real import of his arguments. But there are other reasons. Whilst his commitment to the structural ideal of explanation is so complete as to be only expressed in a casual and *en passant* manner, his enthusiasm for his supposed rationalist ancestors is explicit and emphatic. Hence readers tend to miss the point that he endorses only their negative view their rejection of the 'petty accumulation' or 'echo' theory of the acquisition of language, and not at all their positive mentalism ... though Chomsky's own comments on the Cartesians make this plain:

the proposals of the Cartesians were themselves of no real substance; the phenomena in question are not explained satisfactorily by attributing them to an 'active principle' called 'mind', the properties of which are not developed in any coherent or comprehensive way.[59]

So much for mentalism.

Furthermore, people are misled by Chomsky's repeated and indeed relevant stress on the creativity and originality in the human use of language. But this only means the perfectly valid, but negative, assertion that what we say on any given occasion cannot be tied to 'antecedent conditions' of some kind, as the behaviourist (in fact crypto-mentalist) programme would require. It does not in any way preclude structural explanations of a more complex kind, and indeed the whole of Chomsky's approach presupposes that such explanations deserve to be pursued. What

[57] Not all commentators are starry-eyed enough to make this mistake. For instance, Mrs Shirley Letwin writes in quite a different vein (*The Times Literary Supplement*, 26 June 1969), noting angrily the incompatibility between Chomsky's strategies of explanation of linguistic competence on the one hand, and libertarianism on the other, and complains of Chomsky's failure to deal seriously with this stress.

[58] He does occasionally make it explicit, as for instance in connection with the neo-mentalist Gilbert Ryle, who deserves to be classified as such, notwithstanding his own view of his position, in virtue of his characteristic propensity to treat human skills, when successfully employed, as self-explanatory: 'Ryle is content simply to cite the fact that "intelligent behaviour" has certain properties ... these are described in terms of "powers", "propensities" and "dispositions" which are characterised only through scattered examples. These constitute a new myth as mysterious and poorly understood as Descartes' "mental substance".' N. Chomsky *Cartesian Linguistics* (New York, 1966), pp. 12 and 81.

[59] N. Chomsky, *Language and Mind* (New York, 1968), p. 12.

90

the mentalists/humanists fail to see at this point is that for Chomsky, creativity or spontaneity is a problem, not a solution or (as it is for them) a resting-place. It is stressed because it requires explanation, and because it has, most conspicuously, failed to be explained by earlier theories, and not, most emphatically, because it could itself ever explain anything.

Finally, and most irrelevantly, there are the associations generated by Chomsky's political activities. In politics, Chomsky is conspicuously on the side of the radical angels, and radical criticisms of current societies often include the rejection of its mechanistic organisation, education, and vision of man. Hence, by loose association, it would seem to follow that the Chomskian strategy of explanation of human competence must have similar implications . . .

All this is, of course, a set of irrelevancies and misunderstandings. But their consequences are curious indeed. Note that the justified rejection of mentalism (owing to its explanatory emptiness) carries the implication that, in one important sense, *all* ideas are innate. If only structures ever really explain anything (which I believe to be true), it follows that even in the case of an organism which only records external impressions, in an echo-like manner, it is *still* some internal structure which needs to be specified, if that echoing power is to be really explained. (And note that, contrary to the supposition of both mentalists and behaviourists, who in fact are very close to each other, there is nothing whatever that is self-explanatory about a sensitivity which is capable of noting and retaining external impressions. In fact the structure of any kind of 'skin' capable of sensitivity, however passive, probably needs to be very complex indeed.) In *this* sense, it is simply a consequence of a theory of explanation, of the insistence on structures and of the rejection of the illusion of self-explanatoriness of sensibility, that ideas are ever 'innate'.

This universal and indiscriminate (though in its context valid) sense of innateness, tends to get confused, in the minds of both critics and defenders of Chomsky's thesis, with the 'discriminate', specific point about complex intelligences, capable of using finite means for infinite ends, recognising countless original sentences, and in general possessed of those powers which are the starting point of Chomsky's argument. Almost in one breath it is claimed that ideas must be innate$_1$ because only structures explain (and as minds *are* these structures, the conclusion does indeed follow), and also that they must be innate$_2$ because we are very clever and perform tricks which could never be in the repertoire of accomplishments of a machine working simply by a reiteration of stimulus–response patterns. Unfortunately, the argument does not use subscripts and distinguish the two kinds of innateness, each in its own distinct way valid.

The odd consequences of the confusion are as follows. Normally, mentalists insist on our creative powers, and mechanicists on their limitation and reducibility to simple principles. In one part of the debate roles get reversed. The critics of Chomsky's innateness thesis suddenly stress the humdrum, unsurprising nature of our powers in an attempt to avert some hidden-structure explanation. This is, in effect, an attack on the argument derived from the rich complexity of our powers. It is the result of the error of supposing Chomsky's insistence on our complex achievement to be a premiss of his general 'structuralist' explanatory strategy; were this so, the strategy might be undermined by pointing to the fact (if such it were) that there is nothing remarkable about our capacity to learn languages. ('Why, in Paris every concierge speaks fluent French!') But actually this *general* strategy of Chomsky's is quite independent of this specific premiss or his findings. The complexity of our competence is only relevant to the *kind* of structure that is to be located, and not to the question of whether we are to seek structures at all, a question which is (quite rightly) prejudged in favour of the need to presuppose such structures. That only structures ever explain, and hence that we must look for such localisable and thus 'innate' structures, is given *prior* to the inquiry; what specific, concrete facts concerning our linguistic competence show is that in our case those structures happen to be very complex ones. But all this leads Chomsky's critics into the weird position of saying—but our powers are really not all that remarkable, and *therefore* we are not machines! (In the past, the argument for exempting man from mechanism had the opposite form.) But even if it were true that our powers are not remarkable—and it is only true in the sense that these amazing powers are widely shared by humanity—this would still only be evidence about the *kind* of mechanism involved, and not at all relevant to the issue of whether mechanism is present at all . . .

So much for the issues confused by the conflation of the first two questions. There are also the confusions arising from the intrusion of the third, epistemological issue. Here again, Chomsky is not entirely innocent. Partly, he is at fault in taking empiricism as a theory of the validation of knowledge *so* much for granted, that he cannot conceive of anyone doubting it, and hence takes no precaution against seeming to contradict it. This indicates a curious failure of historical imagination, in one who has written at some length on the history of ideas in his own field.

Here again, his enthusiastic identification with the Rationalists is also to blame. For them, the theory of innate ideas was not merely a tool in approaching the actual mechanics of mind, but also—and sometimes, primarily—an attempt to answer the pressing question of how claims to truth and knowledge were to be validated. This is not the role it plays in Chomsky's thought, of course; but a careless invocation of the slogan of 'innate ideas' cannot but suggest an apriorist *epistemology,* especially as this general confusion is still very widespread. How many people still feel attracted to behaviourist psychology simply under the impression that it constitutes the only defence against apriorism and dogmatism?

But the situation is complicated further by the fact that although Chomsky mostly takes for granted epistemological-normative empiricism, the view that our ideas must be checked by facts and experience, there are also occasions when he has doubts about it. The doubts arise from the fact that our capacity to find true theories, given the paucity of facts and their compatibility with endless theoretical possibilities, is nothing short of miraculous. (Popper for instance deals with this by stressing the miraculous, lucky nature of scientific discovery, the fact that it is never simply a matter of reading the Book of Nature, and be reminding us that these lucky dips are ephemeral and rare.) It is natural for Chomsky to be interested in this fact, for it is of course very analogous to one of the main supports of his theory of 'innate' grammar: the linguistic material placed before a child is too limited and fragmentary to constitute adequate evidence for inferring to the grammar of a language; hence the capacity to 'acquire' an internalised, operational knowledge of that grammar goes vastly beyond the 'evidence' and is, in that sense, an amazing piece of luck, as are successful scientific discoveries. C. S. Peirce was interested in this problem, and invented a term, 'abduction', to name the way the mind has of limiting the number of possible theories covering a given set of data. 'Abduction' thus protects us from the excessive richness of intellectual possibilities, a richness so great that 'the facts' could never really prune them down to manageable proportions. Why should we trust this inner selection procedure? ' ... the reasoning mind is [it] self a product of [the] universe ... [Its] laws are thus incorporated in his own being.' Chomsky, who quotes this passage from Peirce, comments on his solution as follows:

Peirce's argument is entirely without force and ... offers little improvement on the pre-established harmony that it is presumably meant to replace.[60]

Quite so. It is absurd to argue that because mind is part of nature, any principle it employs in the interpretation of nature must therefore be sound. Sociologists however will be amused by the similarity between Peirce and E. Durkheim. In *The Elementary Forms of Religious Life,* Durkheim established to his own satisfaction the social nature and origin of our categories, but nevertheless in the end had to face the question of why or whether we should also trust the concepts which are thus instilled in us. His final answer is also Peirce's ... society is also, like mind, a part of nature, hence its concepts will also be true about nature ... !

There is thus in Chomsky a slight tendency to flirt with epistemological apriorism, at least to the extent of being highly sensitive to the force of Peirce's (or Popper's) problem—how, amongst infinite possibilities and given only the most fragmentary data, do we ever hit on true theories? Might there be something in Peirce's idea that we possess some built-in guide to the true ones ... ? This speculation is entirely marginal to his central argument, but it does alas provide encouragement to those who would mis-read his insistence on locating adequate explanatory structures

[60] Chomsky, *Language and Mind,* p. 82.

93

(and this is what his doctrine of innate ideas really amounts to) and who would treat it as a most scandalous revival of epistemological apriorism, of the view that ideas can be true because they are inside us.

The issue is marginal to his central concerns because the question of truth does not arise with respect to our linguistic powers, as much or as immediately as it would in other spheres. As Chomsky observes, 'language has no objective existence apart from the internalised grammar . . . Hence the doctrine of an innate grammar, unlike the doctrine of innate ideas, does not immediately lead to the mysterious claim that the world out there must conform to what is built in inside us—simply because grammar does not refer to anything out there. It constrains not the world but only our speech.

To sum up: in one sense, *all* ideas are innate, quite irrespective of whether our competence is great or limited. This simply amounts to (or is a corollary of) the correct view that *only structures explain*. And in the end, a structure must be *somewhere*. The place which houses the structure which explains *my* powers, *is* myself. Hence the explanation is, in *that* sense only, 'inside'. This remains true whether I am an imbecile or a genius, and to stress how many hours it takes me to learn a language and internalise a grammar does not either strengthen or weaken the case.

Secondly, there is the enormously important question concerning just how complex the structures are which need to be invoked to explain the kinds of competence which in fact we possess. The non-technical part of Chomsky's work, and its philosophic import, seems to me precisely the highlighting of how very great those powers are, and how very inadequate were the earlier models for explaining them.

Thirdly, there is the question of identifying the ultimate cognitive sovereign, who is to sit in judgment over our competing claims to knowledge. Innatism in this field amounts, in the end, to the intolerable view that some systems of ideas confirm themselves, simply in virtue of being located within the minds or the hearts of some men, or within the conceptual stock of a given tradition, or whatever. It is fairly obvious that Chomsky is not an innatist in this sense, but those who have supposed otherwise can find some excuse, in the tangential remarks about 'abduction', in the wilfully paradoxical self-characterisation, and in some irresponsible ancestor-snatching. (In fact, the Cartesians were not Chomskians.)

But my main point here is this: the turbulent cohabitation of the ghost and the machine, of the empiricist limitations on data or on the assessment of truth, and of the structuralist ideal of explanation (quite freed by now of any dependence on heavy materials, or any materials at all), can be observed both in Chomsky's work, and in the debates occasioned by it. So can the confusions which arise, if the distinct questions that can be answered by each of these pervasive philosophies on turn, are not clearly distinguished and separated.

94

It is worth quoting at length one passage in which Chomsky indicates his attitude to mentalism:[61]

I have been using mentalistic terminology quite freely, but entirely without prejudice as to the question of what may be the physical realisation of the abstract mechanisms postulated to account for the phenomena of behaviour or the acquisition of knowledge. We are not constrained, as was Descartes, to postulate a second substance . . . It is an interesting question whether the functioning and evolution of human mentality can be accommodated within the framework of physical explanation, as presently conceived, or whether there are new principles, now unknown, that must be invoked . . . We can, however, be fairly sure that there will be a physical explanation for the phenomena in question, if they can be explained at all, *for an uninteresting terminological reason,* namely that the concept of 'physical explanation' will no doubt be extended to incorporate whatever is discovered in this domain, exactly as it was extended to accommodate . . . entities . . . that would have offended the common sense of earlier generations. [Italics mine E.G.]

The fascinating and most debatable point contained in this passage is the suggestion that the extension of the notion of 'physical explanation' was 'merely' terminological and somehow arbitrary, with the consequence that the ubiquity of physical explanation—wherever there is a serious and genuine explanation at all, it becomes physical—is an illusion, and a kind of artefact of a definition. The suggestion that the extension of the idea of the physical to *any* genuine explanation is merely terminological, and hence not very interesting, is a profound error. On the contrary, it highlights a most important point: namely, that what is central to the 'materialist' philosophic intuition has nothing to do with the nature of the stuff or material used for erecting explanatory structures, but a great deal to do with precisely the availability of such structures (irrespective of material used).

The notion of 'physical explanation' would not in fact be extended to *anything,* though it certainly is extended to processes that are not merely repugnant to the common sense of earlier generations, but which also in our time need no longer be tangible, visible or visualisable. The elasticity, *and* the limits on the elasticity, of the notion of 'physical explanation' which Chomsky pinpoints so perceptively, illustrate the main point to be made about the mechanistic, erstwhile-materialistic tradition and outlook: the *mechanism* is essential, whereas the (literal) 'materialism', the presence of push-resisting hard stuff, was a irrelevancy, an accretion probably due to conditions of primitive technology in which structures tend to depend on heavy materials. Nowadays, structures are

---

[61] Chomsky, *Language and Mind,* p. 83.

quite independent of them.

But this does not mean that 'structural (or mechanical) explanations' have no antithesis, no rivals. Within science, they may have none, but within human life in general, they emphatically do have them. There are so-called 'explanations' which invoke simply familiarity, or fitness, or a place within a social or semantic system. Chomsky seems to under-rate or simply avert his gaze from the social significance of these rival styles of explanation and the philosophies which have been erected in their defence; in any case, he treats them in very cavalier manner. The extension of the notion of 'the physical' marks the retraction of the self-evident, of that which is explained by a simple appeal to familiarity. This change is no small matter.

He himself applies very high standards: even notions which other people tend to consider to be parts of science, such as 'evolution', are dismissed as vacuous[62] because they do not specify anything precise, concrete, or conceptually tangible.

We can now better understand the real nature of this bewildering debate. Note that it is somewhat paradoxical. In the past, those who wanted to say that man was an automaton, stressed the crude aspects of our behaviour, with the implication that more complex conduct only represented more intricate variations on the same basic themes. By contrast Chomsky *seems* to reach his own version of a 'structuralist' position (i.e. the view that hidden structures and they alone explain our competence) from a stress on the complexity and richness of our behaviour. The argument seems to say—look how very very clever and complex we are—*therefore* what we do is the work of hidden impersonal structures!

This is paradoxical a number of times over. If only our conduct were simpler, if in fact it were susceptible to explanation by the crude tools of the behaviourist, would we then be free angels instead? (This *seems* to be the implied contrast. It could hardly have been the wish of the behaviourists to establish *this*.) Well, no.

The paradox arises as follows. The mechanical or structural ideal of explanation is *simply taken for granted,* and rightly so (just as Chomsky also takes for granted the empiricist norm requiring explanations to be ultimately subject to the test of experience). The norm of 'structural' explanation is imposed by the very nature of explanation, and *not* specifically by the nature of the material. Whether our behaviour be simple or complex, whether in our linguistic competence we make infinite use of finite means, or merely parrot-wise use finite means for finite ends —either way, *only* a structure can explain, and as it is extremely unlikely that the structure is already explicitly present to consciousness, it follows that either way we are to be explained, in that sense, mechanically and heteronomously. (And if the structure were already present to the

[62] Chomsky, *Language and Mind*, p. 83.

96

unsophisticated consciousness, this would only be a piece of good fortune, and its existence and adequacy would still require further confirmation—the sheer presence in consciousness could never validate the structure—and thus this unlikely contingency would also not really affect the situation.)

What the *specific* material does establish is that the competence, the range of behaviour to be explained, is very complex and wide, and consequently that only structures of a certain (and in fact very high) level of complexity *can* explain that behaviour. This part of the argument really runs—complex behaviour, therefore a complex structure.

But this argument gets superimposed on and conflated with the other, more abstract, presupposed previous argument, which runs—only structures explain anything, therefore our conduct (complex or simple) can only be explained by structures (which could only contingently be mirrored in consciousness; and in any case, consciousness as such explains nothing).

The two arguments are superimposed and confused both by the critics and the defenders of the position; hence the total and unholy confusion. The critics invoke both the vacuousness of the innateness hypothesis—not strong enough to explain the phenomena—and the alleged feebleness, so to speak, of the phenomena—does anything much need to be invoked to explain something so common and familiar? And indeed, the innateness hypothesis was once quite vacuous; a 'thinking substance' explains nothing. And indeed, mental phenomena are very familiar, and if *that* is your criterion, they require no explanation.

The confusion is of course also much assisted by those who, far from setting up to be critics of Chomsky, would be only too eager to invoke him as the prophet of some new spiritualism. The effectiveness of his demolition of behaviourism delights them, and his insistence on creativity, on our infinite use of finite means (not to mention all those Rationalist and romantic ancestors) encourages them further. (And there is also the tacit but, I suspect, influential argument, to the effect that anyone so vigorously on the side of the angels on politics must also be on the side of the angels in philosophy.) But they should beware. The stress on creativity is concerned to map its mechanics, and not to invoke the evidence for our escaping all mechanical explanation altogether.[63]

The paradoxicality disappears once the two levels of the argument are clearly distinguished. 'Innateness' is both a way of insisting on the universal, undiscriminating fact that only structures explain (argument 1) *and* a way of insisting on the much more specific fact that the particular

---

[63] In a footnote of *Cartesian Linguistics* (note 18, p. 81), Chomsky goes out of his way not to exclude the possibility that La Mettrie's mechanistic programme 'may be in principle correct'. In brief, the facts of linguistic 'creativity' are invoked to destroy the over-simple model of the behaviourists, and *not* to deny the possibility of 'mechanical', hence impersonal explanatory models.

structures erected by behaviourists, are inadequate for the specific purpose of explaining human linguistic competence and the ability to learn (argument 2).

This is how Chomsky is read by some. Others prefer to see pseudo-argument 3: we are not machines at all, because our capacities are so amazing.

Pseudo-argument 3 arises from an unwarranted extension from the demolition of simple models (therefore, it seems to these expositors, *no* explanatory models at all!), coupled with all that suggestive talk about Cartesianism. Pseudo-argument 3 arises from taking a premiss from one argument and a conclusion from quite another.

To summarise the situation:

Argument 1: we are in some sense machines anyway, because the very nature of explanation makes us so. If subject to scientific explanation *at all*, that explanation will always invoke impersonal structures, which are not necessarily also present to consciousness. (Consciousness being present only contingently, it is the structures alone which are essential to explanation.)

Argument 2: our minds have very complex structures indeed, because the amazing range of our abilities shows this to be so.

Both arguments happen to be valid. Their superimposition on each other, due to expository carelessness by both Chomsky and his critics, leads to confusion and the unintended appearance of the absurd arguments:

Pseudo-argument 3: we are not machines, because our abilities are so very amazing!

Or, by reaction to 2, pseudo-argument 4: we are not machines, because there is nothing remarkable about our powers, really.

THE POLITICS OF FAMILIARITY, OR THE HUMAN USE OF HUMAN BEINGS

The really objectionable thing is the failure to see the problem at all, the failure to see that human competence, in its richness and variety, requires explanation. At the centre of Chomsky's thought there is an acute awareness of a problem others either ignored or grossly under-rated.[64] The problem in his case is that we possess the capacity to utter and to understand an unlimited number of sentences. Almost everything in his approach then hinges on this, plus the requirement that the explanation be in terms of a precisely specified structure, which shows just how that which is 'generated' or understood comes to be so (rather than making do

---

[64] Consider for instance his comment on C. F. Hockett: 'Among modern linguists, Hockett is unusual in that he has at least noticed that a problem exists.' Hockett's proposed solution to the problem of the utterance and comprehension of quite novel sentences is that we do it by 'analogy'. Chomsky, *Cartesian Linguistics,* p. 82.

with schematic behaviourism or mentalism).

It is understandable enough that, through lethargy and laziness, that which is familiar should be treated as self-explanatory. But here one might ask—once the problem is highlighted, why should people resist awareness of it? In fact, they do—and for quite an interesting reason. Any explanation of human conduct or competence in terms of a genuine structure is morally offensive—for a genuine structure is impersonal, it is an 'it', not an 'I'. Chomskian structures are also known to be, in part, well hidden from consciousness; he himself lays great stress on this. If this be the correct strategy in the study of man, then the *I* is ultimately to be explained by an *it* (alas). The Freudian *id* was beastly but, when all is said and done, it was cosily human in its un-housetrained way; at worst you could say it was all too human; it was human nature seen in the image of conscious man, but with gloves off. (Like us, but without the advantages we've had, if you know what I mean.) The explanation of our unthinking, quasi-automatic competence into explanatory schemata, outlining structures which are not normally accessible to us at all, is far more sinister. This kind of *id* is not violent, sexy and murderous, it is just totally indifferent to us. In the case of the Chomskian programme, the impact of this awareness is mitigated by the fact that only language is at stake (in the first instance) and language is, morally speaking, fairly neutral. People are less distressed by a 'heteronomous' account of their linguistic competence than they would be by a similar account of other skills. But in fact, Chomsky's central point applies throughout the field of explanations of human competence, and not merely within the field of language which happens to be his main concern.

All the same, we can now see why the lure of the self-explanatoriness of that which is human should be so very strong. It is not merely a logical error, it is virtually a socio-political programme. It is a kind of populism, a defence of the adequacy of ordinary notions against more high-powered styles of explanation, which would deprive those ordinary notions and their users of authority. Generally this defence takes the form of putative demonstrations of the impossibility of more fundamental explanations in these fields. (Recently, the doctrines of the self-explanatoriness of human powers and of the self-sufficiency, the ultimacy of ordinary discourse, went hand in hand. Roughly, each kind of discourse corresponds to some human 'faculty', as they used to be called, and the self-justifying status of the kind of discourse corresponds to the self-explanatoriness of the human competence.) People are even more reluctant to admit that *man* explains nothing, than they were to admit that God explains nothing. (Laplace was wrong to say that this hypothesis was unnecessary. The point about it is that it is grossly *insufficient*.) It is the mentalism, not the transcendence, of theological explanations which makes them objectionable; and this mentalism is shared by 'humanist' explanations.

The resistance arises from the feeling that if human powers were not self-explanatory, then they are explained and hence controlled by something else, and thus we become parts of nature and not our own masters. The pejorative name for such a view is 'scientism', which generally refers to unpalatable implications or presuppositions of science. We shall see that subsumption of man under impersonal explanatory schemata is not a specific finding or an arbitrary research attitude, but a consequence of the very nature of explanation.

The alignment and disposition of parties on this disputed field is somewhat complex, and superficially confused. One can, however, learn to identify and understand the parties and their order of battle, their affinities and oppositions.

To begin with, the struggle is triangular, between reductionists, humanists and behaviourists. It is the behaviourists who are partly responsible for this complication. It is of course customary to class them with 'scientistic' reductionism, as mortal enemies of 'humanism'; it is thus that they see themselves, and it is thus that their enemies see them, and this aspect of theirs scares many, or gives them half-agreeable *frissons*. But all this is deceptive. Behaviourists are sheep in wolf's clothing. It is true that they abjure the use of consciousness, either as a source of evidence or as explanation or both (when they are lucid enough to distinguish these two aspects), and, in their extreme form, they deny any meaning to the very term; it is true, and more significant, that they are inspired by an ideal of impersonal, general explanation. But, unwittingly, through their misapplication of the restrictive empiricist principle, they insist that the explanatory theory be couched in something that is, in fact, most familiar and 'intelligible' and *inward,* namely, *association.* This, if their vision of man were valid, could not be counted as an unqualified victory for 'scientism'. On the contrary: the human image of man would be preserved, in as far as our conduct and our ability would be explained in terms of something very human indeed and 'internally' familiar. *Man* would remain familiar and intelligible, if somewhat impoverished and dull.

But leaving out the pseudo-scientistic, crypto-humanist behaviourists, we are left with the rest of the humanist camp. Within it, there is considerable variety.

Despite the diversity of type of argument used in support, there is also something which gives this party its unity: the conviction that man is not, or not merely, as he is when seen from outside, by the levelling process of impersonal explanation—but that at least part of the truth about him is only articulable 'internally', in terms of the kind of concepts in which we normally live, make our choices, evaluate ourselves and each other, and so forth.

This is the common thread of 'humanism'—humanism as opposed to mechanism or scientism, of course, and not as opposed to theism. What is at issue is the human vision of man, the defence of anthropomorphism in human studies. 'The proper study of mankind' is no longer at issue; what is at issue is the style of explanation, not the choice of area *for* investigation. 'The proper explanation of mankind is human', they might say. The fact that the opponent, the great alternative, is no longer theism but 'scientism', is of course profoundly significant. It illustrates the changing role of the transcendent and the hidden in human life; its invocation is no longer connected with the more-than-human, the divine, but rather, with the less-than-human or the impersonal. From this follows a great transformation of the role of severely immanentist, restrictionist philosophies, which would forbid anything not familiar from our own experience. Once, such recommendations were mainly directed against theology and religion. Now, though they may use tough-minded 'positivistic' slogans, they tend to be anti-scientific.

The issue of the human vision of man is probably the most important one in the philosophy of science. Once upon a time, the sheer viability of science was probably the biggest issue: could scientific knowledge be attained at all? This was Descartes' problem. The question is still central in Kant, though by then it has a kind of retrospective twist: the viability is no longer in doubt, what is puzzling is how one should explain it. That puzzlement still remains, no doubt, but it continues to be an academic or theoretical one: we should like to know the answer, but in practice it makes little difference whether we know it or not. Science plainly does work, and no one is inhibited in the pursuit of scientific inquiry by the reflection that the validity of scientific method (whatever its essence may be) has not been conclusively demonstrated. Might it fail tomorrow? Well, in some sense, perhaps it might; the fact remains that this is a fear that neither inspires nor inhibits any action.

The other problem, on the other hand, is overwhelmingly real, and not simply theoretical. Briefly, it could be summed up as the incompatibility of cognition and identity. It is a cliché of literary philosophers to say that modern man is Faustian, but it is true in a very precise sense. Cognition and identity are incompatible. The price of genuine, powerful, technologically enriching science is that its style of explanation ruthlessly destroys those very notions in terms of which we identify ourselves. In a cognitively low-powered society, the ideas in terms of which identities are forged and life is lived are not in great danger, at least from intellectual erosion. But the salient feature of scientific knowledge is that its explanatory schemata are impersonal, indifferent to idiosyncrasy and identity, and articulated in terms which are socially and morally blind, and which are, indeed, generally unintelligible without specialised and technical training. This means, to put it brutally, that what really happens is quite other than that which we suppose as part of ordinary life; or to put it the other way round, in Gaston Bachelard's words, the world we live in, and the world of thought, are not the same. The *Lebenswelt* loses its status; though we must needs go on living in it, for we have no other, it becomes devalued, and we cannot treat it seriously. When important decisions are faced, we must seek information from more reliable sources, when they are available to us. Cheap consolations, to the effect that science and its concepts are but fictions, devices, without validity outside their specialised context, and without real authority to suspend the dear notions of ordinary life – these are indeed cheap, facile, spurious consolations.

This is one of the central problems of the philosophy of science. It is of course a problem not internal to science or the pursuit of scientific inquiry, but one that concerns the role of science in life (or, in a sense, the other way around—what place remains for 'life', for the *Lebenswelt*, in a world in which the only serious knowledge is scientific?).

The 'humanists' must be seen in the context of this problem. What gives them unity is a shared inspiration, a shared fear, a shared hope of escape. The sense and identification of a danger, at any rate, they share. When it comes to solutions or escapes, they differ a good deal. It is illuminating to list and classify at least some of them.

There is naive familiarism—on the analogy of naive realism. Just as naive realism takes our knowledge of external fact for granted, so naive familiarism takes for granted the intelligibility of our conduct. In daily life, we do indeed take for granted a variety of our own powers—unless they fail, or in some other way depart from the ordinary. Just as there is a host of philosophical theories underwriting naive realism, and giving non-naive reasons (sometimes, indeed, unintelligible ones) to justify naive realism, so there are also many philosophic theories which likewise seek to fortify naive familiarism. In both cases these theories tend to be some-what odd, in that they play a game which, they themselves say, they can win but cannot lose. They give reasons, and hence admit that, in principle, contrary reasons might be stronger, and their case might fail. At the same time, their central position is that the naive vision, as such, is un-impugnable, and they fall back on this conviction if their arguments are defeated. Arguments are legitimate, it appears, but only when used on *their* side. But if the case is so prejudged, why argue at all?

Reinforced familiarism falls into various species. For instance, there is Professor Ryle's open assertion of the doctrine that human mental powers are self-explanatory; psychology is relevant only in the case of break-down:

Let the psychologist tell us why we are deceived; but we can tell ourselves and him why we are not deceived. The . . . diagnosis of our mental impotences requires special research methods. The explanation of the exhibition of our mental competences often requires nothing but ordinary good sense.[65]

This totally mistaken view, to the effect that our mental competences are self-explanatory, is a hall-mark of a whole philosophic school. When applied to our cognitive competence, this principle also 'solves' the prob-

[65] Ryle, *The Concept of Mind*, p. 326.

lem of knowledge: no further need of validation and selectors, for our knowledge in general is self-justifying, though we may need to know in specific instances why we have been misled. The epistemology of the movement does indeed have this form. But the doctrine of self-explanatoriness possesses even greater powers than the solution of our cognitive predicament: it is a camouflaged social programme and a general metaphysic. If our mental powers are self-explanatory and hence self-justifying, then the whole social world which is their correlate–object, which is generated by them as the milieu in which they operate, is similarly self-justifying, in all its messy complexity. Societies are what men do, and if what men do explains itself, and if society simply *is* those concepts which guide action, why then the societies themselves can give rise to no problems, at least intellectual ones.

This is indeed one of the modern forms of pluralism. The argument is pluralist in that it disavows the search for simpler and more general explanations or base-lines of intelligibility, and accepts the mish-mash of principles underlying the vast variety of our customary actions, as the kind of thing which requires no further, deeper, more abstract, less-locale-tied kind of explanation.

An important diagnostic sign of the movement is the tendency to play down the problem of determinism. The issue of determinism is merely the most acute point of the general conflict between the commonsensical view of the world, based above all on taking our own powers for granted and hence as self-explanatory, and a more critical attitude which requires the seemingly obvious to be explained, and *not* as itself. In an interesting paper,[66] Chomsky notes Wittgenstein's proscription of the pursuit of anything other than the obvious and the easily accessible, when seeking an account of our verbal performances. Chomsky is however mistaken when he considers, tentatively it is true, the possibility that this restriction is imposed by Wittgenstein as a corollary of some general empiricism. In the case of Wittgenstein, it is made to follow not at all from empiricism, but from a view of the role of philosophy, as having no other role but that of highlighting the obvious in a manner which would cure us of the temptation to stray away from it. The idea that the obvious is self-justifying, and the non-obvious inherently pathological, and the idea that human competences are self-explanatory, are closely linked in this kind of philosophy, and give each other mutual support.

An interesting variant on the view that our powers are self-explanatory, is the view that *cultures* have this status. The argument is that the manner in which a given culture conceives the world and itself-justifying, ultimate and self-explanatory, because its concepts make *that* world, and there is no other way to make any world, and no vantage point from which to

[66] 'Some Empirical Assumptions in Modern Philosophy of Language', in Morgenbesser, Suppes and White (eds.), *Philosophy, Science and Method* (New York, 1969), pp. 260–85.

103

judge or to explain it. (The view that each kind of discourse is self-justifying, and that our powers are self-explanatory are obverses of each other.) The (much desired) consequence of this view is that there is no way of going beyond the concepts in terms of which we, or each culture, lives its life. This doctrine has a variety of quite absurd consequences, notably for sociological method, any one of which is sufficient to constitute its definitive *reductio ad absurdum*. For instance, it follows from it that no social knowledge is possible other than an inward familiarity with concepts used in a society, such as is possessed by its members. Or again, it would follow that systematic absurdity could never have a social role.

There are also older forms of reinforced familiarism, exemplified by Descartes and Berkeley. The trouble with the Cartesian 'thinking substance' is, of course, that it explains nothing, in which respect it resembles naive familiarism; but 'thinking substance' gives a name and an image to that explanatory vacuity. Thus it is both worse—vacuity is camouflaged—but also very significantly better; the camouflage at least implicitly acknowledges the need of an explanation and thus in some measure stimulates the search for it. Such camouflaged and reinforced vacuity has a merit similar to that of hypocrisy, the compliment of vice to virtue—it is a compliment paid by spurious to genuine explanation.

Ryle's position is interesting in this connection, in the way it succeeds in making the worst of all possible worlds. It is normally seen as a (very) tough-minded, unspiritualist kind of doctrine, and that is certainly the way in which its author delights to present it. But appearances are deceptive. What is really objectionable in mentalism is its explanatory vacuity. *This* is not only taken over, but enthusiastically endorsed by Ryle, as the quotation shows, and reasons are invented why it should be so. In other words, the whole weakness of Cartesianism is taken over; but where Cartesianism at least highlighted the existence of a problem, this crypto-mentalism obscures it. Ryle firmly refused to pay the compliment to genuine explanation. It is covertly mentalistic, yet contains no stimulus to further exploration.

Another old form of the doctrine of self-explanatoriness of mind is extremist empiricism, when used in a Berkeleyan manner to establish a mentalistic theory not of man but of the world at large. Here, mind becomes self-explanatory twice over: data in general, of any kind, escape all explanation, and mind in particular becomes the one basic and ultimate material of which being is made. Curiously, modern logical positivism, at any rate as preached in England, for all its superficial tough-mindedness, is in many ways a true descendant of this vision. Its 'positivism' is but skin deep: there is little enthusiasm for positive science or genuine encouragement for its pursuit. Its central message was that the world is just as we experience it; metaphysics *out*, that is true, but in an important sense, science goes out too: it was legitimate, but it could tell us nothing radically different and supplementary to ordinary experience, of which it was but an elaborate précis. There could be no radical discontinuity between it and the ordinary world, to which it was in any case in fief. This view was reinforced by a grotesque underrating of the technical power of science; its techniques were so feeble, it appears, that any literary dilettante could set up as a logician-handyman-consultant to science, and expect his counsel to be taken seriously.

There is also the daemonic kind of self-explanatory mind. This flourished particularly in Germany in the romantic period, and happily is not so popular in the Anglo-Saxon world. Chomsky when he seeks out the ancestors of his innatist view of language, favours the romantics almost as much as he does the rationalists (a curious conjunction of ancestors, incidentally). But his picture of them is rather domesticated and toned down for the Anglo-Saxon market, so to speak. Naturally he likes them for the activist, 'creative' view of language, which, as such, is much opposed to the 'echo' theory which he rejects so firmly and rightly. But the romantics were a little more sinister than that. They rather liked the idea that '*it* thinks' rather than 'I think', with its suggestion of dark hidden forces operating in subterranean channels, far below and out of the reach of the shallow superficialities of consciousness. But where, for Chomsky, this is rather a technical matter, for the romantics far more is involved than the complexity and inaccessibility of grammatical rules. They derived some profound and perhaps occasionally unsavoury satisfaction from contemplating the deep and dark—not, in their case, necessarily complex or precise—forces within us. (Complexity and precision in the operation of these forces would have detracted from the daemonic terror, hence the depth, of these powers.) This element the generative grammarians have not taken over from the romantics, and one is reassured by Chomsky's own remarks about the ethologists who have cashed in on the recent revival of the enthusiasm for the dark potential of the human heart:

It is no doubt true that there are innate tendencies in the human psychic constitution that lead to aggressiveness under specific . . . conditions. But there is little reason to suppose that these tendencies are so dominant as to leave us forever tottering on the brink of a Hobbesian war of all against all.[67]

But the most basic kind of humanist, in the sense of thinker who wishes to save the human image of man, is he who tries to use science itself to destroy scientism. A brilliant representative of this approach is Arthur Koestler.[68] The central device of this approach is to seek a better scientific theory, and scientific evidence, to show that man is not the robot or machine or whatnot which scientism or reductionism would apparently have him be. The tacit assumption of the approach is, of course, that the reductionist conclusions are just one possible kind of conclusion, contingently true if true at all—and that, happily, they are not true.

The best way of highlighting the weakness of this approach is to

[67] N. Chomsky, *Language and Mind* (New York, 1968), p. 82.
[68] *The Ghost in the Machine* (London, 1967).

imagine for a moment that it is valid. Suppose, indeed, that the reductionist 'scientistic' accounts of human creativity, love, heroism, self-sacrifice were *shown,* demonstrably, by concrete evidence, to be false. As far as available theories go, this outcome is more than likely. We have come to show, let us say, that the basis of the more admirable human traits – intellectual, moral or aesthetic – are *not* to be found in any neural or other kind of mechanism; the tools of no living neurologist, psychologist or sociologist can explain and thus degrade us ...

Suppose that, indeed, this has been shown not only in a negative way (which is easy and common enough), in the sense of showing the failure *so far* to explain specific phenomena on the part of the 'reductionist' disciplines—but that it has been shown *positively*: we have located the source of intellectual or aesthetic creativity, or of moral heroism or conviction, somewhere else. A great moment indeed in human studies.

Alas—if indeed you *have* found it, in the very instant of finding it, you have destroyed what you sought. It is true that *X* which now explains our highest flights may be located not in nerves, nor in reflexes, nor in social structure, nor ... etc. The medium in which the *X* is located may be entirely new, unsuspected, and untainted by the earthy. But if the patterns or structures (inevitable word) located in it really do explain these great human accomplishments ... well then, once again, we are in thrall to heteronomy, to an inhuman explanation of the human ... Chomsky's remark that the 'physical' will be extended to any genuine explanations, whatever the medium in terms of which they are articulated, reflects this fact.

There is no escape: it is not the content, the *kind* of explanation which de-humanises us; it is *any* genuine explanation, as such, that does it. The sooner we realise this, the sooner we shall seek no further spurious escapes. Of course, this last kind of humanist is specially and genuinely likeable; he does not reject science nor employ cheapjack tricks.

He alone, in that camp, does not campaign against explanation and science. (He merely wants them to bring other, more acceptable results, or is convinced that it can and will bring them.) The others invent a variety of rather repugnant, harmful, and inherently absurd dogmas, such as the self-sufficiency of common sense, the self-explanatory and ultimate nature of cultures or 'forms of life', the acceptability of leaving ultimate direction to some impersonal force acting through us, and so on. To protect their world from erosion by science, they invent forces or realms which are beyond the reach of explanation. The cult of self-explanatoriness, in a variety of idioms, is their shared mark.

He who would destroy 'reductionism' by science itself is quite different. (And of course, it is perfectly possible and indeed necessary to destroy *specific* reductions; but, for instance, Chomskian linguistics destroys simple models not for the sake of some *carte blanche* self-explanatory spiritualism, but in the pursuit of *better* models.) But Koestler is a kind of behaviourist inside-out: where the behaviourist smuggles in a spiritualist (familiarist) explanation under the entirely spurious husk of tough-mindedness, the humanist of this kind, by his search for genuine explanation, could only destroy—if he succeeded—that which he wishes to preserve. It cannot be preserved in this manner.

Reductionism, roughly speaking, is the view that everything in this world is really something else, and that the something else is always in the end unedifying. So lucidly formulated, one can see that this is a luminously true and certain idea. The hope that it could ever be denied or refuted is absurd. One day, the Second Law of Thermodynamics may seem obsolete; but reductionism will stand for ever. It is important to understand *why* it is so indubitably true. It is rooted, as Kant made so clear, not in the nature of things, but in *our* ideal of explanation. Genuine explanation, not the grunts which pass for such in 'common sense', means subsumption under a structure or schema made up of neutral, impersonal elements. In this sense, explanation is always 'dehumanising', and inescapably so. This also highlights why the machine ideal of explanation really falls within 'Copernican' philosophy, the shift of sovereignty inwards, to man: though its premiss *seems* to be about the world ('made up of machines'), not about our style of cognition, there is a reason *why* the world is made up of machines, and that reason lies not in the world but in our *practices* of explanation.

SUMMARY

The interrelations of the ghost and the machine are complex and manifold. The use of the ideal of pure experience, and that of a public reproducible structure, as censors of our world, as touchstones of what can or cannot be found in it, can operate both in conjunction and in opposition. And it is really more complex than that.

Either of them can be invoked as the explanation of the remarkable power of science, of that complete transformation of the map of our world and of our cognitive style which the scientific revolution has brought with it. Each is also involved in the as yet unsuccessful attempt to extend that revolution to human studies, and each tends to be invoked, as witness or culprit, in the attempts to explain that failure, to remedy it, or to castigate that attempt.

The miracle of science is not unambiguously beneficial. It erodes and destroys our old vision and our very identity. Much modern philosophy is an effort to save something from this destruction, or to delimit that which may be saved. In the context of these endeavours, the role of the ghost is more ambiguous than that of the machine. The machine tends to be squarely on the side of the devil, though this, as we saw, can be obscured when an author insists on good complex machines as against bad simple ones. (His denigration of bad simple ones may then sound, especially if he

107

is careless in expressing himself, as the denigration of any machine whatever.)

The ghost on the other hand can appear both in the guise of the severe positivist censor, exiling much of the familiar world to the realm of nonsense, or, on the other hand, as the vindication of the experiential world of consciousness as ultimate, relegating mechanism to the status of a mere convenient fiction. The ghost has been prominent on both sides in this battle, and is perhaps not fully compatible with the needs of either.

Provisionally, the situation may be summed up as follows: the old empiricists conveyed an important, and in their day much contested truth —namely, that the truth of an idea may never be supported by claiming it to be 'innate'—by putting forward a genetic psychological theory which, as such, has little to commend it. The valid denial of apriorism was presented and misrepresented as an account of how we actually learn and think. By contrast, we have seen, in our own time, how a more fruitful approach to the understanding of human learning and competence, has been, quite gratuitously, presented in the language of apriorism.

In some rough way, the record of the two great censors could perhaps be schematised as follows:

	Model of *behaviour*	Selector of *ideas and of information*
Ghost:	very poor	of great merit, but the plausibility of his abstract philosophical justification may lead to an over-rating even here.
Machine:	the only plausible candidate	useful, though hampered by curious lack of plausible abstract philosophical justification.

But this is merely a provisional comment. Much remains to be said.

6 A partial convergence

COHABITATION

The fact that the ghost and the machine are each of them suited for a different end, reconciles them in some measure. The image of man generated by empiricism, the island of consciousness, as it were concretises the most important criteria we impose on beliefs—namely, the requirement that the evidence should come separately from the belief *for which* it is evidence, that *no theory or belief should be judge in its own case*, that the evidence should arrive on its own. The empiricist account of the self, assembled from solitary and independent data, is a kind of beautiful and suggestive parable for this practice. (Religions invariably try to be judges in their own case, and are for this reason fundamentally incompatible with empiricism.) The requirement that evidence be free not merely from interpretation by the theory which is being tested, but also from any interpretation at all, is important even if it can never be properly satisfied.

But empiricism is more than the demand that belief-systems should not, in their time-honoured way, be judges in their own case. It is also necessary to give some indication as to who is to be judge instead. If that were left wholly unspecified, if we contented ourselves with a denunciation of circular, self-maintaining systems of thought but refrained from identifying the proper, external judge,[69] we should have no defence against visions which skilfully camouflage their own circularity and self-maintaining character. They can do this whilst apparently accepting external arbitration; they can also contain great flexibility, willingness to change in the light of adverse external judgments. Yet the flexibility, the sensitivity to external verdicts, may be tacitly restricted to pre-selected external judges, and only to such as will not in any serious way endanger them.

For this reason, the empiricist identification of *experience* as the ultimate, crucial, and in the end perhaps unique judge, is of some importance. This judge is less corruptible than the others, less liable to be secretly in the pay of this vision or that, even if we do not accept the myth of his total purity. Above all, his apotheosis and exclusive status prevent the similar absolutisation of anything else—for everything else must, on

[69] Some formulations of Sir Karl Popper's 'critical' attitude sound just like such a position, like an attempt to make the unaided idea of 'criticism' do the work of empiricism, dispensing with the latter. See, for instance, 'Back to the Presocratics', in his *Conjectures and Refutations* (London, 1963).

109

the empiricist view, submit its credentials to him. This is central. Lévi-Strauss pointed out that what matters about incest rules is not so much the prohibition of intercourse with a given category of women, but the obligation implicit therein to hand these women over to some other group. Knowledge has its own incest rules, and empiricism formulates them. It is not the positive characterisation of experience that matters much (that can best be left to Proust or Joyce or impressionist painters); what does matter is that experience is so conceived as to exclude its permeation, its 'penetration' in the espionage sense, by concepts or interpretations in the service of those theories or visions which are to be subject to judgment. As long as this degree of incorruptibility is maintained—and I believe this to be quite feasible—it does not matter so much that there is no such thing as totally 'pure', uninterpreted experience.

Thus what is essential in the empiricist cult of experience as the source of knowledge is the imposition of an obligation to submit to judges who are eternal to, and independent of, the theory that is judged, and the provisions preventing a surreptitious self-validation by 'external' judges whose independence is not genuine. In the prevention of this, the concept of 'experience' is crucial. It is for this reason that the tendency, detectable in Popper's later thought, to stress 'criticism', *any* criticism, and to play down the empiricist ideal (as specifying merely one amongst an unlisted set of other possible kinds of criticism) seems to me misguided.

This is a good point at which to comment on Popper's doctrine of *falsifiability*. When Popper originally introduced this as a criterion of science[70], in opposition to the view that *verifiability* was the really significant index of scientific status, this innovation was justified by a very simple logical argument, which runs as follows: verification is an infinite and interminable process, falsification is a final and conclusive one. No amount of positive 'verifications' of a theory will ever establish it: the sun may fail to rise tomorrow, the next swan may turn out to be black. By contrast, one good counter-example kills a theory for ever. Let one really good black swan turn up, and the theory 'All swans are white' is dead forever. Hence, by requiring theories to be falsifiable, to be such that conditions can be specified which will make them false—by imposing this condition, we are imposing something which can realistically be applied and which does indeed separate the goats from the sheep. The argument is reinforced by the perfectly valid observation that the most suspect kinds of test-evading theories, such as astrology, are conspicuously rich in instances of *verification* ... It is always easy to find instances when the theory did work.

The simplified account of the power of falsifiability has often been challenged.[71] The point is that clean-cut, final, definitive falsifications are

[70] *The Logic of Scientific Discovery* (London, 1968).

[71] See, for instance, Lakatos' contribution in *Criticism and the Growth of Knowledge*, ed. Lakatos and Musgrave.

110

almost as hard to come by as 'verifications'. The existence of an unambiguous instance of a counter-example to a given theory, invariably depends on the tacit or overt assumption of background knowledge which had been assumed in the identification of that sample. That background knowledge is inevitably theory-laden; those theories may also turn out to be false. If they do, the putatively final falsification will turn out not to have been final after all. This is merely an application, to the problem under discussion, of the important philosophic thesis of the 'impurity', the theory-saturation, of all 'experience'.

But the real importance, merit, and above all the historic and social significance of *falsifiability,* does not really hinge on whether it can be a source of these definitive eliminations. Indeed, the history of science and of ideas is not like the Football Cup, with its round-by-round definitive eliminations. On the contrary, it has a strong tendency to re-play matches, quite irrespective of how conclusive the result of the first match seemed to be . . .

The significance of falsifiability lies elsewhere. If we insist that a theory only deserves respect if it is falsifiable, we force anyone who accepts this criterion, to visualise a world in which the theory *can* be falsified. And to do this is to impose a most dreadful and extremely salutary humiliation on that theory. What world-visions, ideologies, most characteristically do, is to construct a world within which their own falsification is quite inconceivable and in which the preliminary steps necessary for such a falsification are blasphemous, and in some way disqualify him who would set them up (sinner, heretic, deviationist, neurotic, man insufficiently acquainted with philosophy in question, displaying lamentable ignorance of its key ideas, etc., etc.). Insistence on genuine falsifiability deprives the theory or world-outlook of this capacity to be a judge of its own truth. The real importance of the criterion lies in this power to take them down a peg.

Note incidentally that 'verifiability' not merely fails to do any effective sorting at all (the test-evading visions are rich in positive, 'verifying' instances, in fact they pervade the world they create so much that verifications are ever underfoot); it actually also penalises the nearly innocent. The only theories which fail to be 'verifiable' are those highly sophisticated and honest modern forms of metaphysics which, far from incarnating themselves in every village shrine, have purified themselves so much that they only preach a genuine, pure transcendence. Such commendable honesty is penalised; whereas the more characteristic, sociologically far more typical sliding-scale doctrines (immanent when verified, transcendent when falsified) escape scot free.

But the main practical effectiveness of the ghost is, as indicated, that it takes belief-systems down a peg by preventing them from being judges in their own case. Final, definitive eliminations, 'falsifications' of theories by one good counter-example may be a myth; it is not in this way that experience asserts its sovereignty. It does so by proscribing the construction of circular, self-maintaining worlds. It achieves this by its sketch of a world composed entirely of atomic data, independent of each other and of all theories, subservient to none.

The machine attains the same crucial goal by other means. Its mechanismic vision is of course in any case in headlong conflict with most (though not all) faiths. What is really important is that if we are to satisfy the requirements of correct explanations which are inherent in the 'structural' ideal, we automatically refrain from giving any vision that privileged, self-maintaining, world-pervading status which faiths strive to achieve. It is in this way that the two great selectors converge, notwithstanding the great difference in their respective images of man. The corollary of the mechanical or structural ideal is that man, like any other object or system, is explicable, and explicable in that impersonal, *repeatable* manner which is the true glory of genuine explanation— conferring power and testability on the explanation and at the same time, alas, depriving the object of explanation of freedom, idiosyncrasy, and autonomy, as the inevitable price of the genuineness of the explanation.

The corollary of the empiricist ideal, on the other hand, is the famous 'bundle of sensations', the 'island of consciousness', the residual pool of my inner awareness, which remains when I think away, when I suspend or 'bracket' the outer and interpreted, hypothetical, permanent, public, 'natural' world.

Truth to tell, this final warm, introspective identity may not be quite the same as Hume's 'bundle', for it has properties which can only with difficulty be credited to that assemblage of sensory grains. The inner self, the inner light, acts as a kind of final, private, secret, personal *conseil de famille,* the hidden forum in which ultimate decisions are taken, ultimate evaluations are made, in great privacy and behind locked doors, without necessarily or generally disclosing the nature of the proceedings to the outside world. This is the captaincy of our soul, the vantage point from which we live, or at least, from which we chart our course during reflective or critical moments. Depth psychology, and other considerations, may make us doubt whether this captain is really so very much in charge of his own ship: the personnel and equipment under his command appear to have tendencies of their own, are often intractable and, worse still, appear to have cunning and devious means at their disposal for influencing his own views and decisions, means he neither understands nor even notices. The captain, as Chomsky and others have shown, does not even properly understand his own powers, and has little or no access to the principles which govern their operation. No matter—sceptical or not, we must needs live our life from this kind of vantage point, for we have no other.

For these various reasons, it seems to me obvious that we shall never find ourselves without either ghosts or machines, or without the tension arising from their joint presence. Knowledge means explanation, and explanation means the specification of a structure that will apply generally and impersonally to all like cases. The mechanistic vision of the world is the shadow of this ideal, *our* ideal, of explanation. Yet at the same time, no particular explanation is ever permanent or sacred; and it is judged by *us*, ghosts.

But any attempt to prove, underpin, somehow establish the existence of this personal viewpoint as a fact out there in the world, co-ordinate with other facts, is bound to be unsuccessful. If it succeeds in locating one further structure, it is of course self-defeating. More commonly, these attempts just invoke empty words. Kant was right when he taught that we must live with this tension and understand its sources, and not try to overcome it.

EPISTEMIC CONVERGENCE

Thus, in the end, the two great selectors are irreconcilable. Neither is eliminable, and we can only learn to see why we can neither dispense with either of them, nor bring them into harmony.

But at certain level, they are in far greater harmony than is normally supposed. The manner in which the two great selectors work on the material presented to their scrutiny—the ideas, practices, the intellectual flotsam and jetsam of our cultures—is such that notwithstanding the profound differences between the two world-pictures they each positively generate, the verdicts they pass tend to converge and reinforce each other.

The reasons are curious and operate with special force in the Western tradition, including of course its diffused form. In as far as I understand them, they arise partly from the general nature of mechanistic explanation, and partly from certain specific traits of the rather special *Western* ghost.

The natural, inherent philosophic tendency of the ghost is perhaps not really towards the scientific, hard-headed, utilitarian temper. This is in fact associated with empiricist movements in the western world to such an extent that the connection has come to *seem* obvious and natural. But it is not. The natural tendency of the ghost, which could be expected to manifest itself if no other special factors were present, is towards either (a) a world-rejecting negative mysticism or (b) what might be called self-indulgent aestheticising connoisseur-ship or *Feinschmeckerei*.

Consider once again the nature of the ghost.

The ghost arises from replacing the selective double-vision of ordinary life, of the 'natural' viewpoint, by a consistent single vision. In ordinary life, we treat that which we experience sometimes as a 'thing', independent of ourselves, and sometimes as part of our experience. We switch from the one viewpoint to the other without consistency and according to convenience. Most of the time, we simply think in terms of 'things', but for various limited purposes, we switch to 'experience'. Most of our

113

vocabulary is geared to things, and we can generally only identify experiences indirectly, through thing-language (a fact whose significance is very much overrated by thinkers hostile to the empiricist vision).

But under the requirement of philosophic consistency, and the impact of the perfectly valid reflection that experience is always *my* experience, and never part of some object independent of me, the world shrinks to the extension of my experience only, and I am left with bundles of my sensations.

What are the natural consequences of such an epistemological sophistication?

One plausible and natural reaction is what one might call the 'Indian' one. It runs roughly as follows: my experience of the world is, alas, only *my* experience. It is not 'the real'. Moreover, the world disclosed in my experience is one of misery, precariousness, insecurity, which ends in old age and death and within which no secure, reliable, undeceptive goods can be found. The flux and precariousness which make it so unhappy a place, also make it *most* ill-suited to be an object of knowledge: knowledge must be reliable, but what reliable knowledge could there be of these fleeting and elusive shadows, as Plato saw them? Hence, the only proper direction for our cognitive and moral endeavours is to learn to ignore and despise this veil, to learn to penetrate it and flow into the constant, stable, liberating nothingness beyond.

In brief, an epistemological orientation starting out from the perception that the world is only *my* world can very naturally lead to a loss of interest in that world, in the specific but elusive patterns of the flux.

The 'Indian' utilisation of epistemic sophistication does of course have one distinguished, though only partial, Western representative—Arthur Schopenhauer. The attitude to the 'world as idea' which Schopenhauer expresses retains, in his case, cognitive curiosity: the world may be neither real nor allow of hope, but it allows knowledge. After all, Schopenhauer lived at a late and developed stage in the history of science, so that even if he abjured social hope, it would have been odd to abjure hope of knowledge as well. Nevertheless, his use of the epistemic vision was directed towards a kind of passive aestheticism. In politics, this can be used to justify a certain quietism, as Thomas Mann noted.

The Platonic utilisation of epistemic sophistication has marked similarities with the 'Indian' one, though the differences are as important. The contrast to the private, sensory flux, unworthy of cognitive attention, is not a blessed Nothingness and ultimate dissolution, but another and higher world which, thanks to the stability of its objects, is worthy of the attentions of the cognitively and otherwise well-born. Plato has his own selectors, but they are not those of the modern world and do not here concern us.

The 'Indian' solution advises the ghost, on realising his ghostly status, to try and become even more ephemeral and if possible free himself from his illusions altogether, thereby also escaping existence and its ills. This solution is not the only natural and plausible one. Another is the hedonic or epicurean solution. The name of course bears witness to the availability of this solution in classical times. If there is no reality beyond the sensory flux, ought we not to cultivate our palate, our sensitivity within the limits of which we are so firmly confined, and abjure the ideal of transcendence, of a rigorous knowledge which can hardly be satisfied anyway. One can agree with Plato to the extent that the sensory world is not cognitively worthy without, for all that, foreswearing it altogether and seeking another: one may simply abandon that eager and unplausible cognitive ambition, or any other, but retain interest in this world of sense, though in the spirit of the connoisseur rather than of the scientific explorer. (Given the enormous success of natural science in the modern world, it may be difficult nowadays to empathise adequately the plausibility of this despair concerning the world of sense as a candidate for scientific investigation. Perhaps one can still feel this in the social sciences.)

Thus the ghost argument could very naturally lead to a cognitively and politically unambitious, unadventurous, resigned attitude, content to cultivate that palate which on this view is, after all, the limit of our world. (Schopenhauer, officially an 'Indianist', also has a strong element of this attitude in his philosophic make-up. More ironically, when logical positivism was introduced into Britain, it also had a distinct aroma of the *Feinschmecker* about it. Formally, the arguments, which were taken from thinkers such as Schlick and Carnap, were not at all of this sort, but rather of the puritanical, science-engendering kind. But the local version of these views did not in fact encourage or promote science, say by encouraging its extension to social matters; it was rather visibly directed against the hierarchial and injunctive attitudes of the Oxford idealists, as if intended to promote a liberation of dilettante enjoyment, a romp through the garden of experience unhampered by synthetic a priori fences or transcendental restrictions.)

The really fascinating and historically important feature of the Western ghost was the manner in which (in the main) he eschewed either the Indian or the *Feinschmecker* implications of his own premises, logical and natural though they be. The ghost was almost never used for abjuring either cognitive or reformist ambition, in this fluid and elusive world of the senses. On the contrary: Locke and Russell, the two giants of the empiricist tradition, both sought, literally with passion, stable cognisable structure that could somehow be reached through the qualitative sense-data available to the ghost. Locke thought that, through his distinction between primary and secondary qualities, he actually achieved this. Russell was less sanguine about his achievement, but there can be no mistaking the passion in his longing. If he accepts or starts out from the ghost position, it is from cognitive puritanism and conscientiousness: this is all we have, and it would be wrong to pretend that we have any stronger premisses. But all his attempts are to build much, much more on this base and reach a solider world of structure, such as can be the object of science. And neither of them was at all given to thinking that this world was beyond the reach of improvement.

ETHICAL CONVERGENCE

The persistent and continuous preoccupation of the ghost theorists with problems such as causation, confirmation of extrapolative theories, and so forth, is most vivid testimony to the socially activist and cognitive-in-this-world orientation of our special ghost. There are few if any signs here of either resigned otherworldliness or a passive aestheticism.

Obvious though this is in the philosophy of science associated with empiricism, it comes out even more conspicuously in the ethical theories typically engendered by Western empiricism and characteristically associated with it. The real significance of the movement known as Utilitarianism is that it endeavoured to work out the ethical implications of empiricism. The premisses were all in Hume. The social terms of reference were provided by the industrial and the French revolutions. Given that there are quite a few important options in how we run this society, and given that the world is as empiricism says it is, what criteria shall we, can we, possibly apply? The answer was worked out by Bentham and James Mill and John Stuart Mill.

Consider their premisses in the abstract. The most important among them is that nothing exists beyond sensation. Matter, from this viewpoint, notoriously is but the permanent possibility of sensation. How consistently and ruthlessly Bentham worked out the implications of this view! How hard J. S. Mill worked to smuggle in some high-brow valuation of poetry and such, endeavouring not to violate the premisses! These were serious thinkers indeed, who were in earnest about their own premisses, and did not shuffle the pack according to convenience.

But if we look only at those premisses, and ignore for a moment the personal character of the theorists, it is striking—how very easy it would have been to reach very different conclusions. The experiment is not at all fanciful, for these were men who were quite tough enough to follow the wind of argument wherever it led them. Well now, consider that one crucial premiss, from which all else really follows for them, and which simply put is: *nothing exists except sensation.*

If this is so, what should our ethics be? Should we not live exclusively for and through our sensations? If we must waste our time changing anything, should we not reserve our time and energy for increasing our sensibility and exploring new, preferably ecstatic forms of it? And note— nothing exists outside, so there is no conceivable authority or principle in terms of which we could prohibit or even grade our experiences other than by those satisfactions that are internal to the experiences themselves.

116

Translate these abstractly formulated principles concretely and you have, naturally, a kind of Hippy ethic. The idea was not, in itself, unthinkable or even implausible in the country, period, and background of these theorists. Drug-taking was not at all unknown among the poets of the time. And of course the critics of the utilitarians were always pointing out that this was an ethic fit for pigs. Logically, *it should have been*. The interesting thing is that it wasn't.

These were, let us repeat, consistent, serious and courageous thinkers, quite capable of both understanding and following the implications of premises once they had endorsed them. Given all this, consider the fact that logically and naturally, the view of the world as constituted by sensation, leads to what might be called a psychedelic ethic. Yet none of them took this road. Why not?

The answer is that the ghost model of man and the world, whose ethical implications they explored and formulated with such brilliance, had covert features in addition to the overtly formulated ones. Just as in epistemology, there was, in the empiricist tradition from Locke to Russell, a persistent and determined attempt to reach and justify *structure* through or from the flux of experience, so in ethics, the whole focus of interest and attention was on the evaluation of consequences of alternative actions and policies *in this world*. The world may be just a screen woven from sensation, but there was to be no leaning back into passive, cognitively unambitious contemplation. What power we have to affect events on the screen we must use to the utmost, and we must be guided by the most rational, publicly defensible criteria. The job of ethical theory was simply to work out what those criteria for endeavour were to be and to do so without fear, favour or superstition. What admirable values they conjured up from their elegant and simple premises, which however did not, in pure logic, altogether warrant them. But no one needs to preach to *them* about the need to understand *and* change the world.

How ruthlessly they used the ghost in carrying out this task! The job of the atomistic empiricist world-picture was to dissolve all existing associations, to subject them to scrutiny, and readmit them only if sound empirical evidence sustained them. No existing association of fact and value could hope to survive simply in virtue of its past prestige. The programme implicit in utilitarianism was a set of draconic death-duties on past associations, on past evaluations, transforming them as fast as compatible with not disrupting society altogether, and readmitting, without permanence, new ones only when warranted by carefully checked evidence. Our society still lives on their programme.

Formally, what the utilitarians said was this: the criterion for social institutions and codes and policies must be their contribution to human happiness. Many critics have rightly pointed out that 'happiness' was used simply to mean 'whatever men in fact desire'—so, as this concept of happiness was very pliable, was there not a danger that this ethic was vacuous, and could not distinguish between one policy and another? Not at all: one of the important ways in which vacuity was avoided was precisely at this point. The utilitarian vision, in terms of which this ethic was articulated, was thoroughly permeated by the sensationalist-atomistic manner of seeing the world, which consists of seeing the world made up of our experience, and the experience as broken up into its elements. From this followed a powerful and most discriminating, non-vacuous injunction —when assessing important policies, institutions and codes, before you work out the felicific accounts, break up the items on the balance sheet into their ultimate constituents. The accountancy must not be in terms of the old package-deals; all items must be broken up. And this is enormously important: for the manner in which traditional ethics convey and maintain their values is precisely by looking at experience through those package deals: the concepts of a given culture or society generally are not at all 'atomic' or ultimate, they cluster whole bunches of experiential (and indeed other) elements under single notions, which are not normally broken up and inspected in isolation. It is just in this manner that a traditional ethic perpetuates itself and evades questioning. Utilitarianism was a powerful force for change precisely because it prohibits this strategy. It was not the semi-vacuous 'happiness' which was crucial; it was the empiricist manner in which that happiness, whatever it be, was to be assessed. And that manner was, of course, simply a way of applying the 'ghost' vision.

Thus the utilitarians' perception of their guiding ghost was highly selective. They used him to attack traditionalism, the prejudicial package-deals of traditional culture, and not at all to abjure the world, whether for the sake of mysticism or of aestheticism or, as in the case of Schopenhauer, for both. They saw only the ghost's puritanical, as it were Fabian aspects, his selector role in assessing generalisations about this world or strategies for changing it. His other philosophic potential largely passed them by.

PIGS AND PLATONISTS

There is a curious postscript to the story. Despite all the logically manifest implications of their views, drug-taking, orgiastic sensuality, and the like, simply were not parts of the life-style of Bentham or the Mills. We need not fear, or hope, that some new historical discovery will indicate the contrary. It is unlikely that any orgy was ever graced by the body of John Stuart Mill.

But, as is well known, their philosophy ceased to satisfy as the century progressed. There was distinct feeling that it was not sufficient high-minded. Nor was it. Its abstract premises were very earthy. It clearly did not allow for or pay sufficient heed to the values attached to fine pictures, especially when privately owned, or beautiful friendships, and other such manifestations of a refined sensibility.

No one caught the spirit of discontent with crude, sensualist utilitarianism better than G. E. Moore, rightly called a Cambridge Platonist. Around the turn of the century, he replaced it by a much more edifying doctrine, Ideal Utilitarianism, which made ample provision for collecting pictures or cultivating exquisite relationships, though it rather left out the institution-revaluing aspect of crude, rough utilitarianism.

Moore retained the model which requires us to maximise good, but altered the ontology within which this was to operate, so that the balance sheets were allowed to take note of more edifying elements. As the notion of happiness with which utilitarianism had operated was pretty elastic, this on its own need have made little difference. It merely ratified something which most of the utilitarians were quite willing to honour anyway. They weren't really very piggish, in fact.

So, in practice, the Platonic raising of the tone by Moore only ratified Bloomsbury goings-on which (ironically) might well have shocked the crude, epistemologically sensualist, 'piggish' utilitarians. At the same time, Moore diminished the social relevance of utilitarianism. Its cutting edge had always depended on its empiricist atomism, in the requirement that institutions face judgments in a dismantled state, so to speak—that old and customary conceptual clusters not be allowed to pass as package deals. Moore's insistence on the organic unity of complex carriers of value gave them *carte blanche* to continue to do so. The consequence, which Moore spelt out, was that one need not expect much in the way of reform of substantive morals from his system. Indeed not—not because the wisdom of the past is so much beyond correction, as he supposed, but because, if you tolerate conceptual and institutional package deals, you inhibit judgment and criticism.

J. M. Keynes left us a characteristically brilliant account of what Moore's *Principia Ethica* meant to his generation.[72] Here at last there was a charter for their finer sensibilities, a philosophy worthy of them, and one reflecting their refinement. But, by a curious historic irony, we can no longer be quite so confident that no records will turn up showing that the wilder sensuous indulgences were outside the range of this coterie. Mr Holroyd's biography of Lytton Strachey would seem to suggest the contrary.[73]

In the conceptual armoury of simple utilitarianism there had been nothing, nothing to inhibit such conduct, but its upholders were not guilty of it. The logical riches of Moore's schema were designed for greater fastidiousness, for the trascendence of the famous piggishness of utilitarianism. So the most ruthless, brutal, uncompromising philosophic sensualism of the early utilitarians bred puritans; whilst the toffy-nosed

[72] J. M. Keynes, 'My Early Beliefs', in *Two Memoirs* (London, 1949).
[73] M. Holroyd, *Lytton Strachey*, 2 vols. (London, 1967/8).

ethereal Platonism of Moore's *Principia Ethica* was used to ratify quite the reverse.

The irony of the historic consequences of crude and ideal utilitarianism, respectively, is not only amusing, but also symptomatic. It may help explain why the sensualist ghost, who reduces the world to experience, is nevertheless not content with just savouring it, but does his utmost to seek out orderly cognitive understanding and meliorative control of that world. The sensualist ghost was already so imbued with expectation of intelligible structures in the world and the possibility of manipulating them for the improvement of the world, that he only applied those ideas which were congruent with this, rather, than those which were in conflict with it. Knowledge and change was taken for granted, and empiricism was used to give an account of *how* knowledge was possible and *what* the criteria of change were to be—not whether either was possible at all.

The logically surprising puritanism of the ghost is analogous to a central theme in a famous sociological account of how the modern world came to emerge. Just as one should not, *a priori,* expect the sensual ghost to be puritanical, so one would not expect the puritanism of the Calvinists to be this-worldly: one would expect their piety to lead them to look to the other world. But Max Weber showed that one must look at the situation in two dimensions: asceticism/non-asceticism, this-worldliness/other-worldliness. The protestant ethic was ascetic and this-worldly and hence led to restrained, orderly, 'rational' conduct within this world. Similarly, though one might normally expect sensualism to be indulgent, one does in fact need two dimensions here: empiricism/transcendentalism, and puritanism/indulgence. Normally or plausibly, transcendentalism may be invoked to ratify demanding ethics, whereas empiricist sensualism would confirm permissive ones. But the normal connection, if such it be, was here reversed. Puritanism and empiricism came together, generating a vision which seemed to perpetuate the protestant ethic in a secular idiom.

THE MANNER OF THE CONVERGENCE

The contention is that the natural potential of the ghost, in the field of ethical and cognitive endeavour, did not play itself out in the course of Western history. Its natural bent was not for puritanical, orderly world-reform and cognitive exploration, but rather for aestheticism or mysticism, or some combination of the two. This natural bent was distorted, providentially perhaps, because the implications of the ghostly principles, of the reduction of everything to experience, were mainly explored by people who *already* took for granted, who simply assumed as part of their very terms of reference, the possibility of effective cognition and of social reform. They *knew* that knowledge was possible, and so was social improvement. The question they typically asked was not, feebly, *are* they possible—in which case a possibly anticipated negative answer would have justified resignation, quietism—but rather, how is it that we *do* know so much, and *in which direction* should we exercise those remarkable powers for altering life, which plainly we do possess. (This last was *the* characteristic question asked by the utilitarians. The very question already prejudges their own determination to do good, which is not at issue, and only asks for a rational criterion for the direction of endeavour. These were their terms of reference. Failure to see this leads to the commonest misunderstandings of their position.)

So most of those who worked out the philosophy of the ghost were unwittingly, and most beneficially, prejudging or rather limiting the kind of consequence they were willing to see flow from the premises. Still, the interesting question remains, by what devices were they able, for instance, to extract a kind of cognitive optimism and activism, from premises which do not really lend themselves to such conclusions? It was not easy, and in fact the naturally pessimistic, quietistic bent of those premises sometimes reasserted itself: Hume's philosophy, for instance, is frequently thought of as a *sceptical* one.

But even in Hume, the scepticism is ambiguous and ambivalent. Hume cannot quite bring himself to accept his own conclusions. He knows full well that we know a lot, and if that knowledge cannot altogether find an objective basis, he tries at least to base it on the habits and constitution of our own minds.

If we are to see *how* the ghost in practice managed to lead not to quietism, but on the contrary to something highly convergent with the ethos of the machine, the belief in the feasibility and usefulness of 'structural' explanations, we must first of all remember one of the central themes of the present argument: both the ghost and the machine are primarily censors, selectors. Secondly, we must look at some general features of the material which is normally submitted to them for censorship, for approval or rejection.

The mass of material subjected to the verdict of these judges consists of the numerous and manifold ideas, practices, assumptions and so forth which are part of the cultural stream in which we live, plus perhaps any inventions or new combinations which any one of us may think up, or borrow from some other stream.

Now the important thing is the constitution of these streams and the ingredients within them. On this point, modern positivism unwittingly insinuates a most disastrous and misleading error.

The error is this: that our conceptual equipment, the sum of ideas handled by our minds, consists of two parts: an inner, healthy part, healthy because the ideas in it have empirical content, and satisfy the this-worldly criteria of positivism; and second, a kind of accretion, an outer stream of empirically vacuous ideas. The task of positivism is then to encourage us to slough off the second lot.

Were it so simple! In fact, of course, the transcendent is not added to

121

the stream of ideas or a given idea, the way milk may be added to tea. On the contrary, as anyone knows who has ever tried to disentangle systematically the beliefs of any society, it is constitutive, deeply entwined in the 'ordinary' notions, with their empirical or at least operational involvement in concrete activities. This is an elementary, but very central and important fact about all cultures and societies. Modern positivism would not actually deny it; it would merely treat it as a sociological contention which is not in its province, and claim, mistakenly, that the myth of two separate streams of ideas, however unrealistic sociologically, is a permissible fiction or simplification for philosophical purposes. But it is not.

The point is that transcendent notions are deeply mixed in with ordinary ones. A given term will have an 'ordinary', operational, empirical sense on weekdays or in the mouths of the laity, and a quite different, 'deeper', transcendent sense on a holy day or in the mouths of the priesthood. This is but a simple example. And the significance of the example is that we cannot say that it is just a case of homonym, of the same word possessing multiple senses or uses. The functioning of the society may hinge precisely on this link between the earthly and the other.

This being so, the empiricist/positivist injunction, derived from the ghost model, has a very peculiar impact. It does not simply give differing evaluations of two *already* discrete and distinct sets of ideas. It enjoins, above all, a sensitivity to the distinction between that which is publicly verifiable by experiential evidence and that which is not, a sensitivity which is low or even systematically obscured in traditional culture. It creates a distinction where it barely existed. This new sensitivity has an important corollary: the imposition of a kind of dissociation of those complex notions which contain both elements, and also the prohibition of what might be called boundary-jumping—the habit notions have of being empirical in some contexts and not so in others (empirical on weekdays but not so on Sundays, as above, or, more commonly, empirical if confirmed but something else if not). A well-developed sensitivity to the great boundary inhibits these practices. But they are extremely important and widespread, and their inhibition through the newly acquired sensitivity makes a truly enormous difference.

Thus the really important social impact of the ghost philosophy is the injunction 'Be sensitive to the boundary, and impose consistency with respect to it'; the secondary injunction, 'Down with the transcendent' (*Burn the books containing it* according to Hume, or *Call it technical nonsense* according to Ayer) does not matter much. If the first injunction is well observed and implemented, for all practical purposes the second is already performed and prejudged. In social contexts in which the first is well diffused and respected, it is perfectly possible to play down and, at a superficial level, ignore the second in the interests of courtesy, kindness, tact or antiquarianism. It hardly matters.

But now we can also see just how, by what devices, the ghost could and did do the work of the machine. The habit which the ghost inculcated most strongly is a kind of *esprit d'analyse*, the habit of breaking things up into constituent parts. This habit of dissolution works both laterally and qualitatively, so to speak: it leads people both to separate one sensation or experience from another, to be aware that the two are but contingently conjoined, to see how it would be if each had come with a different neighbour; and it also leads them to separate, within each experience, various conjoined qualities from each other. The test imposed by the great censor then has to be endured by each element in isolation: *no block bookings for the Last Judgment*! Or, if some notion does wish to appear as a complete package, the test requires that the contents of the pack be consistent. The notion either does or does not contain certain elements, it cannot (as is so customary in traditional thought systems, which would never satisfy this test), be different when used by the Master and when in the mouth of a suspect disciple.[74]

Understanding alone does not count: the 'inner change' must be authenticated as well. The operational definition of such inner changes is of course endorsement by the Master, which is unlikely to be granted without submission to his authority. No device could be simpler.

It is through its insistence on both the lateral and the qualitative breakups of package deals, and through its insistence on equal and symmetrical treatment, that this ghost helps the work of the machine. (The ghost must insist on equality and symmetry; there is nothing in the model which would provide a basis for making exceptions.) The imposition of these standards, requiring that ideas come before the bar at which they are to be judged without any special charters or privileges, leads in the end to a situation very similar to that produced by the requirement of 'structural' or mechanical explanation. (In theory, the ghost is less stringent, scrutinising only evidence and the notions in terms of which evidence is characterised, but making no demands on explanations other than that they should cover the evidence. In practice this makes little difference.)

But in a society not already imbued with a fair amount of cognitive optimism, the ghost philosophy could hardly work as a censor. It would then underscore the view that not much knowledge can be had anyway; this being so, why waste time on careful scrutiny of our concepts? This perhaps helps explain why some cultures combine a sense of the

---

[74] A delightfully simple modern way of operating this device is to say that a truth does not count unless it is also effectively therapeutic, really at work in the soul of him who utters it. Empty mouthing by one impure of heart does not count. The test of purity at heart is of course reverence for the Master. A neat system ... actually commended (and quite correctly credited to Freudianism and Wittgensteinianism) by an American philosopher: 'Because the breaking of such control is a constant purpose of the later Wittgenstein, his writing is deeply practical and negative, the way Freud's is. And like Freud's therapy, it wishes to prevent understanding which is unaccompanied by inner change.' S. Cavell, *Must we mean what we say?* (New York, 1969), p. 72.

illusoriness of the world with amazing credulity within that world. Whilst everything is an illusion, they no longer note that some illusions are much more so than others. The salutary censoriousness only seems to come when cognitive hope and confidence have already been raised high. By then, the ghost-censor works similarly to the machine-censor, however dissimilar their premisses.

THE REGULARITY OF NATURE

For the ghost, the regularity of nature is a great problem. Indeed, for the ghost tradition of the West, it becomes an obsession, as well it might. By contrast, in the machine tradition it is not a problem, but a postulate, the very starting point of the whole position. The machine *is* that which is regular, that which is repeatable under similar circumstances, by steps which are unmysterious, and follow from the universally present, agreed properties of the materials employed. So the machine *is* order: order is what defines it, and it cannot constitute a problem for it.

For the ghost, the situation is quite different. Order not merely does not follow from its premisses, it seems rather to contradict them. At least, the picture elicited from those premisses is one which can give one no *a priori* expectation of regularity whatever.

The argument from the ghost to the positive expectation of *dis*order has two main forms, one entirely *a priori,* the other involving a rather abstract appeal to facts. The pure *a priori* argument runs as follows: nothing exists other than the sensory screen. There is no beyond. The data on the screen are absolute and final. They are only 'explained' in the sense in which a summary, a mnemonic device, reminds one of the data it conveys; for they are never really the consequence of anything *else.* This being so, we can never have any reason for arguing from data already in our possession to data which are not yet available to us, for no link can bind them. If the future and the past obey similar laws, then this just happens to be so; it can never be the corollary of some wider premiss with some independent corroboration. For what would that premiss be about? There can be no non-circular justification of scientific inference.

There is also the slightly more specific argument, invoking not so much the ultimacy of sense experience, but rather certain very general and conspicuous features of it. Just contemplate for a moment your stream of consciousness. Is it not utterly chaotic, confused, fragmentary and discontinuous? Are not the elements in it devoid of sharp edges, do they not fuse and separate, emerge and disappear, transform and disguise themselves with bewildering rapidity? One thing may have a thousand forms and distinct things may appear in similar form. Life is not just a dream but a nightmare. The idea that order might be imposed on the flux of appearance is an absurd one indeed. Such order as is occasionally found belongs to other realms—the starry heavens, or the pure con-

124

structions of geometry—but not to the world of sense.

Both arguments are powerful. Historically, most formulations of the ghost position no doubt articulated these consequences as straightforward conclusions, as views to be embraced, perhaps with regret. What is so distinctive of the Western ghost is that these arguments are put forward not as conclusions, but as problems or paradoxes. For everyone knows that knowledge *is* possible, that scientific extrapolation does work. What is puzzling is why and how it works, and whether we can show that it must work. Or must we look at it, as long as it lasts, as a kind of continuous windfall?

There is something faintly comic about those worthy and often powerful thinkers who labour so seriously at the task of finding a proof that will guarantee scientific inference, and underwrite an orderly and regular nature, which can then be relied upon to continue to obey some laws, thus making itself intelligible and predictable for us, as long as we know the right laws. We ought not to laugh at these thinkers, for what they seek would benefit all of us, if only they found it. It would make all of us more secure; in proportion to the soundness of the proof they found, we should be shielded from the danger of *chaos*.

All the same, one cannot help smiling. It is all rather like those old 'proofs' of the immortality of the soul. Little will they avail you when you die. Of course, you will not be there to know you were deceived. Similarly, how much would any proof avail you, if suddenly orderliness and regularity of nature ceased to hold? Would you wave a paper with your proof of the uniformity of nature, whilst you, and the paper, dissolved? Would you go down into cosmic quicksands shouting the Principle of Sufficient Reason, like a political prisoner dragged away shouting his constitutional rights?

But the exercise was not pointless, though the point it did have was quite different from the one it seemed to have.

Chaos is not an option. No society, no culture or language, either does or can exist, which operates on the assumption of a chaotic nature, of a world not amenable to conceptual order. We have no way of proving the falsity of such an assumption of chaos, and we do have some sinister intimations that it may be true; but there is little we can do about it. If it is true, we are helpless.

One might say that the frontier with chaos is an indefensible one. It is also uninhabited; there is no society, no group of people, who live on the assumption of chaos. As we look across this frontier, we see only an empty land.

But our society, which is based at least to some significant degree on the assumption of a regular and orderly nature, in effect a bureaucratised nature, amenable to control and manipulation and prediction, does have other frontiers which *are* inhabited: the frontiers with what may be called magical or participatory societies. Our own society, indeed, was of that kind at some point in the past. Not all societies live on the assumption of an impersonal nature, subject to abstract, impersonal laws. On the contrary, most societies conflate the human and the natural order, interpret the one through the other and perceive a kind of 'meaningful unity'. So this frontier *is* inhabited: here there is a genuine option. Chaos is not an option, but *magic* is.

Whether there exists a 'proof' that the world really is of one kind or the other, that it is really of the orderly disenchanted kind, or that on the contrary Enchantment is justified, and the 'meaningful' vision, which conflates the natural and moral orders, is legitimate—whether such a proof exists, in one direction or the other, one may well doubt. Some proofs have certainly been offered, but their absolute cogency is not above suspicion. But there are certainly considerations which can be adduced, and the question is not an empty or an academic one. It is a very real one. This is also part of the battle between 'humanists' or romantics or populists on the one hand, and reductionists or modernisers or what have you on the other. The choice is a genuine one, and perhaps the most important ones which societies can ever face. It thus differs from the choice between order and chaos, which is unreal.

We can now appreciate the real significance of the mental fight, as Blake might have called it, with chaos. Our society and its relatively orderly outlook has two frontiers, one with chaos, and the other, roughly speaking, with magic. The frontier with chaos is indefensible and also, happily, quite uninhabited. We could never defend it but, providentially, no enemy is there to attack us. Nevertheless, philosophers have laboured hard to erect defences along it. Their labours are noisy, their edifices visible and conspicuous. But was it useless, seeing that, for all their efforts, this frontier could never be defended?

No. Their work was so noisy and conspicuous that it can easily be seen and heard from that other frontier, along which there *is* an option and an enemy. And the weight of their preparations had a most powerful moral and deterrent effect all along that *other* frontier. They could never have averted chaos, had it threatened to engulf us; but their defences against it could and did deter *magic*. The noisy and formidable preparations along one border, by a kind of moral impact, tipped the scale at the other one.

To speak non-metaphorically: all the preoccupation with demonstrating the orderliness of the world, proving regularity, the principle of causation or of sufficient reason, against the rival supposition of orderless chaos, could never really attain its aim. If the world were such that we could not know and understand it, that would be that. No one will ever find a proof showing that it *could not* be so. (Personally, I am always surprised to find the world at all intelligible.)

But we have no option in that direction. The supposition of an unintelligible world dictates no course of action, other than, perhaps, resignation and despair. But we do have an option in another direction—

126

whether we act on the assumption of a world regulated by orderly, impersonal law, or on the assumption of a cosy, 'meaningful', personal world.

What 'proof' is available to support the first supposition? Only a kind of negative, left-handed one: if powerful, communicate, cumulative, manipulative knowledge is available *at all*, then it must be of this 'regular' or bureaucratic kind. The growth of knowledge presupposes its communicability, storage, public and independent testing, independence of anyone's status, identity, moral or ritual condition, and so forth. This is what makes such knowledge powerful, and it is also what makes it 'cold' 'disenchanting', 'mechanical'.

This is the only 'proof' which, in the end, is available. We choose a style of knowing and a kind of society jointly. All in all, mankind has already made its choice, or been propelled into it in truly Faustian manner, by a greed for wealth, power, and by mutual rivalry. We can only try to understand what has happened.

But the interesting thing is the role of the famous regularity or uniformity of nature in philosophy, under its various names. This is the machine vision of a bureaucratised nature, which responds in a responsible, regular manner to like circumstances, as does the ideal bureaucrat. Those who wished to *demonstrate* that the world must be of this orderly kind, that some principle of sufficient reason obtains which decrees that nothing happens without good reason, faced an impossible task. But in the course of trying to perform it, they nevertheless did achieve a great deal in that other contest, the conflict with the *magical* vision of the world. Whilst appearing to fight the spectre of chaos, in fact they discouraged Magic, 'the enchantment of the world'. Propaganda is all the more effective if it denigrates a certain viewpoint *en passant*, as unworthy of rational opposition, in Jane Austen's phrase—and all the more so, if this contempt, whether justified or not, is manifestly sincere. The contempt of the major philosophers for the magical vision on the whole did have this sincerity: chaos they deemed a worthy opponent, the enchanted vision less so (even if Kant did deign to argue against Swedenborg). But their eagerness to prove the regularity assumption as against *chaos*, and their correspondingly less heartfelt concern with defending it against *magic*, made its point plain: the magical vision was not a worthy rival.

This casual contempt perhaps did more to discredit the more or less covertly anthropomorphic vision than a frontal assault would ever have done. Chaos is not one of our options, but magic is. The philosophers' preoccupation with chaos and neglectful disdain of magic did much to discredit the latter. This was their contribution to the mechanical ideal of explanation, and it converged with the empiricist proscription of sliding-scale, undisciplined, boundary-hopping concepts. And in ethics, the machine ideal, insinuating an ordered, intelligible, manipulable, reformable world, did a good deal to give empiricism a puritan backbone.

127

7   Skeleton and backlash

There may be philosophies which bloom rarely, but when they do, do so with rare splendour, or at least with panache. There may even be such as can bloom in great glory once only before they perish. Empiricism is not of this kind: it has flowered often, and may confidently be expected to do so again.

But the philosophy of logical form, which I have called skeletalism, is on this heroic, self-immolatory kind. It is true that throughout the history of thought, it had often appeared here and there, making its contribution to the colourful patchwork of ideas; but never till the early part of this century perhaps did it bloom in *pure* form, in its full glory. That was its great moment, and I suspect it was also its last.

The underlying idea of what might be called logicism is that the form of thought is also the form of reality. It is a tempting idea, and I suspect that, once it is clearly articulated and followed out to its full implications, it also becomes visibly untenable.

Perhaps one should allow the method to be characterised by the words of one of its greatest practitioners, the youthful Bertrand Russell:

> ... I shall try to set forth ... a certain kind of logical doctrine, and on the basis of this a certain kind of metaphysics. The logic which I shall advocate is atomistic, as opposed to the monistic logic of the people who more or less follow Hegel.
> The reason that I call my doctrine *logical* atomism is because the atoms that I wish to arrive at as the sort of last residue in analysis are logical atoms and not physical atoms. Some of them will be what I call 'particulars'—such things as little patches of colour or sounds, momentary things—and some of them will be predicates and relations and so on. The point is that the atom I wish to arrive at is the atom of logical analysis, not the atom of physical analysis.[75]

The basic idea is—reality is identified through 'logical' analysis. Russell supposed that because he possessed a logic superior to that of the Hegelians, he consequently had access, through it, to a better kind of metaphysics, a better account of reality.

The reasons why this style of thinking should have experienced a revival early in this century have already been indicated. A contributory fact was that the Hegelians spoke one variant of this kind of language which was natural enough, given the intimate relationship between

[75] Bertrand Russell, 'The Philosophy of Logical Atomism', re-published in *Logic and Knowledge*, ed. R. C. Marsh, pp. 178 and 179.

thought and being according to that philosophy, and those who reacted against Hegelianism tended nevertheless to take over the idiom of their opponents. They merely inverted what was being said within that idiom. If the Hegelians had their reasons for supposing that the world was 'one big comforting thing', they in turn were inclined to seek reasons, formulated in a similar style, for why the world consisted of many disconnected and morally rather neutral things.

More important still were the developments in logical theory and notation. It was only in the nineteenth and early twentieth centuries that logic made the transition, so to speak, from Latin to Arabic numerals— from a clumsy to a genuinely operational script. As Bertrand Russell observed:

a good notation has a subtlety and suggestiveness which at times makes it look almost like a live teacher.[76]

This particular almost-living teacher did indeed inspire, suggest and teach a very great deal. Logicism was always, as its name implied, inclined to seek inspiration in logic; but now logic was, all of a sudden, very much more powerful and inspiring than it had ever been before. No wonder that this was the moment when a philosophy inspired by it truly flowered.

It flowered in a kind of pure and final glory; and the purity and the termination were intimately connected. The purity meant that the principle underlying this kind of thought could be seen in isolation, its operation neither aided nor hampered, and above all not obscured, by any other principle. This logical purity enabled it first of all to generate a philosophy that was, very nearly, all of one piece, with an aesthetically gratifying simplicity of line and design; and secondly, it made it possible to become fully aware, and hence also fully critical, of that chemically isolated principle, and to reject it with a vehemence which had never been directed at it before, when it existed as but one of a whole sheaf of intellectual devices.

The story is a curious one, and though it took place largely within the confines of academic philosophy, it had repercussions in the wider intellectual world.

The principles of logicism, if we may call it that, were that the forms of reality are also the forms of thought, and that the forms of thought were in turn manifest in good logical notation. A notation which captured the real underlying pattern of our thought thereby also seized the nature of reality! The prospect was enticing and exciting, particularly so in a situation in which a new, elegant, operational, powerful notation was emerging.

The resulting philosophy has been recorded for us above all in Ludwig Wittgensteins's *Tractatus Logico-Philosophicus,* and in Bertrand Russell's *The Philosophy of Logical Atomism.* What is the world disclosed by this

[76] Introduction to L. Wittgenstein's *Tractatus,* p. 18.

philosophy? What is that skeleton of reality, revealed for us by the X-ray of sound logical notation?

A curious, aseptic, hygienic, cold world. The fact that it is the fundamental principle of the 'propositional calculus', that all atomic propositions are totally independent of each other (i.e. the truth or falsity of any one of them leaves the truth or falsity of any other totally unaffected), is reproduced in the philosophy as a vision of a world of 'atomic facts', each proudly and totally independent of all others. Whatever pattern the mosaic of the world may display is contingent and accidental: the constituent pieces know nothing of it. Anyone with a strong sense of the ultimate unity and interpenetration of all things—a sense sublime of something far more deeply interfused—must feel dismayed by this theory. But the thinkers who were proposing the theory did not suppose that they were putting forward one *optional* vision, a colder and restrained style in metaphysical decor, as against the cosier, more *gemütlich* vision of the poets. They were, so they supposed, conveying a demonstrable and exclusive, objective truth, and there was nothing deeply interfused about that.

The internal structure of those lonely atomic facts also reflected the notation employed by current logic. That notation had been developed in response to the requirements of certain of the more abstract parts of mathematics, which deal amongst other things with the manner in which unspecified attributes are distributed amongst unspecified 'objects' or classes of objects. (That is to say, it provided a notation capable of recording the distribution of unidentified attributes amongst unidentified objects, and operationalising the deduction of consequences of any such distribution.) Hence the 'atomic facts' of which the world was said to be made up were envisaged in the image of this model. As the notation was capable of working with attributes of one object, or of two objects ('relations'), or of any number of objects ('multi-term relations'), the atomic facts were not circumscribed in their internal complexity.

Needless to say, it was very hard actually to *locate* those atomic facts, and the 'objects' incapsulated in them, in the real, familiar world, though Russell thought he could do it. A piquant aspect of the story is that at roughly the time when physics was abandoning the atomic vision of ultimate, hard, colourless billiard balls as the final and irreducible furniture of the world, a logic-inspired philosophy was reintroducing this very image.

The vision had other oddities and difficulties, in addition to the fact that the items whose reality, indeed whose ultimate and exclusive reality it postulated, were desperately hard to find or identify in the world as we actually know it.

This cold and atomic, so to speak summative world, had no room for value, purpose, 'meaning'. It was an icily cold world. This was not necessarily a snag from the viewpoint of any and all consumers of

130

philosophy: some may long for such an aseptic world, derive some satisfaction from it, or find pleasure in having their worst fears confirmed by such rigorous, impartial reasoning.

But the situation is really more complex. The vision does not necessarily exclude value, meaning, and so forth. All it necessarily does is exclude them from thought proper. Admittedly, it lays claim to a monopoly of articulated, expressed, explicit thought. But there might be another kind—the ineffable, mystical. So in fact the vision allowed a kind of option: either some Bazarov-like tough-mindedness, or an utter and uncontrolled mysticism, quite separate from ordinary norms and constraints of thought, hence free from danger of criticism; or, finally, a position suspended with deliberate ambiguity between these two possibilities, partaking of the benefits of each. (Russell, one should add, was never so guilty of this.)

So, from the viewpoint of the potential clientele, the apparent total proscription of meaning- and cosiness-conferring styles of thought was not necessarily a disadvantage. The vision may, instead of curbing all mystical yearnings, on the contrary free them from all restraint. This was important.

But to return to the original skeletalist vision. In its pure form, it is blind not merely to 'values' and the 'meaning of life', but also to history and to any sense of radical differences of culture. And this blindness, unlike its attitude to mysticism, was straighforward and total, rather than ambivalent. Roughly speaking, the logical atoms are timeless, and cultural or historical variations are parts of those accretions which logical analysis tries to cut away. This skeletalist non-theory of history was not even explicit and conscious. Rather it was assumed and quietly, unreflectingly taken for granted. (One must again add that although Russell worked out a philosophy of logical atomism, his own state of mind never exemplified its spirit.) If it were clearly asserted, it would no longer be quite so unreflecting, absolute and assured. Its negation would then also be articulable and thinkable.

Hence it is puzzling for a skeletalist that any specific and contingent discovery within the world could ever be philosophically significant. Wittgenstein for instance always found such a notion repugnant.

The Darwinian theory has no more to do with philosophy than has any other hypothesis of natural science.[77]

Philosophy was about the form of all thought, and hence beyond or before the content of any specific thought; the content of discovery ought not to be able to affect it.

This error is of course connected with the blindness to concrete and socially diversified forms of thought. The reason why a specific empirical doctrine such as Darwinism *is* philosophically relevant, is manifest: it

[77] Wittgenstein, *Tractatus*, 4.1122.

131

contradicts, and if true refutes, any rival vision which happens to contain corollaries such as the immutability of species, or the creation story. Philosophies and general visions, including those that are 'religious' in the literal sense of the term, happen to be in the same line of business, namely that of picturing the concrete universe, often in great detail, and hence in fact they are and must be rivals. This is something that pure modern skeletalism finds it hard to understand.

But the blindness to history and social diversity, and hence also to the problems of radical social change and to the criteria for judging it, were, just like the *carte blanche* to boundless unrestrained mysticism with which they came to be so intimately connected, very important for the understanding of the appeal of skeletalism. The position is found, in all its purity, extremism, blindness and mysticism, in Wittgenstein's *Tractatus*.

THE BACKLASH PREPARED

We have thus, in skeletalism, or rather in logical atomism, as the particular form of it in fashion early in this century was called, one particular and very curious species of a selector philosophy – in other words a philosophy which believes itself to be in possession of a criterion of truth, a touchstone of valid opinion, and one which is universally valid. Such a philosophy then enables one, indeed compels one, to treat all other opinions, other cultural systems of faith, as either sunk in hopeless error, or as unwittingly in possession of part or whole of that same unique universal truth which is revealed by its own touchstone. This may turn the holders and possessors of the key into an arrogant, cognitive master race *if* they are conscious, pre-occupied with the diversity of belief and society at all; alternatively, **if** the type of problem with which they are concerned is not at all close to the issues of history and society, their effortless superiority may remain latent, implicit, unconscious, and inoffensive at least to the extent of being neither articulated nor stressed.

The skeletalists of this period were rather of this latter kind. They were contemporaries of Max Weber's and were, as he was, preoccupied with nature and criteria of rationality. But there the resemblance ends. In fact, there could hardly be a greater dissimilarity than that which exists between their *Fragestellung* and his. He was aware of rationality as a socially *differential* problem; why did some forms of social organisation possess more of it than others, or possess it in a different form? They, on the contrary, were interested neither in any possible social basis it might have, nor in any differences in its incarnation. They were interested in rationality, thought, logic, language, *an sich,* in some universal and undifferentiated essence. The possible failure of this essence to manifest itself in all places and at all times in undistorted form was a problem which impinged on them only tangentially. It was considered only in an abstract, shorthand and dismissive manner:

132

The silent adjustments to understand colloquial language are enormously complicated.[78]

That is all. Never has the diversity of human cultures been dismissed so briefly. Under those two words, 'silent adjustments', i.e. the accretions to the underlying universal logical essence, there lies all human history.

Bertrand Russell was the greatest mind to represent this logicistic outlook, but, very much to his credit, he never represented it in its pure form. He was ever aware of other realities, and there was no tendency in his thought to use the aridities of pure logic as a gateway to mysticism. With him, a sense of other realities invariably kept breaking in. For purposes of exposition and exemplification, it is generally preferable to choose as pure and 'ideal type' as possible, and Russell was never a very pure type of this style. Wittgenstein, on the other hand was always willing to follow the consequences of some obsessive insight with total, logical ruthlessness—even, or especially, the alleged insight which obsessed him in his later years, namely the unitary vision that all unitary visions were mistaken as such and the source of all error.

Skeletalism thus had an inherent tendency to be blind to history and to human and social diversity, and Russell did not share this blindness. Bertrand Russell was, as many have pointed out, a man of the eighteenth century, of the Enlightenment. The characteristic Enlightenment view did not ignore the past and history, it merely viewed it somewhat *d'en haut en bas*. This, with wit and an addition of a degree of compassion and fear greater perhaps than the Enlightenment proper ever knew, was basically Russell's attitude. In any case, Russell's formal philosophy of knowledge and reality, and his social thought, were not really welded into any kind of unitary whole.

For such a tight integration, we must look to the more exclusive, single-minded, ideal-typical skeletalist, Ludwig Wittgenstein. His philosophic temperament was far more monist, extremist, uncompromising; it was he who was to end by rejecting monism in a truly monist spirit. He did believe in the rigid apartheid of the two spheres, pure philosophy and human attitude, and ironically this doctrine of a rather special and total separation of powers was itself pregnant with social and human implications.

The skeletalist vision is *a* selector philosophy and should be seen as one species of that genus, co-ordinate with the really great and historically far more important selection doctrines of empiricism and materialism. But it is not in the same class as they, either in terms of merit or of historic importance, though it is co-ordinate with them on the chart of possibilities facing the human mind, in its efforts to make sense of our predicament. In its manner of operation and some of its consequences, this option has certain formal similarities with empiricism and materialism, which warrants classing them all together.

[78] Wittgenstein, *Tractatus,* 4.001.

Above all it claims a trans-social or trans-ethnic, independent status for its principles, whose source of validity, whatever it be, is somewhere beyond and presumably above our actual customs of thought, and whose function is, evidently, to sit in independent judgment on those customs.

The actual and specific world-picture generated by the skeletalist principle varies in accordance with the particular kind of skeleton used. The skeleton of subject-predicate logic produces, in Spinoza or Bradley, a unitary, pantheistic world, and in Leibniz, a world of lonely monads. But the particular skeleton of modern logical notation generates an abstract world which can be made to look rather similar to the atomistic mosaic of the radical empiricists. Where the empiricists end up with sensory atoms because experience is claimed to come in the small packages of individual sensations, the 'logical' atomists reach a similar conclusion without, however, initially inspecting experience at all. They reach atomism by quite another route. But when they examine their conclusions and wish to match them with *something*, then experience, or at least experience as described by atomic sensationalism, is the most easily available candidate. This, in a way, is the essence of Russell's philosophy. It is not so much, as is sometimes claimed, that he merely revived David Hume's eighteenth-century vision; he did do so, but he did so on new premises and partly in a new idiom. Russell was basically an empiricist philosopher who wished to use logicist premises or terminology. Whether this makes him preferable to Hume, who supposed that he reached the ghost conclusions by straightforward observation and introspection, or rather the reverse, is an interesting question.

The purity, and consequent extremism, of Wittgenstein's youthful skeletalism is intriguing not merely because it provides one with the closest approximation to an ideal type, but also, and especially, because by reaction it was responsible for a movement of thought which is central to academic philosophy in English-speaking lands in the mid-century. It was 'movement' in both senses—a dramatic shift of vision, a move from one viewpoint to another, and also a 'movement' in the sense of a class of people recognising a shared leadership and distinctive norms, and possessed by the conviction that those distinctive norms were of the greatest importance, inaugurating a new age and bringing a great illumination.

The dramatic move, the shift of vision, was achieved by Wittgenstein—it is the transition from the philosophy of his youth, which was a pure skeletalism, to his 'mature' position—and in all probability it could only have been undergone and expressed by a thinker temperamentally as uncompromising as he. Other skeletalists—Russell in his time, or Quine now—also incorporate other elements in their thought, or simply display a pragmatic, trial-and-error, happy-go-lucky attitude and spirit, which acts as a safety valve, and which prevents that great build-up of steam, the tension, whose sudden release in Wittgenstein's case produced that curiosity of mid-century academic thought, 'linguistic philosophy'.

ON ITS HEAD!

Logical atomism had taught that the world was composed of utterly lonely and disconnected 'facts', which in turn were composed by cold, colourless (sic—cf. *Tractatus* 2.0232) objects, characterised with bland indifference by attributes and relations. On this view, all genuinely significant discourse always refers to this curiously alien world and it alone, even without being aware of this—and other discourse is nonsense. (All else we might wish to say is ambiguously and ambivalently either proscribed, or given total licence, or indeed *both*—by being beyond all articulation, and hence also beyond all restraint. Utmost severity goes with total licence, in true antinomian spirit.)

A curious and unrecognisable world. Yet its existence, indeed its exclusive existence, appeared to follow rigorously from a seemingly innocuous and plausible assumption, namely, that thought or language managed to seize the world by possessing a similar structure, so that the two mirrored each other. The sentence was to be a 'picture' of the fact it asserted. It sounded plausible.

Yet the world generated by skeletalism from this premiss was very far removed from the real daily world in which actual men go about their business and speak to each other. Once again it generates that tension of which the candid student spoke to William James.

Wittgenstein experienced this particular tension with very great acuteness, partly owing to the singlemindedness and determination with which he had embraced his own particular variant of the skeletalist vision, and partly perhaps because of the narrowness of his intellectual interests. And at a given point, the excessive tension led, as excessive tensions do, to a total reversal. The world was *not* the mirror of logical notation, after all! Skeletalism was repudiated with a vehemence corresponding to the fanaticism with which it had previously been espoused. Not surprisingly, the new right-way-up truth was now for him as certain, as indubitable as the old. In fact, Wittgenstein was right (in my view) in his repudiation of skeletalism or logicism, although the refutation cannot really be carried out in quite such a slapdash, wholesale and revelationist a manner. Roughly speaking, it is indeed true that there is no simple and overall parallelism between speech or thought and reality, such that, if only one spoke correctly and omitted the irrelevant accretions and complications, all nouns in one's sentences would refer to 'things', and the verbs to properties and relations, and such that the two systems would mirror each other without residue at either end. On the contrary, the language/reality relationship is much more complex, and the parts of speech do not and cannot correspond, even in an ideal language, to the parts of the world.

135

There are no such parts of the world. The manner in which words can usefully interact with things is very diverse, and never exhausts the richness of things. So be it. Wittgenstein's repudiation of his own erstwhile skeletalism was fully justified, though it was far too summary and total, and in a way was quite unargued. Skeletalism deserves a repudiation which, at least in the initial examination, is prepared to look at skeletalism on its own terms. Wittgenstein, having once refused to look at the world in any other terms, now refused to give them any serious hearing at all. Once again, it was for him an error to be *cured*, not to be argued with.

Nevertheless what was really at fault was something quite different: the totally mistaken supposition that skeletalism was equivalent to *all* past philosophy (so that *its* overcoming was the supplanting of *all* philosophy), and the similarly mistaken view that there was but one alternative to it, namely the curious new vision that was now vouchsafed him.

It is sometimes claimed nowadays that it is hard to identify the real nature of Wittgenstein's thought. It is certainly true that his followers disagree profoundly about just what the hidden gold is. But in fact, his central doctrine is perfectly easy to pinpoint and all else follows from it. It consists of a number of beliefs:

(1) That Skeletalism (logic-reality parallelism) is false.

(2) That all past philosophy was based on skeletalism.

(3) That skeletalism arises from a misguided pursuit of homogeneity in language, in thought, in reality. If we recognise diversity and complexity, we shall free ourselves of this compulsion.

(4) That philosophic problems and doctrines are unnecessary and misguided consequences of the failure to see the truth of the preceding assertions.

(5) That there are also questions of faith and of basic social attitude, but these have nothing to do with philosophy.

(1) is true; (2) and (3) are false; (4) and (5) are also false, but they can be made trivially true by suitable redefinition of 'philosophy', which is what Wittgenstein and his followers in practice did and do: philosophy is defined as that which in fact satisfied the doctrines here asserted. All other questions then are confined to the new residual category indicated in (5). (Philosophy then becomes an empty category, in fact, because in the end all questions fall under the other ramification suggested in 5.)

Diagram 1 illustrates our intellectual world and its options, as in fact they are; diagram 2 the impoverished world of linguistic philosophy, with only two options, and with its curious corollary—all traditional beliefs are vindicated, for lack of any possible external criterion by which they could fail, other than the criterion of skeletalism, which has been (rightly) eliminated. The arrow indicated the movement of Wittgenstein's thought, from the rejected position to the new revelation.

But we must consider skeletalism in the context of the other options of human thought. It is only for this end that it has been re-introduced here.

136

Our intellectual predicament arises from a wholly justified sense of cognitive breakdown, the dissolution of the old certainties and the lack of new ones. One way of coping with this predicament is to attempt to find an independent and trustworthy criterion of truth. Empiricism and materialism offer such solutions, and so, in a much minor and less distinguished way, does logicism.

The discovery that logicism is wrong does not by itself do anything to solve our cognitive problem. The initial predicament remains; and the alternative solutions continue to stand, with whatever merits or failings they may possess. They are quite uninvolved in the crash of skeletalism. Were it an important rival, they would, I suppose, be a little strengthened by its disappearance, in as far as anything is strengthened by the elimination of a rival. But truth to tell, it was not really an important rival.

The error which *was* committed sprang from the totally misguided supposition that logicism/skeletalism was the *only* philosophy, that all philosophies were forms of it, and hence that its denial was the denial, the overcoming of *all* philosophy. This was indeed the way in which Wittgenstein saw it. This was the famous 'bewitchment by language'. And worse: he was blind to the way in which the need for selectors had arisen, that is, through the collapse of inherited belief-systems. He saw only the subsidiary and rather specific cause of skeletalism, namely the supposition that there was a homogeneous language-reality parallelism which explained how speech managed to refer to things, and this he supposed to be the (misguided) origin of all systems of philosophic thought. Just as beforehand, a century earlier, the Young Hegelians had equated Hegelianism with philosophy as such, and hence had supposed that the overcoming of Hegelianism was some universal human fulfilment—reality replacing mere cerebration—so also it was with Wittgenstein and the Wittgensteinians: the overcoming of his own youthful skeletalist error was the overcoming of all philosophy.

This was disastrous indeed. Within the academic philosophic trade, there was concentration on the negative aspect of the thesis, the denial of skeletalism, and the associated conviction that its replacement by a more realistic theory of language, one which saw it as a manifold of human activities in variegated social contexts, would lead to the 'dissolution' of philosophic problems. (Needless to say, nothing was 'dissolved' in this manner; but the doctrine that this should happen had no deadlines, and allowed indefinite delays, and thus had plenty of loopholes to explain failure.)

But if one wishes to understand the social significance of this kind of philosophising, in the context of its time and milieu, it was the positive aspect of these ideas that mattered, the *residue* left over when the one crucial error, skeletalism, was overcome. The ordinary vision of things was the residue: in itself, it apparently presented no problem whatever.

In other words, linguistic philosophy, the anti-skeletalist backlash, was a novel, intriguing variant of a re-endorsement philosophy, a theory which purports to have found reasons for supposing that our normal thought habits are sound after all, that things are as we normally think they are. 'Philosophy leaves everything as it is.' In this re-endorsement lies any social importance that linguistic philosophy may have. It is a new way to reassurance. In itself, it is a minor though very curious episode within the world of professional university thought. But as a species of re-endorsement, it is a specimen of a type of reaction or attitude which, generically, is of very great importance in the life of our society and age.

Diagram 1   Our actual cognitive situation

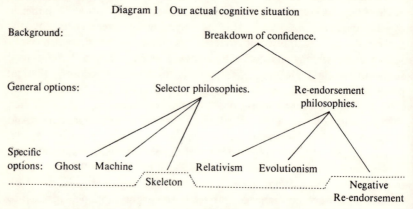

Diagram 2   The restricted world within which linguistic philosophy was articulated. It arises by taking note of only a small fragment of the *real* situation—that beneath the discontinuous line in Diagram 1. The arrow indicates Wittgenstein's development.

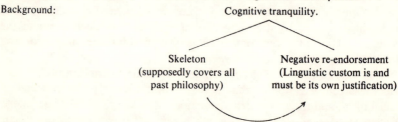

The argument by which the negative re-endorsement position was reached, was simple and fallacious. It presupposes that these two are the *only* options. Then, naturally, the (justified) rejection of skeletalism leads to the only remaining alternative.

Wittgenstein claimed in so many words that these were the only alternatives:

Wittgenstein . . . told me . . . that . . . in the *Tractatus* he had provided a perfected account of a view that is the *only* alternative to the viewpoint of his later work.[79]

[79] N. Malcolm, *Ludwig Wittgenstein, A Memoir* (Oxford, 1958), p. 69, emphasis in the original.

138

Thus the total rejection of a likewise total skeletalism led, by a curious intellectual oath, to a new kind of re-endorsement. The laymen may well be puzzled by the logic of inferences such as that from 'meaning is use' to (say) 'God exists', but the connection is there. One point of the 'use' theory of meaning was its contrast with skeletalism. Its point was the denial of the view that analysis of meaning was a location of those 'logical atoms' which Russell once sought, which would be a kind of ultimate furniture of our world. Instead, meaning was what people did; that is all. Moreover, the skeletalist has thought that the logical skeleton had a kind of authority over people: if they deviated from his schemata, they spoke nonsense. So, by way of *denial* of this view, the participants in the backlash movement maintained that ordinary speech was *not* under the authority of some such logical schema. As no other possibility was considered, it followed that it was its own authority, its own justification. Hence the notions built into it were perfectly in order. If those notions included God, well then that authenticated theology . . . and so on. A lot of leeway was left when it came to just what, specifically, was to be re-endorsed.

Just what was the specific residue that was, in practice, re-endorsed? It is possible to discern several distinct styles.

First of all, there was what may be called common or garden linguistic philosophy. Its members do not really stray from the loose liberal consensus of their time and milieu. They are civilised, moderate men, whose opinions seldom transgress the limits which can be found within the pages of the two quality Sunday newspapers or the reputable literary weeklies. Their views on man, society, God or nature are unlikely to be much further left than the *New Statesman* or further right than the *Spectator*: the spectrum between the *Sunday Times* and the *Observer* will generally accommodate their opinions.

This being so, one may well ask—why should so devious and cumbersome a way be taken to ratify a vision of things which deviated so little from the educated, civilised consensus of the time? Why indeed.

In part, the answer is that this curious philosophic underpinning, whilst having no effect on the content of the *Weltanschauungen* of its upholders (and indeed, it was claimed that it ought to have no such influence), nevertheless greatly affected the manner in which these views were held. It made it much easier to hold them in a complacent, unworrying way. The high period of this philosophy was indeed also a period of intellectual tiredness, and this licence to abstention from general theory or inquiry was welcomed. This outlook provided an end-of-ideology rationale even before the thing was invented under that name. For its upholders, political philosophy was a bit of a puzzle or an embarrassment. How did it ever become part of philosophy at all? How does philosophy, which ratifies all ways of life and all kinds of discourse, get itself mixed up with such a potentially explosive subject? So they tried to say that it really ought to be something called the 'analysis of political concepts'. The practice of this newly discovered craft turned out to be dull beyond all imagining, and not to be endured. The only room left for political thought in this atmosphere was to assimilate it to after-dinner speaking, which, like philosophy, leaves everything as it is.

Apart from underwriting a kind of intellectual somnolence, this negative re-endorsement also had other interesting implications. On the horizon, there was the problem of what came to be called the Two Cultures, and the problem of the co-existence of the technical and the 'humanistic' visions. ('Humanism' nowadays is not something standing in contrast to theological concerns, or to do with knowing Greek and Latin; it is contrasted with knowing science.) This is a very deep and important problem; but it is also an immediate and a practical one for an elite cut off from science.

The linguistic backlash against logicism was a rejection of the pretensions to universal applicability of the notation of mathematical logic; at the same time, it rejected the logical-positivist reduction of all discourse to two simple kinds, modelled on an image of science. It also ratified the familiar *Lebenswelt*, by a seemingly high-powered argument, invented by a man with an aura of authority—had he not made contributions to technical logic? So one had here a most welcome ratification of ordinary thought ('language') against technicist pretensions.

It is for this reason that the majority of participants, despite their ideological non-eccentricity, had cause to welcome this charter of common sense.

Secondly, there was also an inner party of quite a different character. Many have noticed this segment, and it is worth quoting the comments made on it by Professor A. G. N. Flew:

(Wittgenstein's) 'Lectures on Religious Belief' ... have a special interest as Wittgenstein's only application to religion of his fundamental philosophic ideas. These ideas ... would seem to be inexorably this-worldly. It is, therefore paradoxical that so many of those who have been most influenced by Wittgenstein should be Roman Catholics or Catholicisers; although perhaps less so that one or two of the latter should have tried to exploit Wittgenstein's ideas for the obscurantist purpose of putting (approved) fundamental religious practices safely beyond the reach of radical criticism.

The present notes may be seen as lending a certain measure of canonical authority to this last enterprise ...[80]

Let us briefly recapitulate the central doctrines of the great tradition to which Flew refers. They are: absolute truth about this world and another one is available to man. It has been communicated by the creator of this world, and is in possession (the exclusive possession, though this claim has of late been played down) of an organisation which consequently has

[80] *The Spectator*, 16 September 1966.

140

a privileged status within this world, in virtue of a special relationship to the creator. The present leadership of the organisation derives its authority from the fact of institutional continuity with the founder of the organisation, who is also a close kinsman of the creator. The truth in possession of this organisation is not merely so to speak cold information: it is knowledge central to our salvation (as it is rightly called).

The staggering importance of these contentions could hardly be exaggerated. People brought up in this faith can be thrown into deep despair if they lose it. The transformation of European society from one in which this faith was widely accepted, to one in which it is widely doubted, is one of the major intellectual events of recent centuries.

The fact that this faith is now widely doubted proves little. We should be as suspicious of our scepticisms as we are of the dogmatisms of others. Intellectual fashion on its own proves nothing. It would be comic and presumptuous to try and go over the reasons which have led to the loss of faith, in a few paragraphs. What is important for the present argument is only this: affirmed or denied, the faith is of great importance.

It is therefore odd to find that intellectuals who hold this faith are prepared to spend such a large proportion of their professional working-life engaged in philosophical enquiries which, as described above, are certainly trivial in comparison with the concerns of faith. If you really do possess that important faith which so many have lost (for bad reasons, perhaps) surely as a professional philosopher the exposition and the justification of that faith would have absolute priority. Would anything less be justifiable?

One can understand that a man should turn to triviality for diversion after a hard days' work. One can also understand that a man should throw himself into full-time frivolity to escape some deep despair or emptiness. Pascal had much to say about this:

Rien n'est si insupportable à l'homme que d'être dans un plein repos, sans passions, sans affaire, sans divertissement, sans application. Il sent alors son néant, son abandon, son insuffisance, sa dépendance, son impuissance, son vide. Incontinent il sortira du fond de son âme l'ennui, la noirceur, la tristesse, le chagrin, le dépit, le désespoir.

De là vient que les hommes aiment tant le bruit et le remuement; de là vient que la prison est un supplice si horrible; de là vient que le plaisir de la solitude est une chose incompréhensible. Et c'est enfin le plus grand sujet de félicité de la condition des rois, de ce qu'on essaie sans cesse à les divertir . . .

Pensées, 131, 139

Pascal is puzzled that even a king should so demean himself as to

occuper son âme á penser á la cadence d'un air, ou a placer adroitement une balle . . .

Pensées, 142

Pascal's diagnosis of this flight into frivolity is well known: it is an escape from despair, from the human condition, as it is without faith. But we shall have to go beyond Pascal's psychology to explain the phenomenon under consideration, which is even more puzzling than that a king should, instead of taking pleasure in thinking of his own majesty, prefer to think of following a chance step or of placing a ball . . . But here we have thinkers who cannot be fleeing from despair, for they have faith; to compound the puzzle, the trivialities in question lack the charms of either dances or ball-games, and are not known to have tempted anyone other than professional teachers or students.

It would be totally wrong to suspect such thinkers of conscious deception. It would be self-defeating, and certainly would not work if it were conscious and deliberate. But, granting and stressing this, everything suggests that here philosophy acts as a decoy. It is not that they consciously wish to discredit reason and thereby make room for faith; but the objective consequence of their activity is precisely this. It is both a doctrine and a deeply engrained procedural rule of this sub-movement that philosophy and faith are independent. Philosophic reasons cannot touch faith—which means, in practice, that *no* reasons can touch it, for any reasoned arguments concerning matters so fundamental *are* philosophy. So faith is vindicated by default . . .

There is also a third kind of use of 'linguistic' re-endorsement, which differs from the preceding variant above all by openly embracing the relativism which is inherent in its premisses. This sub-movement does not evade the relativism, it glories in it. There are as many valid faiths as there are cultures, 'forms of life', and so forth. The crucial premiss is again the doctrine that because each kind of discourse has its own kind of logic and is to be judged by its own criteria, doubt is in principle misguided . . .

Consider the comments on this position of an author who once embraced it, but has since repudiated it:

[The position which endeavours] to preserve the Christian faith when all its intellectual bases have been removed ... Their central contention ... has been that religion is a specific 'form of life' with its own criteria, its own methods of settling its own questions. So religion cannot be refuted by those sceptics who employ inappropriate criteria, and who try to dismiss religious beliefs because they would be unsatisfactory when they are interpreted as ... scientific hypotheses.[81]

The account is accurate. It is followed however by a puzzling remark to the effect that this attitude turned out to be wrong *because* the intellectual climate which favoured it changed. In fact, this reasoning would be absurd even if that climate *had* lasted.

[81] Preface by Professor Alasdair MacIntyre to the 1970 edition of S. Toulmin, R. W. Hepburn and A. MacIntyre, *Metaphysical Beliefs* (New York, 1970).

142

To say that religious beliefs are not to be treated as 'scientific hypotheses' is just a dainty way of saying that all contentions about the world are to be excluded from them (at any rate when those contentions appear false and doubtful). To claim that such a bowdlerised religion has any similarity to the concrete traditions of faith in the Western world is to say something blatantly false. To make such a claim about the faiths of other traditions is to indulge in irresponsibly *a priori* ethnography which, in any case that is concretely examined, also turns out to be false.

The crucial error here, once again, is the failure to understand the real nature of our cognitive predicament. We do not possess some cosy and viable little island culture to crawl back into, once we abandon the allegedly misguided pursuit of universal and objective truth. On the contrary—we live in a Tower of Babel, and our search for philosophic selectors springs not from Promethean arrogance, still less from a supposed failure to grasp the true nature of language; it arises, inescapably, from the realities of our situation. It cannot be 'cured' by this mumbo-jumbo, least of all by the decoy method.

What are the motives of those who wish to endorse *all* cultures? A part of their motive is, no doubt, a kind of universal benevolence—let a hundred flowers bloom, let all cultures enjoy their own life and their own values. This kind of liberalism on behalf of cultural wholes faces the same difficulty as liberalism on behalf of individuals (but it does not even attempt to face it)—is it to be freedom for the pikes or the minnows? Many traditional cultures are exclusive and intolerant, and oppress sub-cultures within their own territory. Who exactly is to be granted this protected status? It is ironical that those who espouse this position often choose as their exemplar the African tribe of the Azande, largely because of the great literary and expository gifts of the late Edward Evans-Pritchard, whose books provide them with source material. Alas, the Azande are a case in point, which strikingly illustrates the problem:

Azande themselves say that the authority of their leaders was strengthened by war and the increase in numbers of their followers each new conquest brought them. Another consequence has been ethnic intermingling of great complexity. I have listed over twenty foreign peoples . . . who have contributed to the Zande amalgam . . . In the Sudan alone, in addition to Zande, there are spoken in Zande country seven or eight different languages . . .

. . . Zande culture is a thing of shreds and patches.[82]

It is ironical that this culture of shreds and patches, incorporating at least twenty culturally alien groups and speaking at least eight diverse languages in what is but part of its total territory, should have come to have been systematically invoked, by philosophers making facile and superficial use of anthropology, as an illustration of the quite erroneous

[82] E. Evans-Pritchard, *The Position of Women in Primitive Society and Other Essays in Social Anthropology* (London, 1965), pp. 105, 106, 110.

view that cultures are islands unto themselves, whose supposedly coherent internal norms of what is real and what is not real may not be challenged . . .

In practice, those who espouse this universal cultural tolerance are indeed inevitably selective; what they *mean* is nice, cosy, traditional cultures, not as they exist, but as they are pictured in the romantic imagination. And above all, they are interested in selective preservation within their own society. Not surprisingly, they dislike scientism, positivism, rationalism in their own society, and rather ignore the fact that these traits also constitute a culture, and one which, from the viewpoint of their initial and rather abstract starting point, has at least as good a claim as the cosiest of closed societies.

Our real problem is to explain just how we have overcome relativism; it simply won't do to pretend that relativism is a solution, not a problem. (For one thing, this is an affectation which cannot be sustained outside the study—which ought to worry members of a movement which started out from a defence of real-life beliefs against those only held under philosophers' licence.) Above all, the really interesting differences in cognitive power are not within cultures, but between them. The theory of knowledge ought never to be about how we know that sticks-looking-bent-in-water are really straight; it is about how we know that magic is not valid.

The home culture these thinkers in practice favour must owe something to Sir Walter Scott and a great deal to William Morris, with perhaps a touch of Simone Weil, but it is carefully purified, or rather bowdlerised, to exclude superstitious elements:

In Judaeo-Christian cultures the conception of 'If it be Thy will', as developed in the story of Job, is clearly central . . . Because this conception is central to Christian prayers of supplication, they may be regarded from one point of view as freeing the believer from dependence on what he is supplicating for. Prayers cannot play this role if they are regarded as a means of influencing the outcome . . . [83]

Just go and tell any European peasant (presumably a member of a Judaeo-Christian culture), that he does not really consider prayer to be 'a means of influencing the outcome', for this would be in conflict with the view of prayer as a freeing of the supplicator from dependence, to which he is committed in virtue of the Book of Job. Or perhaps those Catholic goalkeepers who cross themselves before facing a penalty shot, do it in this spirit . . . ?

Take a less aprioristic and more accurate account:

Prayer is a form of bargaining; you will see at once that the psychological attitude to the Saint is one of rough familiarity. The tone of voice (that is to say the internal tone of voice—for the prayer is silent though the lips move) is the tone that one would adopt to a recalcitrant child. There is no question of a humble

[83] Professor Peter Winch, in 'Understanding a Primitive Society', re-printed in *Rationality*, ed. B. Wilson, (Oxford, 1970), p. 104.

144

pleading, and a foregone acceptance of refusal; the petition, whatever the request, assumes that it is most likely to be granted . . .[84]

But perhaps the Corfu islanders so described are not full members, or not members at all, of the 'Judaeo-Christian tradition'? If so, one fears that this tradition will be deprived of the great majority of its members, of all but some modernist theologians, philosophers of re-endorsement, and their followers. Note that this argument cannot fall back on saying that the benighted peasants *ought* to understand the Book of Job, and that if they do not, they are ignorant of their own fath. In a sense that is so, of course, for there is generally a disparity between its simple and sophisticated versions, and the latter is highly volatile over time. But the position is intended to justify the simple faith, not to reform it. But whilst pretending to justify it, it distorts it out of all recognition. When this is done for the simple members of distant cultures, it is accompanied by a scandalously irresponsible, scissors-and-paste, selective use of ethnographic material.

In opposition to such views, one must stress that there is an extraneous and independent reality, which makes its inescapable impact on our social and conceptual world in a variety of ways, amongst which the harsh facts of economy and power are the most prominent. In its rarefied, devious and tortuous way, this kind of neo-idealist philosophy is simply an indulgence in phantasy, the phantasy of the *Almacht des Begriffes*, the omnipotence of the concept. Because our world is concept-saturated (which is true), it is falsely and absurdly argued that therefore we are exempt from extraneous causal compulsion or explanation, and that *our* conduct can only be explained in terms of *our* concepts . . . a fairy-tale indeed.[85]

This style of theorising has close affinities with the Instant God School, which indeed it underpins: God exists, because the concept of God is embedded in our thought and language, which are self-justifying, and the boundaries of the real and unreal can only be traced within each language or culture (what proof could be simpler?):

Reality is not what gives language sense. What is real and what is unreal shows itself *in* the sense language has. Further, both the distinction between the real and the unreal and the concept of agreement with reality themselves belong to our language.[86]

[84] Lawrence Durrell, *Prospero's Cell* (London, 1945), p. 32.

[85] 'the central concepts which belong to our understanding of social life are incompatible with concepts central to the activity of scientific prediction.

. . . the conceptions according to which we normally think of social events are logically incompatible with concepts belonging to scientific explanation.

. . . function . . . a quasi-causal notion, which it is perilous to apply to social institutions.'

P. Winch, *The Idea of a Social Science* (London, 1958.) pp. 94, 95, 116. For a criticism of Winch's views, see I. Jarvie, *Concepts and Society* (London, 1972).

[86] Winch, *The Idea of a Social Science*, p. 82.

This just means simply that each language is free to make its own reality and unreality. The corollary is plain: prayer and faith create their own object.[87]

What could be easier than this self-generation of the object by the believer's own activity? The only thing that now becomes odd is that anyone suffered from doubt. Those tormented souls could have been spared all their anguish. As a philosophic procedure, this attitude is summed up by the movement's own principle, articulated by Professor Rush Rees: 'The refutation of scepticism is the whole business of philosophy.'[88] Evidently one knows in advance that scepticism cannot be valid. The re-endorsement logic which guarantees this comfortable conclusion has been explored, and it could hardly go further.

If properly followed out, the relativism of this position is grotesque: whilst God exists in a theistic culture, and many gods in a polytheistic one (and the upholders of this position are really willing to go this far), he also does *not* exist in an atheist one. But characteristically these thinkers avert their gaze from societies whose sense of the real and unreal are unpalatable to them, when they are not bowdlerising cultures they mistakenly consider more tractable. But the God they supply for this society is a very sliding-scale, retractable God, who does not obtrude when He is not wanted, and can cause little logical or moral discomfort.

PEDDLERS OF ANTIQUES AND OMNIBUS POPULISM

As a general style, re-endorsement is quite acceptable when no philosophy is really needed in the first place, and useless when it *is* required. It claims, on the basis of abstract and unsound premises, that all is well with our inherited habits of thought. When these are brought to the bar of Cartesian doubt, there is, on this view, no case to answer. Well, the truth about this world is that our inherited ideas are sometimes viable and sometimes not, and that intellectual crises occur when some important part of them is unacceptable. Hence no general theory to the effect that the bulk of them is *always* sound, can conceivably be correct. We have examined one such theory, which happened to be prominent on our immediate environment; but the others would have proved equally defective.

But there are good social reasons why re-endorsement and in particular the negative variety should be common in our time. For reasons explored with depth and perceptiveness by Max Weber, the traditional visions, in which the natural, social and moral orders are blended and underwrite each other, are eroded under modern conditions. Not only society, but nature too is bureaucratised, subsumed under impersonal rules which make cognition and control possible, but which also operate the great 'disenchantment'.

[87] Cf. D. Z. Phillips, *The Concept of Prayer* (London, 1965).
[88] Quoted in *The Times Literary Supplement*, 27 July, 1973, p. 875.

146

The Enlightenment saw (with delight) the erosion of the medieval enchantment, but it supposed (erroneously) that a new and similarly gratifying synthesis would emerge, with nature, and/or reason, in place of the old superstition. Weber did not share this illusion, for he knew the new vision would not shine with a new warmth, but on the contrary was bound to be cold and comfortless. But it would be an error to suppose that we shall all embrace it, with the same consistency and totality with which it is supposed that traditional man was immersed in his particular social vision. In fact, Max Weber saw this full well with respect to his own contemporaries:

Never as yet has a new prophecy emerged ... through the need of some modern intellectuals to furnish their souls with ... guaranteed genuine antiques ... they play at decorating a kind of domestic chapel with ... sacred images from all over the world, or they produce surrogates ... which they peddle in the book market. This is plain humbug or self-deception.[89]

But it not clear whether Weber saw that such conceptual antiquarianism, the peddling of ersatz 'forms of life' or carte blanche legitimations thereof, would become a major intellectual industry of the age. It was an elite activity in his day. Today, there are cheap do-it-yourself kits available on the market, within everyone's reach. For this is the essence of negative re-endorsement. It revives or justifies a 'tradition' (real, invented, or unspecified) by producing spurious reasons purporting to show why the impugning of tradition (variant: form of life, commonsense, ordinary speech) can never be sound.

But these revivalisms are spurious. The point was made by the medieval Muslim thinker Al Ghazali:

There is no hope of returning to a traditional faith after it has once been abandoned, since the essential condition in the holder of a traditional faith is that he should not know he is a traditionalist.[90]

There are good reasons, particularly in the modern world, why these self-conscious revivals and restorations must be spurious. When a traditional faith was held in the full and literal sense, it was wedded to the best available current forms of knowledge. When it is theatrically revived, in a kind of social inverted commas, it is revived, precisely, by disconnecting it from what is taken seriously as knowledge, and is kept alive only by this artificial insulation, by inventing special criteria and functions for it, which are carefully made distinct from serious cognition. But when serious issues are at stake, when the fate of individuals and communities is at risk, one will not fail to make use of the best available knowledge; so, in any crisis, men tend to ignore the revived 'tradition' and think in the terms which they cognitively respect, rather than in terms of antiquarian conceptual furnishing. So, ironically, the traditional 'faith' is used when

[89] M. Weber, Science as a Vocation.
[90] Quoted in E. Kedourie, Nationalism in Asia and Africa (London, 1971), p. 66.

147

things go smoothly and no faith is really needed, but it is ignored when the situation is grave.

Still, we need the antiquarian furnishings—*as* furnishing. The new cold vision does not generate a complete culture of its own, let alone a warm and cosy one; the idea that it would was indeed the great delusion of the Enlightenment, which thought it was ushering in a new coherent cosmos to replace the old. So by all means let us furnish our houses with antiques, genuine or phoney. (We need them to fill up the detail of our life.) Mostly they will be phoney, because there is a shortage of real ones, which are also often most uncomfortable, and do not look nearly as genuine as does a good fake. So be it. But we must remember—and in any crisis most of us do remember—that all this is not at all serious. The re-endorsed belief will bear no strain, they are useless when decisions need to be made.

Of course, when things go well, it is also natural and reasonable to give a genuine benefit of the doubt to the inherited assumptions. Who wishes to query everything all the time? And even in crisis, we may need to do the same, simply for lack of an alternative. But we then only do it *faute de mieux*. When facing real choices, we prefer real knowledge. We do not always have it, but we do have it sometimes—often enough to know what it is like, and often enough to wish to know its general criteria. It is such because it satisfied the selector criteria; and it is totally unlike the pretty but ramshackle traditional revivals. Re-endorsement is an inescapable, and perhaps not-to-be-decried, style of our intellectual furnishing industry. It is quite good enough for interior decoration, but has no serious claim on our cognitive loyalty.

8 The savage mind

Modern industrial civilisation is unique. One very important tradition of thought, ever since we became vertiginously aware of being plunged into a totally new situation, with enormous potential for good and evil, consists in the attempt to define, delimit, seize and understand this idiosyncrasy. Some have sought the crucial distinguishing mark in the division of labour, some in rationality, in democracy or the equalisation of conditions, in economic organisation, and so forth. For the moment, what concerns us specially are the attempts to locate the great differentia in the style of thought or cognition.

There are two ways of approaching this problem. One is to say that the modern world is based on science and its application, and then to try to define the specific characteristics of scientific thought, as opposed to unscientific or pre-scientific forms of reasoning. This is the problem of delimitation, the *Abgrenzungsproblem*. This was, of course, a preoccupation, amongst others, of the Viennese logical positivists, and of the youthful Karl Popper, and indeed the positivist tradition in the wider sense can be defined in these terms.

Alternatively, one can attempt a positive characterisation of specifically *primitive* thought. This characteristically anthropological orientation in the end springs from the same source as does the interest in the *Abgrenzungsproblem*: from a sense of the uniqueness of our own civilisation. It springs from the realisation that whereas recent pre-scientific or pre-industrial civilisations displayed, in their styles of thought, traits which were partly similar to our own, primitive mentality, 'the savage mind', seems to exemplify principles of thought radically different from ours. If this is so, we can, by isolating these alien principles, come to understand the distinctiveness of our own thought through the resulting contrast. What is the nature and basis of this distinctiveness? Thus one can approach the problem of identifying the secret of the most powerful form of cognition—science—either directly, or indirectly, by looking at that which appears most distant from it and most dramatically contrasted with it.

The first approach singles out specifically scientific thought for explanation or definition; the latter approach aims at a specific characterisation of primitive mentality. If one combines the two approaches, one is naturally left with a large residual region between them, covering the extensive areas of thought and civilisation which are neither tribal-primitive nor scientific-industrial. Hence there is a certain tendency for evolutionary schemata of the development of human society or thinking to end up with a three-stage pattern. This tendency is a consequence of the fact that the very distinctively scientific and the very distinctively primitive are relatively narrow areas, and there is a very big region in between.

Nevertheless, it is my impression that the problem of the delimitation of science, and the problem of the characterisation of primitive mentality, are one and the same problem. To say this is not to deny that the area between them is enormous, and comprises the larger part of human life and experience. But this middle area perhaps does not exemplify any distinctive and important principle. With regard to the basic strategic alternatives available to human thought, there is only one question and one big divide. The mixed or borderline area is enormous, much bigger, and for some purposes perhaps much more important, than the relatively pure areas which may be found on either side of the big divide; nevertheless, it is the basic antithesis which must concern us. Some have approached it from the viewpoint of delimiting science (or even delimiting meaning as such), and some from the opposite viewpoint of seeking to understand the savage mind; but there is really only one problem here. The central question of anthropology (the characterisation of the savage mind) and the central question of modern philosophy (the characterisation or delimitation of science) are in this sense but the obverse of each other. They are two aspects of the same question.

DRUNK OR SOBER

One type of theory of primitive mentality sees the savage mind as somehow steeped in pervasive error. This was Sir James Frazer's approach, or at any rate his overt, official theory, present in the formal summary of his findings. (Quite other theories can be found implicit in his interpretation of his material, or in the manner in which that material is arranged.) On this account, the primitive sought causal connections between phenomena, but he expected them to be somehow logical, to arise from the natural affinities between things. It was only when this expectation was rudely disappointed, that the primitive mind moves from magic to religion, invoking spiritual beings to explain its own previous failure to seize the secret of things, in the hope of at least now being able to influence and propitiate the powers that lay behind events. Spiritual beings on this view make their entry not to account for order in nature, but to account for the previous failure to find order. In this respect as in some others, Frazer was a follower of Hume. He applied to the savage mind what Hume claimed to find in his own. But at either stage, magical or religious, the primitive mind was on Frazer's view in a state of intellectual error. The error, however, was one which we could easily make ourselves,

150

if we found ourselves in the savage's position. Indeed this very point constitutes one of the standard objections to Frazerian anthropology: it proceeds by a somewhat facile piece of *Eindenken*: 'What would *I* think if I were primitive man?' And it goes on to retroject a version of Hume's account of our own thought processes on to the savage.

More interesting, more radical and hence perhaps more profound is quite a different type of theory of primitive mentality, which suggests that the savage mind is fundamentally different from our own: it is not that it possesses the same tools as we do and makes a mistaken use of them, but rather it possesses quite different tools, it is differently constituted. We could not easily make its kind of mistake even if we tried, and conversely, to become as we are, needs more than a mere intellectual correction and accumulation of additional evidence.

The most famous version of this kind of theory maintains, in effect, that the primitive mind is perpetually drunk. This is not the terminology used, but it is what, basically, the theory amounts to. Like the 'Intellectual error' theory, in the end this approach also borrows something familiar from an analogy with our own experience, in order to account for the alien mind; but it borrows not the experience of error, even pervasive and systematic error, but starts from the type of exceptional mental states we know under the impact of alcohol, drugs, fever, drowsiness, or perhaps unusual ecstatic. In those kind of conditions, we have, for better or for worse, a sense of 'something far more deeply interfused' than the discrete, sharply delineated, prosaic objects of sober daily experience. The boundaries between object and object, and more important, the boundaries between objects and self, become hazy, or even disappear altogether. The rules and sense of identity and contradiction are suspended. It need hardly be said that those who put forward this kind of theory do not necessarily or generally put it forward in a spirit of derision or contempt *vis-à-vis* primitive mind; on the contrary, the theory can easily and plausibly be put forward in a spirit of envy and regret, deploring our loss of unity with nature, with each other, with the community, with the cosmos:

Little we see in Nature that is ours;
... Great God! I'd rather be
A Pagan suckled in a creed outworn
So might I, standing on this pleasant lea,
Have glimpses that would make me less forlorn ...

In as far as a schema of historical development is inspired by this kind of theory, it tends to invoke facts such as the wildness and exuberance of primitive art and mythology, and the relative sobriety and restraint of more developed styles of thought and art. On this kind of vision, it was the Greeks, at least in their Apollonian if not their Dionysiac mood, with their restrained art, and the Romans (good orderly lawyers and administrators),

151

who led the western mind from inebriation to sobriety. (The Etruscans, it would seem, were still drunk.)

Recently, the 'pervasive drunkenness' theory of primitive mentality has been out of fashion, at least in scholarly circles. Contemporary anthropologists do not seem to be much given to Wordsworthian moods, at least publicly, and feel little desire to project on to the savage some fusion with nature, whether in admiration or in derision. For instance, Evans-Pritchard's Nuer, though they can discern refractions of the deity in nature, combine this discernment with an otherwise perfectly unimpaired and adequately documented capacity to identify physical objects, especially cucumbers. Professor Lévi-Strauss' *bricoleur*, though he may be distinctive in his style of thought, is by no means drunk. His science may be lacking in abstraction, though apparently it is different in kind rather than inferior to ours, but it *is* science, and experimental to boot. In fact, it is curiously Machian: what on this view distinguishes the savage mind in its scientific constructions is that it draws its categories from the concrete, sensory world, rather than going beyond it. It satisfied the positivist injunction that we should prefer constructions from what we do experience to inferences to the unknown. This has some surprising affinities with Frazer, and above all, it constitutes an interesting inversion of the usual positivistic way of looking at the primitive as uncritically over-indulging a taste for the transcendent.

But all in all, what might be called the 'booming buzzing confusion' theory of the primitive mind is still probably the best known and best diffused theory. There is an element of truth in it, but that element is in fact compatible with the recognition that the primitive's capacity for sensory perception, discrimination and delineation is as sharp as anyone else's. But he does not live in some kind of astigmatic, impressionist haze—however warm and cosy, or however restrictive and inhibiting, such an immersion and participation in the warm flow of undifferentiated Being may seem to us. What then is the correct theory?

SINGLY OR TOGETHER

Thus we are left with the two intimately connected questions: what makes modernity, and what makes the savage? Each of these questions has a strong general appeal. The one makes us gaze in the mirror and hope to catch an innocent glimpse, and see ourselves as we truly are. But we also long for the *frisson* of seeing, or seizing conceptually, the wholly Other, the savage. There is this unmistakeable element of voyeurism both in anthropology and in philosophy. We hope to see what is normally obscured by the decencies, and to find out some truth about ourselves in the process.

The problem of modernity is of course not exclusively, nor even predominantly, a concern of the philosophers. Theories of modernity in terms of industrialisation, bureaucracy or the division of labour, are not the stock in trade of the conventional philosopher. This is rather a mistake on his part, but for better or worse, it is so. The philosophers only take a sustained interest when modernity is defined in the sphere of *cognition*. They are not averse to trying their hand at defining rationality, but they feel really at home when it comes to defining *science*. Hence, by a little extension, it is easy to extract from their work a theory of scientific *mentality*. So, if science is a crucial element of modernity, the philosophers are unwittingly involved in giving an account of it.

As stated, it would of course be mistaken to suppose that the savage and the modern mind jointly exhaust the world, that everyone must needs be either one or the other. Clearly, this is not so. Many schemata of the evolution of the human mind do indeed interpose a middle stage, between (say) the religious and the positive mentality, or between magic and science. Much of human history is taken up by civilisations standing between the two poles, whose privileged and literate classes at least were not savage, though they were not like the citizens of modern, technological society either. One must allow for this middle ground. It covers, perhaps, the most interesting part of human history.

Nevertheless it is for analytic purposes worthwhile to think away this enormous middle ground. It is probably as well to do it knowingly, rather than conjure it away by definition or stylistic sleight of hand. Likewise, it is probably as well to be clear about another tacit assumption which underlies this kind of reasoning: it is only an assumption, not an established truth, that there is one homogeneous kind of modernity. It is certainly not self-evident.

It is interesting to note that C. Lévi-Strauss explicitly adheres to this general two-term approach. He argues[91] that it is essential for us:

to understand how (neolithic or early historical man) could have come to a halt and how several thousand years of stagnation have intervened between the neolithic revolution and modern science *like a level plain between two ascents.* [Italics mine. E.G.]

Just as an evolutionist vision of continuous growth came naturally, almost inevitably, to nineteenth-century thinkers, so the pattern which most naturally leaps to our minds is that of a *flat plain* between the neolithic revolution and modern science. For various reasons indicated, the plain doesn't interest us as much as the precipices at either end of it. Those who lived on that plain often found it rugged, though.

Despite Lévi-Strauss' partial disclaimer,[92] his own approach to the great divide, which remains when we think away the intervening plain, is strikingly reminiscent of Frazer's. Like Frazer, he sees primitive man as seeking *intelligible* connections. According to Frazer, the primitive

[91] C. Lévi-Strauss, *The Savage Mind,* (London, 1966) p. 15.
[91] Op. cit. p. 13.

153

assumption was that the connections had to make a kind of sense; and according to Lévi-Strauss, they were formulated at the level of 'perception and the imagination'—in other words in concrete terms, close to what is seized by the senses. The difference between the two thinkers is not very great; in fact, it could be argued that each of the two positions implies the other. There is more difference in the two thinkers' characterisation of the other pole, science. For Frazer, it is primarily distinguished by experimentation, as opposed to *a priori*, 'sympathetic' plausibility. Lévi-Strauss cannot use this criterion, nor does he wish to do so, for he believes primitive man to be a systematic experimentalist too. So he invokes, instead, *abstraction*, in the sense of formulation of generalisations in terms far removed from sensory perception.

These, then, are the rules of our contemporary game: one kind of savage mentality is seen as confronting one kind of modern mind, and the intermediate ground is ignored as in the end irrelevant. These are but interim conventions, not dogmas. They do however enable us to look, at least experimentally, at what the anthropologists have to say about the savage mind, and what the philosophers say about the delimitation of science, as obverses of each other.

A striking recent effort to pursue this kind of strategy is Professor Robin Horton's 'African Traditional Thought and Western Science'.[93] It is an invaluable starting point. The present attempt overlaps with and diverges from Horton's in a variety of ways.

Horton lists a number of ways in which traditional African thought resembles science, and other ways in which the two traditions stand contrasted. If this were all, his argument would merely present a kind of check-list of traits. But Horton goes further than this. He singles out one differentia as crucial, in that the others flow from it:

in traditional cultures there is no developed awareness of alternatives to the established body of theoretical tenets; whereas in scientifically oriented cultures, such an awareness is highly developed.[94]

Horton goes on to find in *this* the contrast between the Closed and the Open, acknowledging an affinity to Sir Karl Popper's use of these notions, but explicitly narrowing down his own version of the opposition, in contrast to Popper's. Where Popper appears to include individualism and achievement-orientation in his notion of 'open-ness', Horton restricts his own use of the term exclusively to a sense-of-theoretical-alternative.

It is interesting to note that Horton's bibliography includes the name of Thomas Kuhn, whose *The Structure of Scientific Revolutions* justifiably enjoys a great vogue, and has had an enormous impact on contemporary thought. This is slightly surprising, in as far as Kuhn's central point, when formulated in this kind of language, amounts to a claim that science is in

[93] *Africa*, vol. xxxvii, no. 2, April 1967.
[94] *Ibid*. p. 154.

154

fact not nearly as open as is widely believed. On his view, scientific inquiry does not range freely amongst boundless alternatives, as the popular image suggests, but is at any given time constrained by the currently dominant 'paradigm', whose hold is weakened only at the time of major scientific revolutions. The only people whose minds are truly 'open', and who lack a paradigm, are people like social scientists—but the reason is not that they are freer, but on the contrary that their poor discipline is in a pre-scientific stage. For all these reasons, an awareness of Kuhn's work, unless of course it is simply rejected as unsound, should make it harder to find the essence of science and modernity in 'open-ness', for in his view science is *less* rather than more 'open'. Horton does not, in fact, dismiss Kuhn as unsound (though perhaps from his own viewpoint he should do so), but he overcomes the difficulty in somewhat cavalier manner:

(The scientist's) pushing of a theory and his reluctance to scrap it are not due to any chilling intuition that if his theory fails him, chaos is at hand. Rather, they are due to the very knowledge that the theory is not something timeless and absolute.[95]

In the end, Horton's account of scientific conduct seems unlike Kuhn's:

The scientist is, as it were, always keeping account, balancing the successes of a theory against its failures. And when the failures start coming in thick and fast, defence of the theory switches inexorably to attack on it.[96]

So in the end the traditional picture, which enables the scientist to deal directly with an external reality, and dismiss theories if they sin against it too much, is upheld. In Kuhn's disturbing scheme, there is no room for any such direct intercourse with objective reality: the scientist is only capable of checking little theories against the paradigm which is socially imposed, and hence there seems to be no way of checking paradigms themselves against reality, for science cannot function without *some* paradigm. No direct, unmediated, uncensored communication with reality is conceivable. There is no naked paradigm-free reality. (This accounts for some of Kuhn's popularity. His implicit relativism provides an easy other way either to attack or to uphold 'paradigms': to attack anyone else's position, however well-based, and uphold one's own, however arbitrary. Kuhn himself certainly cannot be blamed for this popular use of his ideas.)

It was worth noticing this: despite Horton's complimentary mention of Kuhn, he does not really use Kuhn's conclusion, and on the contrary presupposes its falsity. For Horton assumes the existence and observability of an external reality other than the social perceptions of it, such that styles of social thought can be classified in terms of their stance *vis-à-vis* that independently existing and observable reality. Horton also assumes that this reality is such as to render the 'open' outlook sounder, or

[95] *Ibid.* p. 168.   [96] *Ibid.* p. 168.

at least cognitively more effective, than the closed vision. All these assumptions seem to me most laudable, but it is worth spelling them out, if only so as to be aware of having made them.

Horton's identification of the key property of primitive or traditional mentality seems to me mistaken, partly because some modern men notoriously also have the greatest difficulty in even conceiving an alternative to their own favoured world-vision, and partly because many members of traditional, pre-scientific societies *are* capable of it. Horton invokes Evans-Pritchard's classic work on the Azande:

In this web of belief every strand depends upon every other strand, and a Zande cannot get out of its meshes because it is the only world he knows. The web is not an external structure in which he is enclosed. It is the texture of his thought and he cannot think that his thought is wrong.[97]

No doubt, situations of this kind – conceptual loyalty without any option – do occur. But consider the implications of accepting this as a general criterion of traditional mentality: it means that within it there can be no syncretism, no doctrinal pluralism, no deep treason, no dramatic conversion or doctrinal oscillation, no holding of alternative belief-systems up one's sleeve, ready for the opportune moment of betrayal. Frankly, I do not believe this. Some savages may live in an unique, option-less world. Many do not. They transcend their condition not by reaching out to science, but through syncretism, through the simultaneous use of incompatible belief systems, or doctrinal opportunism. If for in-stance, Professor Edmund Leach[98] is right in his account of the tribes-men of Highland Burma, and some of the Burmese tribesmen oscillate between two quite incompatible visions of their own society, it would follow, by Horton's criterion, that this very oscillation would promptly propel them out of the traditional realm and into the scientific one. Such a conclusion seems paradoxical. One can think of many other examples, many of them not contingent on any daring anthropological interpreta-tion. In brief, not all conceptually plural situations are *ipso facto* modern or scientific ones. The existence of plurality, and the sense of choice which it engenders, may perhaps be a necessary condition of the modern out-look; but it is certainly not a sufficient condition. Even Horton's selection of quotations from Evans-Pritchard's work on the Azande, partly reproduced above, is somewhat selective. Horton invokes those passages which suggest that a Zande cannot escape his own system of thought: 'he cannot think that his (own) thought is wrong.'[99] But Horton omits to quote the sentence which *immediately* follows on the passage quoted:

Nevertheless, (Zande) beliefs are not absolutely set but are variable and fluctuating to allow for different situations and to permit empirical observations and even doubts.

[97] *Witchcraft among the Azande,* pp. 194 and 195.
[98] *Political Systems of Highland Burma,* (London, 1954).
[99] *Witchcraft among the Azande,* p. 195.

Speaking of the ordinary, non-royal Azande, Evans-Pritchard also tells us:

They adapt themselves without undue difficulty to new conditions of life and are always ready to copy the behaviour of those they regard as their superiors in culture and to borrow new modes of dress, new weapons and utensils, new words, and even new ideas and habits . . .[100]

It is, or was, apparently only the royal class who were 'more proud and conservative'. So, as far as the lower orders were concerned, even the Azande faced a plural, and hence 'open' situation. Did they consequently exemplify the scientific spirit? I suspect they did not. Nor could such a claim be made for all those numerous populations who are familiar with conceptual alternatives, through living in frontier areas between diverse cultures, and who often have no difficulty in switching from one 'language' to another, in a deep rather than a superficial sense of 'language'.

It is considerations such as these which make me reluctant to accept Horton's key criterion as it stands. A sense of alternatives, like patriotism, is not enough. The criterion of a 'developed sense of alternatives' does not, in fact, help separate the sheep from the goats in an acceptable manner. Yet one may well feel reluctant to reject his touchstone outright. The underlying intuition seems too valuable. Can it be reformulated and saved?

One related defect in Horton's formulation of his own position (a surprising one in an anthropologist) is its *individualism*. The 'awareness of alternatives' appear to be credited to individuals. This is most regrettable. One consequence is that individual scientists who happen to be unimaginative, dogmatic, over-confident, ignorant of the history of their own subject, and without a nose for new ideas, promptly become excluded from the community of science. Are there no such scientists-vegetables? They may not be good, inspiring, creative scientists, but to exclude them from science altogether would seem not only harsh but also arbitrary. And similarly, not every opportunist guru or dervish, who can switch from one cosmology to another, if his pursuit of a powerful patron or of a clientele require it, thereby becomes a worthy exemplar of the scientific spirit.

The first emendation I should propose for Horton's scheme is that Horton's crucial differentia be credited not to individuals, nor even groups, but to *systems of thought*. If applied to individuals it becomes untenable, for the reasons indicated. This emendation does have an obvious disadvantage: systems of thought, unlike individuals or groups, are an abstraction. They can only be observed as incarnated in the verbal and other behaviour of individuals or groups, and their isolation from the continuum of behaviour may well be question-begging. The observer may isolate one or more such 'systems', which then illustrate his point, whilst a rival observer may choose to isolate quite other units. How could one

[100] *Ibid.* p. 13.

choose between the claims of such rivals?

There are two principal methods normally employed for identifying, isolating a 'belief system': one of them invokes the observer's own sense of coherence, and the other appeals to a corpus of written sources and documents. The possibility of bias or arbitrariness inherent in the first method is obvious. But the danger is clearly not absent from the second method either. The fact that a corpus of writings exists, recording the beliefs and prescriptions of a given social tradition, in no way excludes possibilities such as, for instance, syncretism within that corpus, or, on the other hand, selection and bowdlerisation. In many cultural contexts, the scribes are but one of a number of groups, all of them disputing the cultural heritage and authority within it. What the scribes put down is but one version of the system, not necessarily the 'correct' one. On the contrary, it tends to be one biased towards the set of values normally associated with literacy.

Despite these difficulties inherent in using the notion of a 'system of belief', in place of the individual or group credited with holding it— difficulties for which there may be no formal solution—it seems essential that the great dividing line be drawn in such terms.

But this is not the only emendation I propose. Horton clearly supposes that this one trait is crucial, a key differentia, and that the other differentiae flow from it. It seems to me, on the contrary, that we are faced with two opposed syndromes, and that within each, there is not one but a number of crucial traits. Each of these tends to have a natural affinity with the others in its group, and one could perhaps slant the characterisation of either group in such a way that it seems to 'flow' from one trait. But this might be arbitrary and misleading. I shall sketch the opposition, as it 'really' seems to me to be. Apart from diverging from Horton's in the ways already indicated, and perhaps in some others, it also overlaps with his at many points.

FOUR CRITERIA

There seem to me to be not one, but four possibly crucial differentiae between the savage and the scientific mind. First of all, it might be useful to give them names. The savage displays the following traits:

(1) the use of idiosyncratic norms;
(2) a low cognitive division of labour, accompanied at the same time by a proliferation of roles;
(3) the entrenched clauses of his intellectual constitution are very diffuse and pervasive;
(4) cognition has little or no extra-territorial status.

These four traits are not independent of each other. But they can usefully be considered separately.

158

(1) *A traditional belief system contains at least one general vision of 'what is normal'.* The normal differs from the abnormal in that it either requires no explanation at all, or only requires explanation of a kind radically different from that required by the abnormal. The normal, if explained at all, is explained wholesale by the general belief system and its myths. No specific explanation is required for individual occasions over and above their place in a 'normal' sequence.

This normality is both cognitive (in the sense of having these negative implications for cognitive strategy, by abolishing the need to probe) *and* moral. It defines a social order as well as a natural one. In consequence, it is 'meaningful'—truth and the social order support each other—and rather untidy. It has, so to speak, jagged and complex edges. The language of cognition must be rich enough for all moral nuances. It must be rich and specific enough to articulate the local rules of etiquette. Explanation does not fall on the just and unjust indifferently. On the contrary, it must help define and pinpoint them.

By contrast, the crucial feature of scientific thought-systems is that the notion of normality is not conspicuously present in them. They do, admittedly, distinguish between what does and what does not require explanation, and this might be held to be an equivalent of 'normality'. But this base-line for explanation is very different from the 'normality' of traditional belief systems. On points of detail it is relative, temporary and problem-bound rather than socially entrenched. On generalities it is tidy, symmetrical, with fairly straight rather than jagged edges, as it were. The boundaries of the self-explanatory are general, abstract, and not tied to ‣and repeatable in accordance with a publicly stateable and socially neutral recipe or formula, such that the behaviour to be explained follows than in terms of concrete properties of the *thing* explained. As stated, the most widely favoured base-line of this kind is what is popularly conceived as mechanism or materialism; it hinges on the existence of a structure, built of publicly available materials with no unsymmetrical properties, and repeatable in accordance with a publicly stateable and socially neutral recipe or formula, such that the behaviour to be explained follows from the properties of that structure.[101] It does indeed follow that such cognitive base-lines are *not,* at the same time, the delineation of a moral or social order. On the contrary: the formal criteria they must satisfy, at the time also make them singularly ill-suited for the under-pinning of moral expectations, of a status- and value-system. They tend to be 'meaningless' and 'morally blind'.

---

[101] The importance of the absence of unsymmetrical elements in explanation is noted by Steven Lukes, in 'Some Problems about Rationality', *European Journal of Sociology* (1967) vol. VIII, no. 2, p. 259. Lukes lists no fewer than ten senses of rationality, and this one is given the fourth place in the list. His own words for this type of irrationality are that beliefs are so irrational if 'they are situationally specific or *ad hoc,* i.e.: not universalised because bound to particular occasions'. Lukes rightly hints at the affinity between this kind

Another way of making this point is to say that an important distinguishing mark of science is the mechanistic outlook. (The well-advertised, allegedly non-mechanical features of some parts of modern science are in no way in conflict with this contention.) It is interesting, however, that the best known and probably the most influential tradition in the philosophy of science has *not* adopted this kind of criterion as an answer to the *Abrezungsproblem*, the problem of delimitation. Instead, it has chosen to delimit science, not in terms of the type of *explanation* it tolerates, but in terms of its sources of *information*. It insists, in its most famous formulations, on the availability, in principle of in fact, of verification or of falsification. It leads one to look to the *data*—to whether data of a certain kind (such as would verify, or falsify, the explanatory theory) are, or could be available.

It was argued earlier that, in as far as the verificationist or falsificationist criteria actually succeed in defining any boundaries, in segregating the scientific sheep from the goats, they do it by covertly employing the kind of mechanistic criterion indicated above. (By as it were asking each concept to show its credentials, it forces them to be consistent, symmetrical, in their application. Explanatory models erected through such concepts have the same properties as 'mechanical' ones.) One important tradition in sociology sees the crucial feature of modernity as 'bureaucratisation'. The central idea in the notion of bureaucratic conduct is the orderly treatment of cases in accordance with fixed rules—the ethic of rules, as opposed to the ethic of loyalty. The mechanistic world-picture is, in this sense, simply the bureaucratisation of nature. This deep underlying affinity is of great importance. Kant's account of morality applies best to the ethics of cognition: *tolerate no exceptions*! For him, the essence of sin is the making of exceptions. Similarly, only symmetrical, 'universalisable' concepts, whose compartment does not vary from case to case or individual to individual, are to be allowed in a real science.

of cognitive rationality and ethical theories formulated in terms of 'universalisation'.

He fails, however, to comment on the connection between this kind of rationality, and his rationality no. 1, defined in terms of avoiding inconsistency, self-contradiction, or invalid inference. In as far as a society does tolerate unsymmetrical, context-bound concepts, it can, if it is concerned with saving face, always *appear* to satisfy rationality no. 1 (consistency), simply by means of hiding all inconsistency under irrationality no. 4. An inconsistency can be hidden by inventing an *ad hoc* term for the situation, as required. Inconsistency is then hidden: the concepts create a difference between two situations, which exempts us from treating them alike. Such asymmetry can easily be built into the local concepts and thus camouflaged. In brief, what really matters is the type of criterion a society applies to distinguish acceptable from unacceptable concepts. If concepts leading to asymmetry are condoned, the society has little to fear from any requirement of formal consistency. It can evade consistency whilst seeming to satisfy it. If on the other hand they are not condoned, formal consistency is already presupposed. This highlights the importance of philosophies whose effective social role is the censorship of concepts, and which impose orderly behaviour on them.

160

(2) *The division of labour.* Philosophers do not generally believe the division of labour to be their special concern. Yet the most characteristic form of modern philosophy—the form in which it also makes the greatest impact on the general public—is as a set of doctrines which in fact concern the intellectual or cognitive division of labour. Typically, it consists of a classification and characterisation of broad types of knowledge (or uses of language). These types are generally defined in terms of the criteria of validity employed within each of them. Thus, in one of the best known and simplest forms of this kind of theory, assertions are classified into four groups: those which stand and fall in virtue of factual checking, those which stand and fall in virtue of formal calculation, those which stand or fall in virtue of consonance with the speaker's feelings, and those which have no basis or anchorage at all.

What requires note is this: theories of this kind make a really powerful impact not so much through the specific detail of what they teach (i.e. through the manner in which they list and define their particular categories of knowledge or of discourse) as through the general point and approach which is shared by all of them, and which is largely taken for granted—namely, the assumption of *specificity of function.* By habituating people to the idea that there is indeed a single, simple criterion and function, governing the evaluation of any one given cognitive or verbal act, they profoundly modify their outlook. What these theories really inculcate is what sociologists are liable to call functional specificity. Of course, these thinkers do not deny that, in life as it is actually lived, or in language as it is actually spoken, various purposes or functions are very often conflated and confused. But this is dismissed as accident or shorthand, a compromise with the hurry and untidiness of daily life. The various functions are seen as 'really' distinct.

On this view, complexity and conflation are only there on the surface; underneath there is neat specificity. In fact, of course, this is a covert value-judgment of the utmost importance. What is presented as an analytic, neutral requirement or interpretation, in fact prejudges the question of the distinction, and the relative merits, of the savage and the scientific mind. It is of the essence of the savage mind, as it is of savage institutions, that there is little functional specificity. The tacit but persistent propaganda by modern philosophy, in quite a broad sense, on behalf of functional specificity (which however is introduced 'innocently', as a neutral analytic device), in fact insidiously favours the mechanistic, disenchanted vision of the world as against magical enchantment. The enchanted vision works through the systematic conflation of descriptive, evaluative, identificatory, status-conferring and other roles of language. A sense of the separability of the various functions, on the other hand, is the surest way to the disenchantment of the world.

At this point, the present argument is in complete harmony with Horton's. Horton puts the same point as follows:

One theory is judged better than another with explicit reference to its efficacy in explanation and prediction. And as these ends become more clearly defined, it gets increasingly evident that no other ends are compatible with them. People come to see that if ideas are to be used as efficient tools of explanation and prediction, they must not be allowed to be tools of anything else.[102]

All one needs to add here is that this consequence does not follow specifically and exclusively from the pursuit of the two special ends singled out by Horton (explanation and prediction): it follows from the clear specification of *any* isolable ends or criteria. The world is not so conveniently arranged that one can generally serve two or more at once. It is not only God and Mammon who cannot be served jointly. And philosophers are in error when they suppose that what matters most in their arguments is the particular way in which they define the various ends or criteria of types of knowledge or language. Those scholastic details are generally too abstruse to be remembered, or to have such real effect on habits of thought. The part of the lesson which *is* retained, and which some of the philosophers, quite mistakenly, suppose to be merely part of their preliminary scaffolding, is precisely the requirement that the various criteria be clearly distinguished and separated. (Descartes, unlike many contemporary philosophers, was not guilty of this misunderstanding. He very explicitly spelt out this very requirement.) And part of the reason why this lesson could be learnt so effectively and retained was of course its consonance with other aspects of modern life, which also display, in opposition to intimate traditional society, a tendency towards orderly division of labour and specificity of function. The fact that the doctrine was introduced as a neutral, innocuous, unprejudicial and apparently preliminary device, of course made it far more effective than if it were *argued*, and thereby admitted to be contentious.

This brings us to a further mistake of the philosophers and of empiricist philosophers in particular. Here, once again, the mistake arises from ignoring the social context of their own reasoning. Empiricists are generally concerned with drawing and stressing the distinction between what is empirically testable and what is not so testable. So far so good. They go on to presuppose a certain picture of the manner of co-existence of the empirical and of the transcendent, especially of the way two species are believed to cohabit in the minds of those who do not observe or respect their key distinction.

This tacitly presupposed picture of the empiricist philosophers might be called the accretion model, and it could be summed up as follows: there is an inner circle of the positively observable or the scientifically testable. This is shared ground, as it were, for the empiricist and the metaphysician. But the metaphysician sees not merely this charmed circle (the Island of Truth, as Kant called it in one of his more lyrical moments), but he also, impelled by a religious, aesthetic or other need, *adds* to it further and

[102] 'African Traditional Thought and Western Science', p. 164.

162

wider circles of transcendent, untestable Being. The empiricist then averts his gaze with embarrassment from such uncritical, cognitive self-indulgence and expansionism. He at any rate knows that these wider areas must either be ignored and eschewed altogether, or if, like other addicts, you find your will-power insufficient to impose such restraint, you must at least not take them seriously.

The trouble with this picture is its total lack of sociological realism. An individual or society which is *already* capable of distinguishing clearly between the inner circle of the testable, and the outer circle of transcendent accretion, is already much more than nine-tenths of the way towards the acceptance of the empiricist ideal. It is precisely in this way that the severely transcendentalist adherents of a pure and hidden God, scornful of divine conjuring tricks and of any day-to-day interference in the details of His creation, prepared the way for an orderly and secularised vision of the world, as Weber stressed. It is the segregation, and not so much the exclusion, of the transcendent that really matters. A society which is truly immersed in the transcendent does not see or recognise such orderly lines of demarcation. Quite the contrary.

In such a society, the really important feature of the behaviour of concepts is that they habitually and constantly dart across this boundary, and that the boundary itself is barely perceived. It would be idle in such a society to ask to have concepts separated into two camps—those which have an empirically operational role, and those whose reference is transcendent. There may be specimens of such pure types; but the interesting and characteristic examples are concepts which are, so to speak, semi-operational, which have both empirical and transcendent reference according to a locally recognised sliding scale, which is part of their very life and meaning, and the working of which dovetails neatly into the rest of local life and its ends.

The significant change achieved by three centuries or so of empiricist propaganda has not been the proscribing or the discouragement of the transcendent; it has been the systematic inculcation of a sensitivity to the existence of the boundary between that which is testable and that which is not. It matters little whether this boundary can always be traced convincingly on the tortuous ground of our actual conceptual and scientific world. (Often, it cannot.) It matters little whether or not that which is beyond the boundary is proscribed, or whether some items which seem to lie beyond it are tolerated because they prove that they are indispensable – emotionally, socially, or for the services they perform for concepts lying on the other side of the border. What does matter is that an increasingly touchy and insistent sensitivity to the existence of such a boundary discourages systematic conceptual boundary-hopping, or the habit of living astride this border; it becomes increasingly difficult for a notion to be empirical when successful, but something else when it is not; to have one status in the mouth of a priest and another in the mouth of a peasant, one significance on a weekday and another on sabbath day. Orderly and regular conduct is exacted from concepts, as it is from people. No unsymmetrical privileges, no sliding-scale status, are easily tolerated.

This (and not some restriction of our life to the Island of Truth) is the real and effective achievement of empiricist propaganda. This explains how, appearances notwithstanding, this propaganda really served the cause of the mechanistic, disenchanted, orderly vision of the world, and in practice converges with mechanistic 'materialism'. It did so by insisting on orderly, sober, consistent conduct on the part of concepts.

But what really matters here is that empiricist epistemology inculcated sensitivity to the division of labour applied to cognition, and the requirement of functional specificity encourages orderly behaviour on the part of concepts. This helps us understand the affinity between empiricism and the orderly, 'mechanical' ideal of explanation, and the profound, non-accidental reasons which make empiricism and materialism such faithful if occasionally uneasy companions.

(3) *The pervasiveness of entrenched clauses.* The stock of ideas or beliefs available to a given individual or society can be divided into the 'entrenched constitutional clauses' and the rest. The distinction is a crude and simple one, but important.

I can, roughly speaking, divide the stock of my ideas and convictions into those which can be denied or replaced without significantly disturbing my total picture and composure, and those which can only be budged at the cost of a widespread dislocation and disturbance. If for instance I discover, at the last moment, that the train which I have been counting on to reach home is no longer running, this is a considerable inconvenience— but, without claiming any remarkable imperturbability, I can say that my general composure remains unaffected. If, on the other hand, a man is convinced one day that the identity of his parents is other than he had been brought up to believe; or that the political movement he had supported all his life is in fact criminal and immoral; or that the interpretation of recent history officially put forward by his nation is fraudulent— discoveries or conversions of this kind cannot leave him unmoved. So much else is implicated in these crucial, favoured, and entrenched convictions that if they go, much else also topples.

It is an interesting and important sociological truth that there is *no a priori* way of delimiting the area in which these crucial, entrenched convictions are to be found. Of course, one can do it by means of a camouflaged tautology, which boils down to the assertion that what is important for a society is what is important for it. But there is no non-question-begging way of doing so from the outside. In other words, there is no special, privileged type of basket into which all societies place their most valuable eggs. You cannot say, for instance, that in any society the world-foundation story, or the rule of selecting political leaders, or theology, or the rules governing sexual behaviour, will be singled out for special reverence and so cross-tied to all other institutions that they cannot be shaken without everything being shaken. Some areas are, indeed, more plausible candidates for the location of the sacred than others; but no area is necessarily predetermined for it, and no area is excluded from it. The sacred may lurk in most unexpected quarters. Sometimes, indeed, part of its impact hinges on the shock produced by its location.

But there is a systematic difference in the distribution of the entrenched clauses, of the sacred, in this sense, as between savage and modern thought-systems. In a traditional thought-system, the sacred or the crucial is more extensive, more untidily dispersed, and much more pervasive. In a modern thought-system, it is tidier, narrower, as it were economical, based on some intelligible principle, and tends not to be quite so diffused among all the minor aspects of life. Fewer hostages are given to fortune; or, looking at it from the other end, much less of the fabric of life and society benefits from reinforcement from the sacred and entrenched convictions.

This important trait of traditional belief systems is, of course, a kind of obverse of a trait stressed earlier—the tendency to rely on a socially idiosyncratic notion of the normal, which determines what does and what does not require explanation. The diffusion of the entrenched is also the delineation of 'normality'.

Here, once again, we can observe the marked distance between the latent and the manifest meaning of much modern philosophy. Modern philosophy writes about knowledge in what purports to be the indicative mood: knowledge really 'is' this, that or the other. But the picture of knowledge which it offers is in fact an idealised and simplified model of a belief system, in which the entrenched clauses have been reduced to a kind of formal minimum. In reality, this is a commentary on an *emerging* cognitive order, and its endorsement. Consider, for instance, the empiricist theory: it describes our view of the world as a kind of mosaic, in which all individual pieces are quite independent of each other and can be replaced without disturbing any of the rest. The only thing which is entrenched, which could really shake the composure of the theorist were it undermined, is the 'formal' fact of the existence and nature of the mosaic's framework itself. This vision is shared by classical empiricism and by skeletalist doctrines such as 'logical atomism'.

Once again, if we approach this with a modicum of sociological realism, we see that this picture is not at all a generally usable account of how belief-systems or visions of the world actually work, (or, indeed, of how any of them could possibly work), but a simplified, overdrawn, stylised account of *a* feature of certain (i.e. 'modern') belief-systems. But the sustained propaganda for this feature, presented as a neutral, universal characterisation articulated in the indicative mood, in fact greatly helped to legitimate that particular kind of world-picture—the kind which reduces and minimises the extent of its own entrenched clauses, which

165

discourages their proliferation and dispersal.

Perhaps I should say that I do not object either to this propaganda or its success, though I do try and understand its significance. But it is useful to understand what has really been happening, rather than to be deceived by the manner in which it has been presented.

(4) *The extra-territoriality of knowledge.* In a sense, this trait is the obverse of the preceding one. The important achievement of empiricist propaganda is the establishment of the autonomy of fact. The 'mosaic' model, however inaccurate an account of how knowledge really functions, conveys above all the idea that the individual stones on the mosaic are independent of each other, and indeed of anything else. This means that they or their displacement cannot endanger whatever entrenched clauses may exist, covertly or openly. The important converse of this is that they in turn are neither required nor excluded by any entrenched clauses. Greater and greater expanses of truth acquire an autonomy from the social, moral, political obligations and decencies of the society. This autonomy of truth is even more important than the philosophically much better advertised autonomy of value—though the two are of course, linked, and are jointly corollaries of the cognitive division of labour, discussed above.

In a traditional belief-system, cognition, the discovery or the endorsement of beliefs, is an event in the world, and this means the social and moral world. Hence they are subject to the same kinds of obligations and sanctions as are other kinds of conduct. Indeed when these ideas touch the entrenched clauses they are quite particularly subject to them. Man the knower is not alienated from the citizen and the moral being. At this point, it is in one sense hard not to suppose that in one sense the traditional outlooks are correct: we do not believe that our cognitive activities are *really* extra-territorial, are qualitatively distinct from the rest of our lives. Nevertheless, as Kant pointed out, we assume (contrary to all consistency) that such extra-territoriality does in fact obtain, and our attribution of 'objective validity' to our own thinking hinges on this odd assumption.

The social implications of the assumption are of course of the utmost importance. Here there is an interesting difference between Western liberal societies, where the officially endorsed entrenched clauses of the belief-system have an eroded status and importance (comparable roughly to the heraldic devices inherited from the Middle Ages), and thus facilitate the assumption of autonomy of fact, and those societies which possess entrenched clauses that are still on occasion taken with some degree of seriousness, such as Marxism. The consequence of this is of course that in such societies the autonomy of fact is only partial, and in as far as it exists —as, inevitably, it does—it generates painful strain.

Some traditions of thought in modern philosophy (in very broad sense) had supposed that certain substantive pieces of science were destined to acquire an 'entrenched clause' status comparable to the key religious dogmas of the past. Newtonian physics, for instance, was revered by many thinkers as the very paradigm of well-established, permanent truth. It is interesting to note when Newtonian physics was tumbled from this pedestal, virtually no tremors were noticed in the rest of the social fabric. Little or no entrenchment had in fact taken place, contrary to what philosophers had supposed.

Other modern philosophers have noticed this relatively limited capacity of the *content* of modern science to achieve such status, and have quite mistakenly inferred from this that science of its content are philosophically neutral. This in no way follows. At the very least, the content of science cannot be neutral, precisely because it is so frequently in conflict with the messy, over-exposed entrenched clauses of the *older* traditional belief-systems. There is of course a major contemporary intellectual industry which specialises in pruning, restating those older belief systems in a way such as to minimise this exposure to conflict. This is the negative or face-lift aspect of the Meaning Industry, to be discussed. Every traditional faith nowadays has a kind of modernist shadow, a pruned replica which repeats the past version in a way which cuts out or restates all parts which could conflict with science. These are given a double identity, presented according to a sliding scale, operated according to the response and the type of audience. This might be called differential or sliding-scale sophistication.

To sum up: the present chapter considered the big divide between styles of thought, and indeed in some measure attempts to defend the viewpoint that there *is* one big divide, that this is the correct way of looking at things. This is not to deny that there are also many and profound differences within each of the two great categories; it is to assert that the big ditch is qualitatively different from the other ones, and gives rise to quite different issues. The problem of 'overcoming relativism' calls for quite different considerations, according to whether we are dealing with the great divide between rationality and (for lack of a better word) tradition, or whether we are dealing with differences within each of the two camps.

The aim was to set up a rough sociologically realistic characterisation of this big divide. This in a way complements the argument of the rest of the book, which attempts to describe the nature and operation of the principles which led to or expressed the great transformation. Very roughly, the present chapter attempted to sketch the outcome, whilst the rest of the argument was concerned with the way it was reached.

9 Identity regained

Power, wealth and knowledge—each of these has grown immeasurably in the modern world, to an extent which makes each of them quite incommensurate with their previous historic forms. Each of them is both coveted and also, on occasion, repudiated as the root of all evil, and each has passed through periods of precariousness, when men were close to despairing of their accessibility. Effective government, economic prosperity, and the advancement of learning—these are three central preoccupations of Western thought.

The three are of course interrelated, though generally it is one only which becomes the central object of concern. Their logic is not entirely parallel. Only wealth and knowledge look as if, even in principle, they could grow indefinitely—though one may doubt whether beyond a certain point further increments could be of value. Political stability, on the other hand, cannot be measured along one indefinite continuum.

From one viewpoint, however, the problem of power is the paradigm for all three. Political thought vacillates between the preoccupation with anarchy, and the fear of despotism. Likewise, theories of economic advancement are notoriously strung out along a spectrum stretching from *laissez-faire*—inspired by a fear of interference—to doctrines of central or collective control, inspired by the fear of economic anarchy. (The concept of the right wing in politics, as it actually crystallised, is an amalgam of social and political authoritarianism with economic liberalism.) Likewise, theories of the advancement of learning stretch from a stress on free inquiry and the importance of competition and the natural selection of ideas, to the contrary stress on the need for the attainment of shared norms and procedures by the scientific community, as a precondition of genuine science. In brief, science, like the economy, has its own political philosophy.

But there are conspicuous analogies in the theories available in the fields of knowledge, wealth and power. Theories can consist of recipes, or of descriptions of perpetual growth. Evolutionary theories are descriptions of an ever-continuous progression, presenting stories of the growth of wealth, of liberty, of diversification or of knowledge. Instead of tracing the pattern, the theory can specify the mechanism, such as natural selection, or inner conflict and its resolution, or perpetual accumulation. It can of course do both things, specifying pattern and indicating its underlying driving force.

Theories of the great transition, of the crucial hump, stand contrasted to the continuity stories. Hump theories are in some ways the most characteristic ones of our age, and the identification and diagnosis of *the* hump tell us much about the preoccupation of a thinker or his age. Modern political thought began with a preoccupation with the hump of order, the establishment of effective and legitimate government, and the overcoming of anarchy, whether this arose from feudal indiscipline or from religious dissension or both. It shifted to a preoccupation with the hump of the establishment of liberty, constitutionalism or democracy. Mid-twentieth century social theory has tended to re-enact the preoccupation, but in terms of the hump of wealth, of 'industrialisation'. Though by no means indifferent to effective and legitimate government, it tends to see it partly as the fruit of successful industrialisation, and partly as its instrumental precondition – rather than seeing it as a thing in itself, against an assumed and static economic background, which was the way in which classical political theory tended to see it. This particular recent preoccupation is a consequence of the realisation that the 'continuity' theories of economic growth, associated with classical economics, are irrelevant in as far as they presuppose a certain institutional framework, which is *precisely* what is generally lacking in underdeveloped societies. Hence the once-and-for-all establishment of that very framework, which constitutes the current version of the hump, then becomes crucial, and the mechanisms of perpetual progress, which might perhaps be expected to take over thereafter, become secondary. It is the hump that matters.

The present book is of course concerned with the hump of cognition, the sources, nature and authority of *the* transition to effective knowledge. Like political philosophy proper, the political theory of science is liable to veer between the poles of liberalism, intended to protect us from the arbitrariness, stagnation and the enforced errors of authority, and authoritarianism, meant to protect us from the chaos, violence and—likewise—the arbitrariness and stagnation of anarchy. It also has its crises of legitimacy. Legitimation in the field of cognition faces dilemmas similar to those which validation faces in all other fields.

It can either appeal to something outside, larger than us, 'objective', which if indeed it exists and is revealed unto us would solve our problem by identifying and guaranteeing our norms and procedures—but it then faces the difficulty of justifying the belief in the existence and accessibility of this great norm-endorsing Other, and of silencing the suspicion that this great Other is only invented in order to buttress the authority and privileges of its self-appointed spokesmen in the here and now, and of their preferred options. Alternatively, validation can be anthropocentric, and appeal only to premises internal to man and his world, eschewing the Other, and seek the justification of our activities in ourselves and in what is visibly accessible. It then no longer faces the problem of invoking premises which claim too much and are liable to provoke excessive

169

scepticism. On the contrary, the premisses are homely, and refer to entities whose existence is not in doubt, such as our own sensations, customs or desires. But it then faces quite another problem—that of building on quicksands. Using *our* custom or *our* desires as the basis of legitimacy may be perfectly in order when everything is stable and not seriously contested—but under such circumstances we have no great need of legitimation in the first place. When, on the contrary, all is in flux, when we have doubts about our very identity, then our own aims and customs are precisely what is most *sub judice* and requires to be chosen, selected from amongst alternatives, and validated; and then of course the 'internal' style of legitimation fails us.

In recent decades at least two outstanding political philosophies of science have been promulgated and have rightly been much acclaimed and discussed. One is Sir Karl Popper's, the other Professor Thomas Kuhn's. They have often been juxtaposed and contrasted, as interesting rivals. But in fact, in as far as these two brilliant formulations contain a partial error, it is in essence the *same* error. The interesting mistake is one they share, and not something which separates them.

The shared error lies in the underrating of the specificity of the great divide, or in the misinterpretation of it. Popper underrates it, Kuhn misinterprets it. Popper, especially in his later work, assimilates scientific method to *any* trial-and-error procedure so much that revolutionary advances in science are somehow lumped together, in the end, with any adaptive solution of any problem by any organism. There is no room within such a scheme for a *specific* diagnosis of one particular revolution, namely the birth of science or rationality at all, the adoption of the kinds of principles of thought which generate an orderly world within which alone falsification really is effective and really does eliminate failed efforts. Indeed it is not clear whether, on Popper's later views, any such event ever could have occurred. If science is trial-and-error, and trial-and-error was always with us, science or rationality has no inception.

Kuhn, on the other hand, is interested in those qualitative leaps between incommensurate 'paradigms' which on this view make up scientific revolutions. But these leaps within science are not at all the same thing as *the* leap *to* science. Kuhn is more aware than Popper seems to be of the extra-scientific world but, possibly because his image of the non-scientific is based too much on the comportment of contemporary social scientists, he sees it as *lacking* paradigms, rather than as having a profoundly *different kind* of paradigm. Thus, for different reasons, we can look to these two thinkers more for (rival) accounts of revolutions within science, than for an account of what distinguishes science as such. (Positivism, which is repudiated by both of them, had the merit of having a very strong sense of this one big divide, even if it gave an incorrect diagnosis of it.)

It might be best first of all to sketch their positions. Popper's philosophy of science is in effect an ethic of falsification; it is the transposition into

170

the cognitive sphere of one of those extreme warrior codes which forbid their devotees to take cover, to use shelter, camouflage or cunning, in effect to do anything other than expose their body to maximum risk. The advancement of knowledge is attained, on this view, by seeking formulations which offer the enemy, namely nature, the most exposed and extended surface. Glory cannot lie in victory, which is a mere matter of luck and can in any case never be long-lived; glory lies only in the fearless exposure to danger.

Popper is of course fully aware that man is, cognitively speaking, addicted to cowardice. Men and societies do put forward theories about the world, but they generally fortify and insure them for all they are worth, and indeed often take great pride in the extent and elaboration of these fortifications. *Eine feste Burg ist mein Gott.* Quite so. Hence Popper's theory is not a descriptive account of humanity's actual cognitive practice, but rather a prescription, an ethic, which at the same time also singles out *science* from the the rest of putative cognition *and* explains the secret of its success. Its success is due not to the fact that it is more certain, as many had mistakenly supposed, but on the contrary that it is *less* certain, that it accepts and rejoices in uncertainty, seeks it out, and possesses devices, such as accurate and unambiguous formulation, which increase the exposure to risk. On one occasion when the Kabyles fought the French, it is said that they chained themselves to each other, so that none should run away. Clear and public formulation of hypotheses in accordance with the custom and conventions of science has the same role and effect as such chains—it makes evasion so much harder when danger strikes.

Thus the ethic of science, like so many others, promises a reward and attributes a status. Those who satisfy the ethic will be deemed *scientists*, and those who do not, perpetuate a moral fraud when they claim this title of nobility. The genuinely noble community will attain cognitive glory, though at the cost of individual sacrifice; other communities will stagnate in safety.

Like other ethics it is ramified, it possesses a stratified system of laxer and more severe requirements: minimal ones which are adequate for escaping outright damnation, and stronger and extreme ones for the cognitive *tigers,* for the élite, the virtuosi. The minimal requirement is falsifiability, the exposure to some risk at least, the price of minimal initiation and membership. But Popper knows that even amongst true scientists, i.e. those who in their professional work satisfy this minimal criterion, there is much weakness—conservatism, lack of enterprise, routine. He recognises this as a *de facto* truth about science, but spurns it *de jure.* The ultimate elite goes far beyond the minimal requirements. Its courage, enterprise and restlessness are such that it never relaxes into a complacent stable state. Instead it comes close to living in a state of permanent revolution. Thus there is an implicit ethic within the ethic, a recommendation within the recommendation.

There is thus both an unity and parallelism, and also an asymmetry and strain between Popper's philosophy of science and his social theory. His social ethic consists essentially of the commendation of the virtue of *openness*, which is the social equivalent of *falsifiability*—the holding of social principles without rigidity, in a spirit which is willing to learn, innovate, experiment and change. Social and cognitive health are analogous, and the wider society is but the scientific community writ large. Thus far the parallelism holds. The Popperian ideal of the *Open Society* is visibly inspired by his account of the scientific community. He endeavours to extend to society the specific merit of science.

But a conspicuous asymmetry also appears. In science, openness implies the taking of maximum risks. In social affairs, the contrary is commended. Rigidity and self-maintenance are indeed excluded, but change, which in itself is praised, is to be piecemeal, and hence inevitably less than fundamental or far-reaching. There is an attempt to deduce this recommendation from the requirement of falsifiability, on the questionable grounds that small changes can be assessed, whereas large-scale ones cannot. (The contrary can easily be maintained. The effects of small-scale changes are, in any society, swamped by the pervasive effects of the unchanged remainder of the social framework, and hence can neither be evaluated, nor be effective. This indeed is the principal argument of the *radical* revolutionary when he attacks the cautious reformer.)

Nevertheless, the Popperian commendation of piecemeal social change can be accepted *in a limited context*—that of liberal societies which do not habitually sabotage reform, which tolerate radical questioning, and do not simply use the cult of piecemeal change as a camouflaged technique for inhibiting fundamental criticisms. In other kinds of societies— tyrannies and totalitarianism of all kinds—which do not tolerate or systematically circumvent peaceful change and persuasion, there often is no alternative, alas, to violent and fundamental disruption of the system of order and authority. Some revolutions, at least, are the least of possible evils, though evils they are. Some revolutions are inescapable. (There are two unutterably foolish contemporary doctrines—one to the effect that revolutions are *never* desirable, the other, that they are 'the festival of the oppressed'. They are never anyone's festival, though they are sometimes, indeed, necessary and desirable.)

There is nothing, unfortunately, within Popper's system of thought which would enable one to draw a line between the two sets of conditions. On the contrary, the line remains conspicuously *un*-drawn, and the praise of piecemeal procedures is in practice uncircumscribed.

This is a very fundamental weakness in his social thought, and it has often been noted before. What has been noted less often is the corresponding weakness in Popper's philosophy of science. The flaw in social theory springs from a failure to distinguish between two quite distinct sets of social circumstances, and the attitudes to change which

172

they call for. There is a similar fundamental distinction to be drawn in the sphere of cognition, between innovation within a viable scientific tradition, and the innovation *which brings a scientific tradition into being in the first place*. Within a scientific community, recognising something like the principles specified above, Popper's diagnosis and ethic can perhaps, especially in a moderate form, and possibly with some qualifications, be allowed to stand. *Dare* and *criticise* is perhaps an adequate ethic, especially if like most ethics it is not honoured too much, but honoured on occasion only. As the recipe for the initial *establishment* of a rational style of thought and inquiry it is inadequate.

Within a rational world—that is to say, a world within which it is clearly understood that explanations apply symmetrically, for the goose as for the gander; within which it is understood that the data which decide the fate of a theory must not also be under its control, subject to interpretation in the light of its dictates—in *such* a world, it may perhaps be sufficient to say that all that is required for the growth of knowledge is that theories be hotly and actively 'criticised'. Such a world, by insisting that acceptable explanations, and the concepts they employ, should observe a certain standard of impartiality (the mechanistic principle, in effect), and by insisting on extraneous, independent checking (the empiricist principle), already ensures fair play.

But most total outlooks by-pass precisely these principles. The outlook, the ideology, permeates, saturates the world within which 'testing' or 'criticism' (if any) take place. And once this is allowed an outlook has little to fear from 'criticism'. It is true that such outlooks are generally rigid and actually proscribe sinful, heretical questioning. But logically they do not really need to do so, and some modernist ones in fact are 'open'.

The great transition between the old, as it were non-epistemic worlds, in which the principles of cognition are subject to the pervasive constitutive principles of a given vision, and thus have little to fear, and a world in which this is no longer possible, is a fundamental transition indeed.

It is far more profound than the jumps between one scientific vision and another, when each takes place within such a rational world. In as far as Popper's later formulations of his philosophy of science tend to play down both empiricism and mechanism, and base the growth of knowledge almost exclusively on 'criticism', he seems to me to be in error. Unless the judges, the canons of criticism, are obliged to act roughly in the way in which 'mechanism' (in the sense indicated) and empiricism require, the criticisms can easily be bypassed.[103]

[103] The spirit of Popper's later formulations is conveyed by the following remark: 'The significance of observation and experiments depends *entirely* upon ... whether they are used to *criticise theories*'. [Emphasis in the original.] The truth seems to me the other way round: criticisms are only effective and contribute to cognitive growth, in a certain kind of world, which by making observations sovereign, makes it possible for them to be used in the spirit of effective criticism.

The associated error is the excessive assimilation of this one great and overwhelming transition—from an unsymmetrical to a symmetrical world, from a world in which cognition is not sovereign to one in which is —to the other fundamental scientific transformations *within* a rational world.

To put this in another way: Popper takes as his very model of cognitive advance, those scientific 'revolutions', allegedly fundamental and radical innovations, which were exemplified by the work of a Newton or an Einstein. But he fails to distinguish between fundamental-fundamental innovation, and the merely relatively-fundamental. Einstein falls into the second class, and so does Newton, (unless one treats him as equivalent to the whole establishment of mechanistic science). And quite different principles apply to the two kinds of 'fundamental' innovation. A very great deal hinges on this distinction.

There is a certain interesting shift in stress in the development of Popper's philosophy, which is relevant to the present argument. His early thought is centred on the idea of falsification, but it also contains a pretty clear indication and delimitation of what *kinds* of falsification are available. (Roughly—conflict with hard fact, and logical contradiction.) It is this identification of the types of available falsification which brings Popper close to the positivist position, though of late he has been very eager to deny and trivialise this affinity.[104] What concerns us particularly in his later position, which stresses the 'critical spirit'—willingness to criticise and falsify—at the expense of any circumscription or definition of what is to count as falsification.

In a scientific community in which this is indeed taken for granted, in which everyone knows the type of evidence that can be allowed to count as a falsification, it is perhaps possible in practice to reduce the maxims of intellectual life and cognitive growth to the simple injunctions—innovate, criticise, treat nothing as exempt from criticism.

But even if adequate, such injunctions are elliptical. They tacitly

[104] 'The fact is that throughout my life I have combated the positivist epistemology under the name "positivism" '. K. R. Popper, 'Reason or Revolution', *European Journal of Sociology* (1970), no. 2, p. 261. Of course there are important differences between Popper's position and positivism, but this kind of exaggerated dissociation obscures the truth that unless a cult is made of 'fact' (=positivism), 'criticism' is powerless.

This article also contains the interesting and relevant self-characterisation by Popper (p. 255): 'And it is a fact that my own social theory, which favours gradual and piecemeal reform, strongly contrasts with my theory of method, which happens to be a theory of scientific and intellectual revolution.' The present criticism is that he does not distinguish sharply enough revolutions within science from the revolution which makes science possible at all. The contempt for 'positivism' hinges on this.

For the development of Popper's thought, see: Bryan Magee, *Popper* (London, 1973); J. W. N. Watkins, 'The Unity of Popper's Thought', in *The Philosophy of Karl R. Popper*, ed. P. A. Schilpp and W. W. Bartley III, 'Theories of Demarcation and the History of Philosophy of Science', in *Problems in the History of Science*, eds. I. Lakatos and A. E. Musgrave, (Dordrecht, 1968).

presuppose, incapsulate, an assumption concerning the court of appeal which is to decide whether a theory has or has not withstood criticism, whether the innovation was a good one. And the best available method for conveying the nature of that court of appeal is still the empiricist metaphysic, the picture of the world as constructed from sensory data. The reason why this picture is so good is not because the world is indeed so constructed, or because there are any such 'pure' data; it is because this picture conveys so well the crucial requirement—that of isolable data *which are independent of the theory that is being judged.* If on the other hand there is no such tacit assumption about the kind of evidence that will be allowed at the court of appeal—if for instance that court were allowed in the end to judge in conformity with some religious, substantive vision of the world, elevated above any principles of the cognitive ethic—then openness fails to be real, however daring, inventive, or intellectually litigous the members of this particular community happen to be.

All this indicates a number of things. Popper is wrong in repudiating or dissociating himself from the empiricist metaphysic and from positivism, for his vision presupposes that picture, or something very much like it. He is mistaken in supposing that the 'critical attitude' can be self-sufficient, and formulated without presupposing something like those rejected elements. The rejection of 'induction' is also misguided. What mattered most in the inductive picture was not so much the specification of an alleged and perhaps mythical inductive process, but the atomistic-empiricist metaphysic in terms of which it was articulated. For this alone, with its effective stress on isolated facts, independent of each other and above all of any pervasive theory, could destroy the self-maintaining, circular, self-validating world which had preceded it. What is crucial is the contrast between a world in which unwanted falsification (hurtful to the pervasive and entrenched myth) can hardly occur, and a rational or scientific one in which it can. The idea of criticism, without the empiricist metaphysic, cannot really characterise or define this difference. A closed world can allow 'criticism' yet be adequately endowed with devices for ensuring that criticism will be silenced, that falsification will be evaded, in its own internal courts of appeal.

It is relevant at this point also to comment on the status of Popper's idea of *falsifiability.* This of course is one of the points at which he distinguishes himself from 'positivists', with their stress on 'verifiability'. But one is liable to miss the real significance of falsifiability if one looks at the differences between it and verification purely from a formal, logical viewpoint, as is often done.

From that viewpoint, the demerit of verification is that it is endless, whereas falsification is final. A positive instance does not establish a theory: the theory may fail tomorrow. But a conclusive negative instance, a well-established counter-example, eliminates a theory once and for all— or so the story runs. In formal logic, in which the conventions of the subject make us a present of clear-cut cases, it is certainly so: the generalisation that 'All *A*s are *B*s' is conclusively and finally shown to be false by one *A* that is not also a *B*. So, if science works by such elimination, this enables Popper to dispense with the dubious process of 'induction', for the elimination of the above-cited generalisation by a counter-example falls well within the rules of ordinary, relatively unproblematical 'deductive' logic. This was indeed part of what he claimed as his achievement.

But, as many have pointed out, the matter is not so simple.[105] The trouble is that, outside the conventions of formal logic, it is not so easy to get hold of a really unambiguous, final and definitive counter-example for a generalisation. This hinges on the much-invoked truth that 'facts' are theory-saturated, and that the theories presupposed by any given single fact can be brought into the open and challenged. Hence refutations-by-counter-example are final only as long as the theoretic assumptions of the example used are not themselves challenged.

But the real importance of falsifiability—and its superiority over verifiability—does not hinge on this formal logical consideration, and does not fall with its weakness. What really makes the criterion of falsifiability so powerful is this: if you insist that a believer specifies the conditions in which his faith would cease to be true, you implicitly force him to conceive a world in which his faith is *sub judice,* at the mercy of some 'fact' or other. But this is precisely what faiths, total outlooks, systematically avoid and evade. They *fill out* the world of their adherents, the world they in a way create, and they interpret the processes of cognition in such a way that all verdicts must, in the end, be returned in their favour. Note that they have little to fear from a requirement that they be 'verifiable': generally speaking, they pervade the world they create so completely that verifications abound—here a verification, there a verification, everywhere a verification. Ironically (but this is not uncommon in law) the verification principle penalises only the *honest* faith, which segregates and candidly admits the 'transcendent', unverifiable elements within it, like the honest traveller who admits to all his purchases that are liable to customs duty. Those who systematically mix up the transcendent with their other luggage have little to fear from a customs examination by the principle of verification.

But our main point here is that Popper's entirely admirable stress on falsifiability, which really works by forcing the believer to shift from his faith-pervaded world into another one, only works if that other world meets the empiricist-mechanistic requirements; and the difference between a world which meets them and one which does not, perhaps the most important distinction which we make in our intellectual lives, cannot

[105] See, for instance, the repudiation of 'naive falsificationism' in I. Lakatos, 'Criticism and the Methodology of Scientific Research Programmes', *Aristotelian Society Proceedings* (1968/9).

be assimilated, as Popper seems to be inclined to do in his later views, to the transformations, however great, which take place *within* the rational world. This rational or orderly world, in which alone falsification or criticism works, only emerges at some point (which can of course be historically a very diffuse 'point'): it is not something inherent in any and all worlds! We had to acquire such a world, to achieve the kind of thought which 'makes' such a world. It was not our birthright, it was not given us on a plate.

This rational world emerged thanks to the great Selectors. Its emergence, its precariousness, is underrated or perhaps even ignored, especially in Popper's later work. Hence his willingness to dispense with 'positivism', and his willingness to suppose there is a kind of continuity of trial-and-error method from the amoeba to Einstein. The difference is more important than the continuity, if continuity there be.

Kuhn's philosophy of science is in various important ways different from and opposed to Popper's. The most crucial point at which this opposition arises concerns the ethic of science. Kuhn, with emphasis, refuses to accept the extreme version of the Popperian injunction, the requirement to aim at continuous and near-total revolution. His opponents are somewhat outraged by this—is he, then, commending ossification and dogmatism? Not quite. In his case as in Popper's the injunction is tied to a delimitation, diagnosis of science, and derives its authority from this fact. When obeying the injunction, you are thereby emulating and joining the elite of science. The prescription claims also to be the description of the best *actual* practice.

But the injunction and the delimitation of science is not the same as the one we find in Popper. Kuhn does not locate the defining essence of science in free, unbounded criticism, which may include or even concentrate on fundamentals. He does not consider the pre-Socratic Greek philosopher to exemplify *science*. On the contrary, their ding-dong controversies concerning the nature of things, free, critical and untrammelled, seems to him the very model of a pre-scientific stage, so characteristic of philosophy, and in our time also so plentifully and richly exemplified by the social sciences. This is the early stage in the life of a subject when it lacks a shared 'paradigm', to use the term which has, in this sense, acquired a wide currency through Kuhn's work.

In this early stage, fundamentals are constantly and freely discussed. And indeed, in science as in ethics, fundamentals are never really secure. They are ever open to challenge, their foundations are never beyond question. Scientific progress occurs, on the contrary, when some paradigm is widely accepted, when a scientific community adopts it as its reasonably firm norm, and works *within* it. This produces 'normal science', an activity in which the individual 'normal' scientist does not challenge the paradigm, but is required to display ingenuity by squaring his problem and his findings with the paradigm. It is he, not the paradigm, who is on trial . . .

There is of course also 'abnormal' science, those traumatic revolutions which take place when one paradigm replaces another. The problem facing Kuhn's philosophy are well known: given that, as he stresses, rival paradigms are mutually incommensurate, it is difficult either to evaluate or to explain these fundamental shifts of vision. To do so we should need to have as our vantage point some third, neutral, absolute world—and this is precisely what, on his assumption, we cannot have. Given that we can apparently know nature only with the aid of *some* paradigm, it would seem impossible for us to attain that paradigm-free awareness of some facts, which alone would enable us to judge whether a paradigm is or is not acceptable. In other words, Kuhn's philosophy would seem inevitably to lead to a relativism and a repudiation of empiricism. His own emphatic rejection of these inescapable implications of his views would seem to be a sincere enough expression of his personal temperament and position, but to lack much logical relationship and coherence with his central argument, though this is something of which he is not fully aware. A most remarkable footnote in his 'Reflections on my Critics',[106] clearly conveys his failure to appreciate the difficulty of combining his position with empiricism. He describes how a friendly colleague observed to him, after the appearance of his book: ' . . . it seems to me that your biggest problem now is showing in what sense science can be empirical'. Kuhn comments, trying to convey despair at being so grotesquely misunderstood: 'My jaw dropped and still sags slightly.' In fact, it is the colleague rather than Kuhn who could claim permanent astonishment at such incomprehension: if, as Kuhn teaches, we can *only* apprehend reality thanks to the mediation of some 'paradigm' or other, it is not clear in what sense any paradigm could be closer to reality than any other. In order to pass such a judgment we should first of all need to be able to see reality as it is on its own, without *any* paradigm—a possibility which, of course, dramatically contradicts Kuhn's central doctrine. This central problem is never adequately faced by Kuhn.

The arguments which can be invoked in support of a Kuhnian code of cognitive conduct are obvious and powerful. A scientific discipline in a state of permanent and universal revolution, in which everyone was imbued by a thoroughly 'critical' spirit, and which everyone refrained from internalising any paradigm, and preferred instead to behave in accordance with the extreme, heroic, elitist version of Popper's ethic, would be in a state of utter chaos. No genuine testing or cumulativeness would be possible then. Kuhn would seem to be right, both descriptively and normatively, in his insistence on the need for 'normal science'. But our task here is not to pass judgment on the issue which separates Kuhn and Popper, but to highlight an error which they *share*.

The relevant question to ask in the case of Kuhn is—just what is it that

[106] In *Criticism and the Growth of Knowledge*, ed. Lakatos and Musgrave, p. 264.

178

stands contrasted to the possession of a 'paradigm'? Just what is it like to be in a pre-paradigmatic or a non-paradigmatic stage in the life of a given discipline?

On internal evidence, it seems reasonable to conclude that Kuhn's experience of social scientists was most important in helping to crystallise his views:

Even more important, spending a year (1958/9) in a community composed predominantly of social scientists confronted me with unanticipated problems about the differences between such communities and those of natural scientists among whom I had been trained. Particularly, I was struck by the number and extent of the overt disagreements between social scientists about the nature of legitimate scientific problems and methods. Both history and acquaintance made me doubt that practitioners of the natural sciences possess firmer or more permanent answers ... Yet, somehow, the practice of astronomy, physics, chemistry and biology normally fails to evoke the controversy over fundamentals that today often seems endemic among, say, psychologists or sociologists. Attempting to discover the source of that difference led me to ... 'paradigms'.[107]

Kuhn's account of the state of play in most of the social or human sciences is perceptive and accurate. Their failure to achieve really convincing and cumulative progress is not due, clearly, to stupidity, lethargy or dogmatism. These qualities may not be wholly absent, but equally one can find intelligence, inventiveness, brilliance, enthusiasm and determination, and free, untrammelled inquiry. What is true of the pre-Socratics is also true of contemporary social scientists: they do argue about fundamentals freely and even rationally.

Kuhn's conclusion is well known. It is consensus, and not freedom, which distinguishes science. Thomas Kuhn is the Thomas Hobbes of the philosophy of science. The fear which the English civil war engendered in Hobbes' breast was awakened in Kuhn's by his experience of social scientists, with their dreadful freedom and near-total anarchy. In the social sciences, the lives of ideas and of procedures are solitary, poor, nasty, brutish and short. And they die to no avail. Their martyrdom serves no cause. They are selected for it at random, and not by some wise natural (or, for that matter, planned) selection, which would systematically guide the surviving population in some desirable or desired direction.

Well, so it is. Or at any rate, this sombre picture is not sufficiently removed from the truth to make it worth while criticising Kuhn on this score. His error lies elsewhere.

It lies in the assumption that social scientists of the twentieth century (or, for that matter, Greek pre-Socratic philosophers, especially as interpreted by Popper in his own image) provide the general model for the cognitive condition of mankind in the pre-scientific or pre-paradigmatic stage. In fact these social scientists, with their anarchic freedom and their habit of ever challenging each other's fundamentals, are highly untypical.

---

[107] Kuhn, *The Structure of Scientific Revolutions*, Preface, p. x.

179

It is wrong to infer from their condition, as Kuhn tacitly seems to do (for he does not explicitly formulate a general sociology of pre-scientific cognitive life), that what is typical of the age prior to scientific consensus and order, is a general free-for-all. Here, once again, he resembles Hobbes.

Social anthropology has shown, conclusively, that in the political sphere a Hobbesian state of nature does not generally obtain (though the contrary myth, that of primitive man totally enslaved to social norms, a retrojected *Brave New World,* is not valid either). Similarly, there is no reason whatever to suppose that anarchy obtained in the intellectual, cognitive sphere. In fact, this view need only be made explicit to be seen to be highly implausible. *Intellectual* anarchy presupposes social conditions which are seldom present—conditions favouring the free articulation, elaboration and criticism of theories.

The view that a kind of intellectual *laissez faire* is the main and most important contrast to the existence of scientific paradigms, can only be held if it is not properly examined. It survives in a semi-tacit form, mainly because the central concern of Kuhn and his critics is with science, rather than with its absence or its contrary.[108] The intellectual life of non-scientific cultures is not his official business.

But the significant contrast to science is not a free-for-all devoid of all agreed paradigms: it is not the absence, but *a different kind of paradigm.*

We attempted earlier to explore in some measure the most general features of those pre-scientific paradigms, of the 'savage mind'. They are characterised by a failure to separate cognitive functions from others, by the fusion of nature and culture, of knowledge and of social charter. They generate a world which is 'meaningful', cosy and human, rather than cold, mechanical and unhuman.

The world of regular, morally neutral, magically un-manipulable fact, which some of us are now in danger of taking too much for granted, and which is presupposed by science, is in fact not at all self-evident. Far from representing some kind of normality, a natural starting-point, historically it is a great oddity. It is separated from most or all other worlds in which men have lived by a profound chasm. Both Popper and Kuhn, in their different ways and for different reasons, underestimate this chasm. Popper assimilates it to later and indeed to earlier chasms, to any major advance in knowledge, all of which however supposedly share the same underlying principle (trial and error). For Kuhn likewise it is either one shift of vision, no different from any of the others, or it is assimilated to the difference between having some paradigm and having none at all,

[108] There is another and closely related error, which Kuhn's manner of exposition, itself dictated by the nature of his concerns, seems to imply, and which it certainly encourages amongst his readers. He seems to find the main distinguishing mark of science in the presence of a paradigm. So baldly stated, this would seem to suggest that *any* paradigm will turn a field of inquiry into a science. But this most emphatically is not so. Even if the distinguishing mark of a science is the presence of a paradigm, this can only be part, and not the whole of the differentia of science. Not all paradigms are scientific.

180

living in a kind of intellectual *fronde*. (But that is a very special phenomenon, occurring in sophisticated rather than traditional contexts.) In
each case the specificity of the shift from the pre-scientific *kind* of paradigm to the scientific one, from (roughly) a projective world to a rational,
orderly one, is underestimated.

Kuhn, highly sensitive to, not to say obsessed by, the difference
between anarchy and order in cognition, is haunted, in his Hobbesian
way, by the ever-present threat of chaos. We re-live it, according to him, in
each of those dramatic Gestalt-switches which make up a 'scientific
revolution', when the cognitive sovereign dissolves and no reasons remain
to which one could appeal. As order seems to be reborn anew from chaos
on each such traumatic occasion, there is no need to give special attention
to the first occasion. It was not different from other and later such events,
apart from constituting the first such occurrence in time. But qualitatively
it does not, in his view, differ from its successors. All this does indeed fit
with the Kuhnian vision, and it is not surprising that his thought shows
no sign of preoccupation with the distinctive nature of the *first* revolution—or, to put it in qualitative rather than ordinary terms—with what
distinguishes the boundary between science as such from non-science,, as
opposed to the boundaries between successive, incommensurate,
paradigms within science.

In the case of Popper, the failure to consider the supremely important
distinctiveness of the first great transition has quite other sources.
Popper's originality as a political thinker springs from his preoccupation,
not with the fear of anarchy, but on the contrary with the fear of our
excessive longing for order. It is our deep longing for the cosy social
womb of the Closed Society which underlies totalitarianism, in his view.
The liberation comes from *criticism*—whether in science or in society. It
is sufficient to *criticise*, and to be able to continue to do so, for progressive
science, or the Open Society, to be born. The first opening-up is no
different in kind from subsequent occasions, though it is perhaps more
heroic and more surprising, for it lacked precedent. But it is not different
in kind. The enemy is always the tendency to *close* our vision, whether in
science or in society. It was so at the start, and it remains so. Nothing has
fundamentally changed.

But this is a mistake. It is not *any* criticism which either makes or
sustains science. At the very least, it is only criticism which submits to a
certain kind of court of appeal, that of an orderly, symmetrical world of
man-independent and lonely fact, fact which is not itself permeated by and
tied to the very vision which is supposedly on trial. Criticism within a
world which tolerates magic, in which there is one truth for the ritually
pure and another for the impure, and so forth, would be powerless. In such
a world, you could have 'criticism'—in the sense of intellectual change,
justified by who knows what criteria, an unstable succession of beliefs
which to participants might seem rational or somehow progressive—but it

181

would not be science as we know it.

Despite the asymmetry between his cautious, conservative social philosophy, and his ultra-revolutionary theory of science, Popper's thought in both fields suffers from the same weakness: the tendency to underrate both the uniqueness and the difficulty of the great and fundamental divide, and to assimilate it to other 'revolutionary' situations. The attainment of a rational, non-magical, non-enchanted world is a much more fundamental achievement than the jump from one scientific vision to another. The latter may perhaps be simply characterised as just daring innovation and criticism; but the former, which concerns the establishment of criteria of what is to count as successful criticism, is more difficult either to achieve or define. Similarly in sociology, the problem of the establishment of an order within which the liberal recipe can work is much more basic and difficult than the characterisation of the liberal procedure *within* a context, which makes it possible at all.

One can find support for this diagnosis not merely in the general structure of Popper's thought, but also in a very interesting *en passant* remark, when he rightly attacks the

... Myth of the Framework (which) is, in our time, the central bulwark of irrationalism.[109]

Quite so. The myth of the framework has indeed become the last refuge of scoundrels. The idea that we are, all of us, prisoners of our 'framework', enables them to discount ideas of their opponents, and to stick to their own, without seriously examining *either*. But Popper goes much too far in the other direction. On the same page he observes:

I do admit that at any moment we are prisoners caught in the framework of our theories ... our language. But we are prisoners in a Pickwickian sense: if we try, we can break out of our framework at any time.

And if we do break out and then find ourselves in another: ' ... we can at any moment break out of it again'. *At any time*? A thinker who asserts this without qualification, twice on the same page, is open to the suspicion that he gravely underestimates human bondage. It was not *so* easy. Not at *any time*.

Popper seems to suppose that an open society was always within our reach: for all his comments on the psychological appeal of the Closed Society, he underestimates the difficulties of establishing an Open one. The single commandment, 'criticise', simply is not enough. Kuhn, by contrast, envisages the antithesis of the ordered scientific community on the model of contemporary intellectual *frondes*, and mistakenly sees it as a kind of Hobbesian state of nature. But the pre-scientific world was not paradigmless; it had a very different *kind* of paradigm. Neither 'criticism' nor the possession of a 'paradigm' is sufficient as the distinguishing mark of a

[109] *Criticism and the Growth of Knowledge*, ed. Lakatos and Musgrave, p. 56.

rational world.

The present argument is concerned with that big divide; it attempts to sketch out its general features. It contends that this is what, in effect, the knowledge-oriented philosophy of the past three centuries has been doing. It tried to codify and justify a new cognitive ethic (even if it did so in a misleading, seemingly descriptive idiom). One might add that positivism did have one great merit: it had an acute sense of the fundamental and unique nature of this great divide. That indeed was its starting point. It failed through its excessively simple characterisation of that chasm. On one side, it said, was respect for hard fact; on the other, irresponsible *accretion,* addition of cognitive claims not based on observation. This, as many have stressed, ignores the extent to which *any* perception of the 'world' is permeated by interpretation. Philosophers of science such as Kuhn on the other hand do have an acute sense of the diversity of visions ('paradigms') within science, of the way in which basic styles of interpretation permeate the supposedly 'empirical' material, and of the way in which these diverse styles are incommensurate; but they tend, in their reaction to positivism, either not to be very interested in the general problem of the demarcation of science as such, or to assimilate it to the chasms within science (for these interest them most), or to mis-diagnose the great divide (when they suppose that those on the wrong side of it are lacking in any paradigms). What is required is a fusion of the positivists' acute sense of the importance and uniqueness of the great barrier, with a more sociological awareness of what may lie on either side of it.

What is at issue here is the correct way of stating the problem of relativism. One cannot deal all at once with both the big ditch, and the minor ditches in the two lands either side to it. The argument of the present book is concerned with the nature of that big ditch, the differences between its two shores, and the nature of the reasons and causes which explain or justify our firm location on one side of it.

This problem is quite distinct from the question arising about the minor ditches in the lands on either banks. (By all normal criteria, those chasms may be enormous and important; but they are different in kind, and also, I believe, less important.)

The land on the 'traditional' side of the big divide may, for all philosophic purposes, be left to relativism. Even there, it is not true: it is unlikely that all illiterate tribal societies are similar in cognitive power, and downright absurd to say the same of all pre-scientific civilisations. Nevertheless, to grade them is a fairly pointless exercise.

By contrast, relativism plainly is not valid on the 'scientific' side of the big ditch. The manifest paradox of Kuhn's position, for instance, is that he is both aware of the fact that some paradigms are better than others—yet does not possess, within the conceptual armoury of his position, *any* means of justifying or even saying it. This is a problem which concerns the philosophers and historians of science.

Recent efforts in this direction are interesting. Lakatos' approach, for example, could be summed up as follows;[110] once upon a time, under the influence of the early Popper, the philosophy of science believed in the immaculate bull and the elegant toreador. Hypotheses arrived in the arena of science like a prize bull, clean and splendidly groomed, initially faultless. The great scientist dispatched the bull like a master toreador, with a clean and definitive blow. The stone-dead hypothesis was then dragged out, feet upwards, from the arena, never to be seen again.

We now know this is not so. The bull arrives filthy and bleeding. (All hypotheses *start* with many black marks, falsifications, against them.) Toreadors are seldom if ever elegant. They poke here and there, never really striking any vital organ. When the gore and blood is more than sight can stand, and some other bull takes the bullfighters' fancy, the bleeding bull is dragged out, alive and kicking, to be sent back on its next comeback.

A sordid but more convincing story. The Lakatosian strategy when dealing with this situation is to try and devise a blood-flow indicator—a conceptual device which will assess the amount of punishment a hypothesis or a 'research programme' has taken, and indicate just when it is rationally justified to drag it out of the arena. I rather doubt whether anything resembling a formal criterion, outside and independent of the theories that are being tested or bled, could be found or devised; but we can leave this problem to the philosophy of science. Our concern is with how the arena came to be set up at all, and not with the rules which govern its internal procedures.

THE GREATEST THINKER OF THEM ALL

On this side of the great chasm, there is a distinctive world: one amenable to science, to public, progressive, cognitive exploration, but one which, on the other hand, is not available to be the charter for social arrangements. It provides no warm cosy habitat for man. The gain and the loss are correlative: the impersonality and regularity which make it knowable are also, at the same time, the very features which make it almost—not quite—uninhabitable. It is possible to live and survive in its icy climate, but only just.

The major philosophies of modern times—the ghost and the machine traditions—are basically the explorations of the inner structure and the limits of this very distinctive world. We have seen how the ghost came, rather surprisingly, to serve this end. The empiricist vision, in its atomising manner, isolates each 'fact' or 'datum' not merely from its fellows, but also, and above all, from those theories which these facts or

[110] Cf. I. Lakatos' contribution to *Criticism and the Growth of Knowledge*, ed. Lakatos and Musgrave.

184

data are to confirm or to refute. The facts come alone, and not in the retinue some vision of the world, as was their wont. It is essential that theories/visions be not allowed to fill out and control the world, as they try to do, but that instead they should be judged *in* a world which they do not themselves control. But *which* world? Empiricism helps us construct such a world. It is one in which theories are not allowed to be judges in their own case. The insulting, isolating action of empiricism ensures that that data come to judgment alone, blindfolded, segregated like some murder jury, and hence uninfluenced—or not *very* influenced, not sufficiently at least to pervert them reliably, to make them handmaidens of some social myth. They may not be wholly pure, and indeed they are not, but they are not *reliably* corrupted and at the service of some vision. The end result is very similar to that which is achieved in a more direct. and manifest way by the 'materialist' or 'mechanist' insistence on a world which excludes 'meaningful' interpretations, a world in which our spirit can come to rest only on explanations which are resolutely symmetrical and hence 'inhuman', which allows explanations only in terms of structures and their general properties, where these are quite blind to the human personnel who erect or specify them.

No philosopher has explored this situation from the inside better than Immanuel Kant, and it is this which makes him the greatest of modern philosophers. He was a philosopher both of the ghost and of the machine.

The great irony of Kant's critical philosophy is of course that it is simultaneously inspired by two fears which, superficially, one might expect to make each other redundant. The first fear is that the mechanical vision does *not* hold; the second fear is that it *does*. The first fear is for science, and the second for morality. Kant's greatness is reflected in the fact that, quite rightly, he felt both fears, and tolerated no facile arguments which would play down their importance. If the machine hypothesis does not hold, then science is impossible—for science is based on the assumption that genuine explanations are available and are there to be found. On the other side—if the machine hypothesis does hold, then, in virtue of a very familiar argument, human freedom, responsibility *and* the attribution of validity to our own thought, all fly out of the window. Either way, disaster. Kant never stooped to the silly supposition that accepting either one of the two disasters would evade the other. He attempted to prevent both.

Kant's manner of validating the mechanical vision is notoriously left-handed, and therein lies its great merit. He does not foolishly suppose that we could somehow find an argument which would prove that things, of their very nature, 'in themselves', could be constrained and shown *a priori* to be necessarily 'causal', i.e. amenable to orderly explanation. Any such 'proof' must necessarily be circular and question-begging, and assume in some covert way that which is to be proved. What he did endeavour to prove was that our thinking, our concepts, *must* be such as to conform

185

with this model. *If* we are to have proper knowledge at all, then we must think in this manner. The proof constrains not nature, but our concepts.

The mechanism of Kant's proof is interesting and, under the formidable-looking jargon and terminological scaffolding, simple. His starting point is this: it is a central and essential feature of our vision that we distinguish between subjective and objective sequences, between things which happen to the world and those which happen to the perceiving subject. This is essential; without such a distinction, we should have neither a world nor a self. But the manner in which events, changes, are allocated to either of the two realms always depends on the prior assumption of *some* causal properties. It is done by placing them in a *sequence*—that is, a causal sequence. Unless things were orderly, rule-bound in their behaviour, we could not allocate them to one side or the other of this divide. We can distinguish between a rotating room and an observer rotating in a stable room, only through assuming some causal regularities which, on that particular occasion, allow the one but not the other. It is not that we can know a priori any *specific* causal generalisations; but unless we assume that some such generalisations do hold (though we don't always know which ones), we could not distinguish between the 'external' and the 'subjective' in the way in which in fact we do, and which is presupposed by our ideas both of the world and of self.

The proof could be put another way. It is not that we first of all know an 'external world' and *then* come to decide whether or not to assume that it obeys causal laws. By the time we 'see' an external world at all, we have *already* assumed a causal orderliness in it—those causal sequences which enable us to locate, to place, objects and events in the positions they occupy. Causality and objectivity stand and fall together.[111] The *placing* of objects already presupposes that they are orderly. Causally unbound objects would have no fixed location. There is no sense in asking about a supposedly un-caused event—*where* is it? Or how big? It can only be located an measured through processes which are inherently causal. The assumption of causelessness also frees the object of which it is made from those other characteristics which make up an 'objective world'. The *Gedankenexperiment* which imagines a world of uncaused events, but leaves the world otherwise unchanged, similar to the one we know, makes no sense. We must have causation and objectivity together, or neither.

It is a merit in the proof that it does not seek, absurdly, to offer us some guarantee against the dissolution of the world. All such guarantees must

[111] It is often claimed that Kant's doctrine of the universal applicability within nature of the principle of causation has been disproved by certain much-publicised developments in modern physics. But these developments in fact confirm his insights. For it appears that the point at which determinism is replaced by probability is also the one at which interference by the observing mechanism makes it impossible to determine all at once both the location and the speed of a particle. Objectivity and causality lapsed together, which is precisely what Kant taught: his proof of causality overtly hinged on the assumption of objectivity.

186

be worthless. Kant shows rather that constraints operate inexorably in our thought, compelling it to seek and assume order. *We* are constrained, not nature.

But having so constrained ourselves—providentially, from the viewpoint of the viability of science—we only impose another and as grave a problem on ourselves. Properly understood, without facile evasion, a world which is eligible for scientific understanding, *ipso facto* also leaves no room for freedom, responsibility *and* validity of thought. The world is amenable to scientific explanation because it is assumed to consist of repeatable structures, whose behaviour follows inexorably from the properties of the materials they are made of, and from the manner in which they are put together (roughly speaking). But in such a mechanistic world, where is there room for freedom and value?

There is no room for such things in it. Kant's solution of the problem is well known. He falls back in the fact that it is not the nature of things, but the nature of our thought, which had imposed this inexorable order on the world. But if this is so, he argues, and if we find that our humanity requires that we have at least a partial exemption from this cold world, may we not grant ourselves such an exemption? *We* imposed the order; it was not in the nature of things. Why should we suffer from a vision imposed by ourselves?

This is a desperate remedy, and Kant does not use it lightly. It is only because, without such an assumption, and without such an exemption, all morality and freedom would disappear, that we must in his view assume, in the interest of preserving this absolute minimum which gives meaning to our lives, that we are indeed exempt from the vision we have ourselves imposed. Only such great need justifies this step; and only the previous discovery that causal necessity was man-made also makes it permissible. Without this, it would be impermissible, *however* great the need might be.

Kant is of course not a materialist in the sense of supposing that materialism/mechanism gives us the truth about the absolute nature of things. But he was one, in the sense of supposing that the machine tradition tells us what the world is like in as far as it is available for understanding, for cognitive exploration, *by us*. The kind of explanatory structures that we can work with, can only operate on the assumption of a certain kind of material.

He placed this firm awareness in the context of a wider 'ghost' philosophy, of the circumscription of our knowledge by *our* experience, and an insistence on its sovereignty. He differs from the pure empiricists by his concern with the form in which these data are arranged by our style of explanation, and his awareness that this style imposes the 'machine' vision on those data. He differs from the pure materialists in his sensitivity to what is lost by this cold explanatory vision, by his awareness of the fact that its roots are in our vision rather than the nature of things, by his determination to save something (freedom, morality) from this cold projected vision, and his scrupulous fastidiousness in saving only what is strictly necessary, and no more.

He retains only the absolute minimum of what is required, in his view, to save our human identity. If we were simply machines, or simply bundles of sensation—these being basically the two rival theories of man —then no sense could possibly be attached to ideas such as freedom, responsibility, obligation, and the validity of thought. A machine does what it is programmed to do: it does not think truths because they are valid. A bundle of sensations and feelings cannot be under an obligation; it either does or does not contain an impulse in some direction or another, but if it does not, there is no possible sense to saying that it *should* strive in that direction. Hume was willing to accept this consequence.

Valuation, obligation, validity of thought, freedom—these were the kinds of minimal equipment, for Kant, which needed to be saved from the encroachment of the mechanical world if we were to remain human. What is remarkable about him as a thinker is not that he tried to save them, but that he tried to save so little. His severe restraint stands in contrast with the greed or self-indulgence of later thinkers who faced the same predicament. Kant did not suppose that we could take with us, when entering the cold cognisable world, *all* our luggage, whole lorry-loads of conceptual furniture. He took the absolute minimum to save our humanity, to make us more than mere *things*; the rest he spurned. Our modern re-endorsers show no such restraint. He was like a refugee from a catastrophe who arrives, nobly carrying but the two or three beings dearest to him. They, by contrast, arrive with several wagon-loads of rubbish. Everything, but literally everything, is to be retained, it seems. 'Philosophy leaves everything as it is.' They manufacture by the dozen spurious proofs purporting to show that all our favoured conceptual furniture may be retained. On their account, you need fear no inconvenience at all.

Kant, despite the noble economy with which he refrained from taking anything but that which was of ultimate value, was mistaken in supposing that he was dealing with a universal human predicament rather than a historically specific one. In a way he did not think we were leaving anything *behind*, for on the literal interpretation of his official view of man, we had never possessed it, and so were not losing it. Nor should we covet it. Our real moral vision had ever been 'autonomous' and had spurned ratification by external echoes. In this noble view of man he was mistaken. We did once possess a great deal more in the way of such illusion, and we *do* still covet it. This is the big conceptual divide, and we have made the move across it.

KANT AND WEBER

Max Weber is the sociologist of rationality and disenchantment. Strictly speaking, there is no *and*: we have here not two themes, but one. Rationality and disenchantment are intimately connected. A rule-bound society ('bureaucracy') and a rule-bound nature are bound to be disenchanted, simply in virtue of being rule-bound: enchantment works through idiosyncrasy, uniqueness, spontaneity, a magic which is tied to the identity and individuality of the participants, and all these are excluded by orderly regularity.

And rationality is in the end closely connected with regularity. Weber's treatment of rationality has not always been held up as a model of lucidity,[112] but what the issue finally amounts to is this. There is the rationality of the bureaucrat or the impartial judge, which amounts to treating like cases alike, to the elimination of bias and arbitrariness: 'No differentiation without justification.' On the other hand, there is the rationality of means and ends, the free selection of the most efficient available means for a given end, on the best available evidence, and without regard to precedent, to traditional or extraneous consideration. Weber was close to Marx in seeing this as the central trait modern production: the use of formally free wage-labour, employable on this or that task in the light of profitability, as opposed to those social systems in which work and production are less elastic, and more integrated with other aspects of life. Like Marx, Weber saw the social price of this principle: he was inclined to use the term 'rationality' where Marx saw 'alienation', but the difference in assessment is not quite as great as this difference in terminology might suggest. Though not exactly a pejorative term, Weber's attitude to 'rationality' was deeply ambivalent. Like Marx, Weber probably exaggerated the extent to which free-floating wage-labour is a *permanent* feature of modern industrial society, as distinct from being a characteristic of its early and transitional stages. Labour in advanced industrial countries is not notably mobile, geographically and occupationally. Work does seem anchored, once again, to other aspects of life, and to a man's general identity; developed countries tend to be obliged to import labour from backward lands when economic changes call for re-direction of resources, and require labour which really approximates to being a 'mere commodity'.

But let us return to the kinds of rationality. In a covert kind of way, ends-means rationality, i.e. the cold and flexible adoption of any means to given ends without paying heed to tradition, *also* constitutes a kind of regularity. In like circumstances, like ends will call for like means. Equality of treatment, indifferent to the 'human' aspects of the case (i.e. all those not related to the attainment of the isolated, clearly specified aim),

[112] 'The use of the word "rational" and its cognates has caused untold confusion ... in the writings of sociological theorists ... I think Max Weber is largely responsible for this. His use of these terms is irremediably opaque and shifting.' S. Lukes, *European Journal of Sociology*, 1967, vol. VIII, no. 2, p. 259. This is a harsh judgment. Though the formal explications of rationality may not be happy, there is nevertheless an underlying coherence in the use of the notion.

emerges in the one case as it does in the other. Means-ends efficiency is at any rate a species of the rationality of regularity. Conversely, the fetishism of orderliness only assumes its characteristically modern form, as opposed to its scholastic or talmudic variants, when the rules themselves are subject to scrutiny, in the light of their conduciveness to some stated end of policy. So the two things converge.

Thus the preoccupations of Kant and of Weber are really the same. One was a philosopher and the other a sociologist, but there, one might say, the difference ends. It is of course a very significant distinction. They saw the same problem, but Kant saw it as a universal one, which concerned man *as such*; Weber saw it as a differential problem—concerning why *some* men, but some men only, saw the world in a certain way and acted in a certain manner. Each of them was concerned both to explain and to justify; but the justification, above all, had to be very different in the two cases.

Descriptively, Kant supposes he is speaking about the universal structure of the human mind; normatively, the way that our mind works is justified by Kant as the allegedly inescapable consequence of a necessary and universally shared structure. *We can no other.* In as far as, nonetheless, we *do* violate these inherent principles in the sphere of conduct—and Kant was not so blind as to suppose that we did not violate them—we do it under the impact of extraneous forces at work within our own breast: alas, we are half animal, half rational being, and the principles inherent in reason are often overcome, in thought and deed, by the impulses of the beast. But, thought Kant, we only do so against our better nature and regretfully; we could not possibly *identify* with those lower impulses. Even the most hardened villain, he gratuitously goes on to observe, cannot but feel regret and feel the call of law, reason, regularity. And here, of course, Kant was wrong. Leaving aside hardened villains, who in fact can pursue exception-ridden, rule-defying courses without batting an eyelid, whatever Kant may wish to think, it is not merely possible, but exceedingly common, for men to identify with aspects of themselves other than the respect of reason, law, and order.

Of course, Kant *had* to believe all this, for otherwise his whole strategy of justification would collapse. Were it but a contingent identification, one which held for some men only, and binding only for those who choose so to bind themselves—then everything, for Kant, would fall. He was not interested in optional matters of taste of choice, but in obligation in the full-blooded sense, binding on all, as Reason is. And he concluded that man could only identify with that which is universal and necessary to him, reason, and not with that which is contingent and accidental.

Weber's case is different. Descriptively, what fascinated him was not man *an sich*, in general, but one particular and distinct species, *rational man*, in the specific and circumscribed form which he so brilliantly sketched out in *The Protestant Ethic and the Rise of Capitalism*. But

190

Weber's vision of this special kind of man corresponds to Kant's view of man as such. The philosopher Kant was naturally superior in working out the inner logic and strains of the rational vision; but the sociologist was greatly superior in painting the portrait of a life style, *one amongst others,* in its historical setting and its contrasts with other, rival styles. This of course is the heart of Weber's sociology: what were the specific pre-conditions and consequences of this unique kind of man, who was also responsible for that fascinating monstrosity, the modern world? The universal question of Kant's becomes a differential one for Weber.

But he too, contrary to a certain popular image of him, was concerned with the normative validation of this particular kind of man and his vision. Of course the Kantian style of justification was not open to him: a man whose very starting point is that the Kantian rationality is specific and *not* universal, obviously could not appeal to some necessary and hence universal structure of the human mind. But, though in general he did not suppose neutral reasons could be given for the ultimate choice between warring gods, he shared Kant's view that *we,* at least, had no choice in this particular matter.

We were doomed to the rational vision—the alternative was phoney antiquarianism—but not because it was inherent in man as such—on the contrary, it was rare to the point of making its unique emergence miracu-lous—but because it was a necessary pre-condition and consequence of the kind of civilisation we lived in, and to which we are now wedded. In style of justification as in analysis, Weber was a sociologist and Kant a philosopher.

IRONIC CULTURES AND THE MEANING INDUSTRY

There is a certain mistake which Kant and Weber shared. At one point they both tended to overrate human lucidity and consistency. The bleak vision which, for Kant, was inherent in the very human condition and which, for Weber, was instead the specific condition and predicament of our age, is not quite as pervasive as a credulous reader of either Kant or Weber might expect. For Kant the problem is naturally more acute, as his claim is stronger: what can he make of those many un-puritan, un-iconoclastic cultures, whose enchanted visions populate nature with man-like spirits and which, most certainly, do not restrict the irreducibly human to that exiguous minimum postulated by him, which leaves nature to mechanical interpretation? His main doctrine does not quite face this issue.

But even Weber, who is committed to crediting modern man only, rather than man in general, with the disenchanted vision, would seem to have overdone it a bit. Modern societies are not systematically and consistently secularised; luxuriant, self-indulgent, cosy or ecstatic faiths are present in a thousand forms, new, old, or revivalist. It would be most

191

rash to say that they are on the decline. On the contrary, the augmentation of leisure, the diminution of economic pressures, the reduction of authoritarianism in formal education, and a general permissiveness, all seem to combine to encourage a new wave of antinomianism accompanied by emotive, disorderly, near-incoherent doctrines which are anything rather than icily order-bound and disenchanted in their interpretation of the world. The rebellious young of the 1960s, for instance, had little resemblance to those of a century earlier: Bazarov would scarcely have recognised them.

It is, I suppose, conceivable that the whole Disenchantment thesis was profoundly mistaken, and that, on the contrary, the total indiscipline, the uncritical self-indulgence, the luxuriant slush of Californian-style religion and-protest are a real foretaste of the future. Through leisure and emancipation from economic pressure, technological civilisation would perhaps become the base of an anti-technical, sensualist-mystical emotive, and intellectually undisciplined form of life. Though something of this kind clearly is one strong tendency at work on the contemporary scene, it seems to me to constitute only a partial and superficial aspect of it.

The new anthropomorphism of our age, the delusion that the universe can best be understood, and human fulfilment best be pursued, through the sloppiest, most 'spontaneous', least disciplined thought, is in the end but a surface phenomenon. No doubt there are elements in the American tradition which favour it—the populist egalitarianism and anti-intellectualism, the emotional fundamentalism. The rejection of America by the 'protest' movement has a raucous and indiscriminate quality which holds up a faithful mirror to the earlier nationalism and collective self endorsement, and the tone and style of the mid-West preacher were discernible under the Californian rebel even before Jesus Freaks appeared on the scene. But even allowing, as one should, that this movement also has more general roots, apart from the local and specific ones, it still remains true that all this is froth rather than substance.

Weber was of course aware of this tendency, and as we saw commented with some derision on the pseudo-spiritual antiquarianism of some intellectuals of his time. But since his day, the number of those who could indulge this taste has indeed greatly increased, thanks to affluence, and the provision of the means for satisfying it has grown into a very sizeable industry. But that is all.

Why is it ultimately superficial? Society continues to be based on a productive, administrative, and order-enforcing technology which is scientific, which transcends cultural boundaries, and is blind to the new cultures of instant truth and spontaneous, participatory revelation. The new pseudo-cultures continue to rely on this technology for a standard of living to which its members are accustomed and which they are most certainly not seriously prepared to forego. These monks go out to an air

192

conditioned wilderness. It is all rather like Tolstoy re-enacting peasant life in one part of his house and maintaining his habitual standards in another. So many Tolstoys these days ... nowadays, you need no longer be really rich to play at the other thing. Such affectation is now within almost everyone's reach. It is precisely because the basic and assured standard of living is so fabulously high that so many can 'opt out' and sacrifice some marginal benefits. And at this level, those marginal benefits only have a symbolic or status value anyway; and as so often, the status game can be played both ways. Spurning some sign of rank can so often be a better move than visibly reaching out for it. Such conspicuous abstention from these marginal extras is one thing, and a genuine return to the squalor of pre-industrial poverty would be quite another. There is no sign whatever that anyone is genuinely willing to opt for the latter; and that whole populations should *choose* such a course is unthinkable.

And as it continues to live by and rely on powerful, manipulatively effective scientific knowledge, society also habitually turns to it in real need, in any field in which this type of knowledge is genuinely established. (In fields in which it is not yet established, the situation is more complex. For instance, the cognitively dubious practices in areas such as psychiatry, willingly and eagerly assume the garb of science, and thus pay homage to the recognised paradigm of truth, as hypocrisy pays homage to virtue.) It is only in the residual sphere, where nothing very serious is at stake, that the scientific vision has become optional.

Thus in most of our life, there is a complex symbiosis of diverse conceptual styles. The concepts which are part of the serious business of real knowledge constitute one strand, and the many other styles, whose virtues are different—such as to be jolly, entertaining, homely, or comforting—constitute another. It is for this reason that the Weberian disenchantment thesis is in partial error. What is true is that modern cognition does bureaucratise nature, and must necessarily do so; but, serious cognition need not pervade all aspects of daily life. On the contrary, the insulation of various spheres of life, the division of labour and specificity of function, makes it easier to permit any degree of fantasy in those aspects of life which are distinct from the serious business of knowledge. The disenchantment of cognitive life, together with the severe separation of thought from play, can actually liberate the latter from constraint.

This, then, is a very important general trait of modern societies: the emergence of what may be called ironic cultures. By this I do not mean that the individuals involved in them necessarily or indeed generally hold and internalise such cultures and their doctrinal content in a detached, ironic spirit. The irony is not generally conscious, explicit or individual. It resides in the fact that the whole organisation of such cultures, the way in which they are implemented and enforced in life, the limits within which they are enforced, work in a manner which tacitly presupposes and admits

193

that they are not to be taken seriously, as knowledge. They contain claims, assertions, which *sound* cognitive, and which in other, non-ironic cultures would indeed have been such; but here, it is somehow understood that they are not fully serious, not commensurate or continuous with real knowledge. Real knowledge is to be found elsewhere; and it does have the cold forms which Kant and Weber discerned and anticipated. But more colourful, human, cosier worlds and thought-styles are at the same time available to envelop our daily life, and they have reached their quiet accomodation, their tacit division of spheres of influence, with the island of truth. The world in which we think is not the same as the one in which we live, in Gaston Bachelard's memorable formulation. The colder the one, the more fanciful the other, perhaps. The world in which we think seriously, and in which rational decisions of importance are taken, is one world, and all in all, Kant and Weber were right about its general nature. The world in which we live our daily lives is another, and that one tends to escape them. Extensive parts of it become more and not less luxuriant, and conceptually unrestrained.

And it had to be so. To see this is best to reflect on that great illusion of the Enlightenment that there is a rational humanist vision, waiting to reveal itself when the knavish anti-vision of the priests and kings has been torn down—the Heavenly City of the eighteenth-century philosophers, in Becker's phrase. This was an error. Reason does not produce another, and a rival, total and closed picture, as gratifying for man as the old theological ones (or more so) only upside-down. It produces none at all. On the contrary, it merely erodes the old one. It does not uniquely generate some culture, some style of life, with its system of roles and ranks (though it may indeed be incompatible with most or even all preceding ones). The scientific vision, for instance, does not dictate any sartorial or gastronomic style (though it may exclude some). But we must wear and eat *something*: nay more, in the interest of convenient social intercourse and of legible menus, of the rapid recognition of people and dishes, we must have shared customs in the wardrobe and at table. This is quite essential. The experience of the ethnographer, when he tastes for the first time the food of an outlandish tribe, may be exciting (or revolting, or indeed both); but to have this experience at every meal would be intolerable, and would no doubt lead to ulcers. Similarly, a perpetual fancy dress ball would be tedious, and it is of course notorious that those who preach and indulge the wildest sartorial unconventionality also impose, in their own groups and cliques or milieux, conventions more rigid and constraining than those of conventionally-conventional society. Drag is not free of rules, it merely has its own set.

So? A culture, a sartorial, gastronomic, moral style and tradition is indeed adopted and imposed, by the normal methods of shared expectation, education, social pressure and so forth. But now there is a difference. It is no longer continuous with, possessing the same status as, the best cognitive and productive equipment of the society. On the contrary, there is a deep fissure between the two. In a traditional society, the rationale of dietary regulation, say, may well come from exactly the same source as the premises governing fundamental therapeutic, political or productive activities, and hence can have similar status. This is no longer so, and cannot be so. When serious issues are at stake—such as the production of wealth, or the maintenance of health—we want and expect real knowledge. But when choosing our menu or our rituals, we turn to culture and religion. In these frills of life, we may, and indeed we must, use *some* culture or other, and select it in *some* other way. (We must, because our truth no longer generates or selects its own.) But all this is not serious. Most of us do not openly admit that it is not serious, at least in words. Actual practice however indicates that this is so. Culture remains rich and human and is even, in various ways, more luxuriant than it used to be; but it is no longer all of a piece with the serious and effective convictions of a society. These, at any rate, tend to be as Kant and Weber claimed they must be.

THE SECOND SECULARISATION AND 'LE SELF-SERVICE'

The ironic, or non-serious, and in a way free-floating, expansive and liberated culture of modern society may need, and in any case often receives, philosophic underpinning. Probably—who knows—it could manage perfectly well without it. But, whether or not it requires it, it certainly receives it. Many philosophers, of quite diverse schools, fall over themselves to supply it with certificates of authenticity.

These certificates are issued either to specific singled-out and named ways of life, or on an omnibus basis to all of them, or to their cognitive content or to the manner in which it is acquired. In a sense, the very fact that they should seem to need such confirmation may inspire some suspicion. In the days when the *Lebenswelt* was simply the world, *die Welt,* no one felt much need to demonstrate its existence and importance. It would indeed have been an odd enterprise, and one difficult to explain. On the contrary, thinkers and seers tended to specialise in purveying information about *other* worlds, generally such as contained vindications of authority and of therapeutic techniques and of other manipulations in *this* world, and to this day philosophic thought has popularly retained something of this image. By contrast the *Lebenswelt,* though no doubt a predicament, an obstacle and an encumbrance, was not felt to be so precarious as to require proof ... The thinker might be solicited for means and formulae which would bend this world to our will, or which would enable us to escape it, but hardly for reassurance concerning its existence. That seemed too obvious, sometimes painfully so. To *prove* it would seem redundant, perhaps insulting, probably comic. Some thinkers were at considerable pains to preach its *un*reality, though they never had very marked success in persuading men to adapt their actual conduct to this view.

The curious fact that the *Lebenswelt,* the ordinary world in which we conduct our daily life, should become problematical, is symptomatic of a very important development which could be called the Second Secularisation. The notion of secularisation normally suggests the elimination of transcendent religious belief, the restriction of the range of belief to *this* world. But, far more important that the amputation, as it were, of such additional, incremental worlds, is the transformation of *this* world itself. In its natural state, so to speak, it is suffused with 'meaning', purpose, sensitivity; it speaks with a human voice, it dovetails with our life, it responds like a person. The price of cognitive advance, of its intelligibility and manipulability, has been its de-humanisation. More is involved in this than the exiling of the elfs and spirits that once haunted it. The very idiom in which the world is characterised becomes distinct, not just from the idiom in which we might have spoken of the elfs, but also from the way in which we think of ourselves and of each other. The languages of cognition and of life become distinct: and it is thus that the 'ordinary world', the object of ordinary speech, becomes suspect and problematical.

Some philosophies recognise this and attempt both to locate some other world, and to justify the ordinary one in some limited measure by relating it to that more fundamental and trustworthy one. The situation can be conveyed in terms of a celebrated example, that of Professor Eddington's table: was it the hard familiar table of common sense, or the mysterious largely empty space sparsely filled with mini-solar-systems, which is known to physics? Philosophers of 'common sense' have ironised and derided this question, and provided omnibus, *carte blanche* validations of ordinary tables and ordinary everything. If tables are not real, what is?

In fact, to put it simply, if one thing is certain it is that ordinary tables are not real. Of course, the nature of our sensory equipment and the ingrained conceptual customs of our language and culture ensure that, for daily purposes, we shall continue to act and think in terms of tables. But the central point about our contemporary condition is that the manner in which we think in daily life is not congruent with the manner in which we think when something really important is at stake, when the gravity of the issue forces us to shift to an idiom for which we have greater cognitive respect. The *Lebenswelt* or the ordinary, commonsense world of the ordinary language philosophers has become an abstraction, a mere part of the world we really inhabit, of a far more complex and stratified structure. To make that *Lebenswelt* ultimate is, ironically, to violate real common sense, or to give a false phenomenology of our world.

The two great philosophies, the ghost and the machine, have definite things to say about the table. For the ghost, the table is a bundle of actual and possible sensations. For the machine, the table is a congeries of

196

whirling particles. Either of these views deserves respect. The one view which cannot be taken seriously, except as an affectation in the philosopher's study, is that the table is a table.

The ghostly theory, interpreting the table as a collection of sensations, gives us its cognitive genealogy, or rather and above all, its cognitive status: it tells us why and how the table has passed the test which spooks, angels, fairies and so forth have failed to pass, though they also were once part and parcel of our living language and culture. The machine theory, on the other hand, gives us the schema of the kind of explanatory model to which tables are subject, and indicates the direction in which we should look if we had some serious purpose in mind, such as the manufacture of tables. Common sense and its daily table are good enough for the do-it-yourself handyman, who only does it for fun really; for serious purposes, however, we should require the best physical information available about current materials, and this would most certainly *not* be articulated in the language of common sense.

In brief, it is of the essence of our condition that we live, not in the alleged *Lebenswelt*, the world of common sense, but in a wider world of which it is but a part, and a part which has a tense, unstable and in the end subordinate position to other parts of it. The *sursis* has been placed on the ordinary world, not by the fiat of some thinker, not by way of intellectual experiment, but by our objective situation, by the unprecedented and unforeseen fact that cognition has become powerful and autonomous, and has in the course of this process partly eroded, partly detached itself from the 'ordinary world' which had once been its matrix.

Thus Husserl and the phenomenologists are quite wrong when they claim to 'bracket' the ordinary world, to 'suspend' the alleged 'natural viewpoint', in the interest of holding up that world in pincers and examining it for what it is. This is what they claim, but it quite misrepresents the real situation. The ordinary world has *already* been suspended and subjected to examination, for quite some time, not as an experiment but as a necessity. The suspension of our world is not a spectacle but a predicament.

In the course of claiming to 'suspend' it, the phenomenologists have in effect done quite the reverse. The alleged suspension constitutes a kind of vindication, a justification of the ordinary world as such, leading it to be treated as ultimate in its own sphere, and no longer treated as a rival or dated scientific theory. The suspension then in effect says—this is the world you actually live in, and at least *as a Lebenswelt* its standing is unquestionable.

One false claim which is implicit in all this is that there is any novelty in it. Modern man has been practising *epoché* for some centuries, without knowing it, much as he speaks prose. It is precisely because the new science speaks in a strange and 'technical' idiom, referring to a cold and inhuman world, which is discontinuous with the notions of everyday life, and because at the same time the new science manifestly has much greater cognitive power than any contained in the practices of daily life, that daily life has come to be surrounded, as part of its very nature, as part of that which is 'lived', by tacit, doubt-conveying quotation marks. We are not too sure of the status of anything within this ordinary world. Real knowledge, science, may re-validate it—or not. In the meantime, we continue to live in the ordinary world and use its ordinary concepts, for generally speaking we have no choice and no alternative, but we do it with a certain amount of distrust. It has a kind of interim status. So what is really interesting is that the ordinary world, the *Lebenswelt,* has 'brackets' around it already *as part of its natural condition,* incorporated in the 'natural viewpoint' towards it; it does not merely acquire it in consequence of the phenomenologist's new vision. If that vision were accurate, it would have to notice it and end up with a double set of horns, as it were, superimposed on this animal . . .

So what phenomenology really does is not to teach us to hold the ordinary world in special pincers, ready for examination—for that we do anyway; what it does do, by giving it a name, is to reassure and re-confirm its status. Previously, the ordinary world was just the place in which we appeared to live, but which we had learnt to doubt and query; now, by being *called* the *Lebenswelt,* it is in a curious kind of way restored to its full pristine confidence. By so calling it, we imply that at least *qua* 'our world', as a *Lebenswelt,* it is not in doubt. (The mistake is the supposition that 'our world' is necessarily something static, not affected by the wider interpretations surrounding it.)

The phenomenological method tends to yield interesting results only when applied to human or social fields. When applied to inert or unconscious nature, it simply repeats our concepts for us, or at best acts as a conceptual projection test, or remains vacuously programmatic. It is when applied to men and cultures, entities for whom their own concepts are an important part of reality, that the method can be exciting. This is not surprising, for it is in these spheres, when consciousness is as it were reflexive, that it also possesses a structure complex enough to reward the investigator.

But the method then becomes satisfying to its addicts for another and more questionable reason. It contains a most curious device for re-validating our beliefs and self-images. The '*Lebenswelt*' is the world as we live it; that is its 'ontological status'. It is the general nature of man that he is 'consciousness-for-itself', that his capacity and tendency to be aware of himself is central to his nature. So, as this is what we are, and this is the world we live in, what we find in it and the characteristics we appear to have are automatically validated, for no other world has authority over this realm.

What it all amounts to is defining the human as that which is conscious of its own condition, and then proceeding to turn this not unreasonable definition into a warranty of the *content* of that consciousness ... We live in the world which we conceive. Freedom is indeed part of the conceptual furniture of that world: we do think of ourselves as free. But as the world of our ideas *is* our world (phenomenological first principle), so we *are* free ... Q.E.D.

The phenomenological method and this use of it is, for instance, an essential part of later forms of existentialism, such as Sartre's. The consequence of this is the breathtakingly facile vindication of, for instance, human freedom; we 'choose ourselves' because that is how we experience ourselves. Any question concerning whether this experience of ours is truly veridical, which bothered earlier philosophers, is automatically brushed aside, by the implicit or explicit appeal to the phenomenological method, which, at the very point where it claims to suspend belief, in fact re-confirms and excludes doubt.

We are as we experience ourselves, for 'being-for-ourselves' is of our essence. We experience ourselves as free. So ... the *Lebenswelt,* by being so named, is in fact given a realm of its own in which to be sovereign and secure. That realm then in fact includes the basic manner in which we see our own selves, and thus revalidates it.

Sartre is a keen practitioner of this method, which dovetails well with his contempt for natural science and the easy self-spun dogmatism of his psychology and sociology. It naturally leads him into trouble when he endeavours to marry this philosophy and Marxism, for the former teaches that man is inherently, 'ontologically' free, whereas the latter prophetic vision hinges on a liberation which is to come and which is not yet achieved. How can freedom be both our permanent birthright and predicament, *and* a future salvation? Answer comes there none. The dilemma was wittily seized up by J.-F. Revel[113]:

l'existentialisme ... fut le plus souvent considéré ... par les marxistes ... comme réactionnaire, étant donné son affirmation de la conscience comme 'liberté' absolute, indépendente des conditions ... Je parle ici ... de l'existentialisme première manière, ... et non point des rattrapages ... tentés quinze ans plus tard par Sartre, lorsqu'il s'efforca ... d'introduire un peu de determinisme historique dans le *self service* de sa conscience libre.

Of course, the situation is complex. Whilst the erstwhile common sense world is no longer cognitively sovereign, and no longer constitutes the ultimate court of appeal (if ever it did), the fact remains that any reflection about our situation and its evaluation is in the end done by individual men in an idiom which is generally closer to ordinary thought than it is to the formal and rigorous disciplines. Whether this is so in the nature of things, or only in the nature of our age, is a difficult question which we shall evade. But it is certainly so at present. This however helps explain a marked and bitter feature of the situation of the contemporary

---

[113] *En France,* (Paris, 1965), pp. 52 and 53.

philosopher, a feature which could be called Plato-on-his-head.

Plato thought, not unreasonably, that the nature of things, of ways of knowing them, and of social groups, was stratified along proper and reasonable lines. From this it would seem to follow that the more important a topic, the more rigorous the thought within it, and vice versa. Certainly a world in which this were so would exemplify a sense of fittingness and propriety.

Our actual world, regrettably, does not exemplify anything of the kind. The sad truth is—honesty compels us to confess it—that the relationship is the inverse of that which Plato so reasonably expected. The more important the topic, in a human-philosophic sense, the less rigorous the reasoning; the more rigorous the reasoning, the more abstract and humanly irrelevant the topic.

The social consequences of this undeniable state of affairs are sad, notably for the philosopher. He is by profession the man who discusses the most important topics in the least rigorous way.

It would seem that the most dignified reaction—making the best way of a bad job—is to accept the situation, learn to live with it, and try to understand its sources and implications.

TRUNCATED EVOLUTIONISM

Our stocktaking, our surveys of the rational devices available in our efforts to gain some degree of orientation, has on the whole neglected what was the most powerful current of thought of a not negligible century, the nineteenth. The central epistemological ideas of the period which preceded it have been noted with respect, and so have the ploys and devices of the epistemological re-play or second coming which the universities have witnessed in this century (and which does not deserve so much respect). But we have paid less attention than perhaps is fair to that effort which is so characteristic of the nineteenth century, the attempt to seize and understand the general flow of things.

Yet in fact that heroic endeavour is by no means irrelevant to our predicament. What was mistaken was merely its intoxication, its inebriation, its megalomania—the supposition that the predicament of rapid social change in its own time was the culmination, the paradigm, the quintessence of *all* change, of transformation as such, of all development. It was and is nothing of the kind. The megalomania is not merely objectionable on the usual grounds, but also on specific ones: the subsumption of our problem under the question of the nature of all things (and vice versa, really) naturally obscured the *specificity* of our predicament. And what is specific in our problem, in the cognitive, productive and moral transformation of which we are part, is in all probability far more important than what it shares with the rest of the history of mankind, of life, or of being.

200

Nevertheless, a substantial part of the style of nineteenth-century thought remains relevant, if it is re-stated and *is* cut down to size, if it is suitably truncated. The reformulation consists of replacing questions concerning the destiny of man/life/being as such (according to how broad a variant of the old question you favoured), by a question which is imcomparably more specific, though still large enough, concerning the potential and consequences of *the* transformation we are witnessing. Given the new productive, organisational, cognitive bases of society— what are their limits and their consequences?

In this form the question remains relevant, important, and indeed mandatory. Nothing is more absurd than the supposition that just because we are not slaves to some ineluctable laws of historical development, therefore technology imposes no constraints and anything is possible.

To recognise that nineteenth-century thinkers (provided they are thus cut down to size) nevertheless asked one of the proper questions, does not of course oblige us to endorse any of their answers. For instance, the unwarranted manner in which Marx mistakenly extrapolated from certain features of early capitalism to industrial society as such has often been noted. But, to take a later example, the same is also true of Max Weber, against whom it may be objected that he remained far too Marxist. He saw the essence of the new emerging world in a certain rationality, exemplified in the free choice of means, untrammelled by tradition, and this in turn more specifically exemplified by mobile wage-labour, channelled to its tasks by market forces, to ends assigned by an economic rationality which remains unaffected by more diffuse social considerations. Marx called this 'alienation' and disliked it a good deal, whilst Weber called it 'rationality' and remained ambivalent about it. But, under either name and whatever our attitude to this way of running production, it is most questionable whether it is indeed the permanent and essential trait of modern industrial production.

The truth of the matter appears to be that 'capitalism' of this kind does carry the seeds of its own destruction, though not at all in the way Marx supposed. Advanced industry operates with highly trained, permanent and well-motivated labour, rather than with an undifferentiated mass of unskilled muscle-power driven by fear of hunger. The tacit, or indeed written, contract which ratifies labour relations in such organisations must be of the socially multi-purpose kind, respecting a wide variety of 'social' considerations, and thus cannot observe the kind of crude and ruthless ends–means rationality which horrified Marx and which gave Weber such complex *frissons*.

Moreover, 'classical' capitalism is, ironically enough, tied to a fairly low technological level and small productive units, which are small and non-disruptive enough to be *able* to disregard considerations other than narrowly economic ones. They could take their environment more or less for granted. The sheer size and the fundamental nature of the technology of contemporary industry forces it into multiple and political considerations. The Marxist attempt at incorporating such phenomena by means of the label 'monopoly capitalism' is abortive; for it can only do justice to the phenomenon at the price of abandoning most of its own initial premisses.

This, of course, is but one example. There are many areas within which the options and constraints that face us remain unexplored. The knowledge we do possess in this sphere is fragmentary, incomplete and unreliable. No doubt we must endeavour to improve it, but until we do we shall be obliged to use such sociological ideas as we do now possess.

But the general point remains: this kind of 'truncated evolutionism' remains one of the fundamental, most relevant and inescapable ways of coming to understand our situation. It consists of trying to understand the pattern, preconditions, implications, options, of that basic social transformation which made our world and which is irreversible. It resembles nineteenth century evolutionism proper in its justified preoccupation with 'development', but it is truncated in that it does not suppose it to be simply the local version of some eternal and global story. It is not the key to everything, nor is it just the local representative, so to speak, of the great everything. That was indeed a delusion. It is a specific process, with complex characteristics which may well make it highly idiosyncratic.

But if that is understood; if the conceptual megalomania of the nineteenth century versions is avoided, the suitably cut-down-to-size preoccupation with social development must be one of our central concerns. Only it can give us a concrete understanding of the options we face. In other words, we cannot dispense with sociology.

THE ROLE OF KNOWLEDGE

The argument is now complete. We have tried to make explicit why modern philosophy has been largely about knowledge and why it matters.

Fundamental intellectual endeavour, philosophic thought, starts not from a revelation, or a premiss, or a *tabula rasa*. The *tabula rasa* is a good methodological device, but has no relation to a real historic starting point. The real starting point was a justified sense of chaos, of cognitive breakdown. Of course, had there not been a previous more or less viable structure, however questionable its bases, there would have been no mind, no anguish, to initiate the endeavour. Thought begins in the collapse of an old order.

But most often, and certainly in this case, the old order was beyond repair. Conservative philosophers are quite mistaken when they preach that the only salvation is a return to the local 'sources'. They have no good reasons for saying this, other than the argument from total scepticism— because there is not objective, independent truth anywhere, the only succour is to be found in an on-going tradition.

But in fact such on-going traditions as this world contains have long been torn asunder by the extraordinary forces which constitute the modern world. They are poor things in any case, and no modern population would consent to live within their walls. The conservative philosopher can only recommend them because what he in fact concretely commends is some modern compromise, containing far more of modernity than of tradition, though it may invoke the slogans of the latter. But these compromises are as yet unstable, and we must learn to understand, and as far as possible, to assess them. It would be a total delusion to believe that they possess an inner automatic pilot, 'tradition', to whom their steering can best be assigned. This is pure mythology, the reliance on an empty word.

The truth is the very opposite. Just because there is no safety or solution in the available automatisms, we must seek, if not some 'absolute' truth, at least an *independent* truth, which is not just an echo of the accidental and interested *status quo* but can offer some genuine guidance. If the truth available is not as perfect—lucid, self-authenticating, luminous—as some philosophers have hoped, and this certainly seems to be so, then we shall have to accept it.

Modern philosophy is a commentary on this shared condition. Our aim has been to make its real context and role explicit. Our condition arises from the simultaneous collapse and the unprecedented growth of knowledge. The collapse meant that we quite literally ceased to know just which world we lived in. It is true that many faiths, both formally organised ones and informally diffused ones, claim to tell us. But their reasoning is circular, self-interested and suspect. We must use some more impartial touchstones of truth. The theory of knowledge has tried to satisfy this need.

At the same time as we discovered that we knew so much less than we had previously supposed, we also found that we knew much more. The miraculous growth of knowledge known as science is notoriously a revelation, a technological cornucopia, a threat and a mystery. How does it really work, what is its price, morally, conceptually, ecologically?

So the preoccupation with knowledge was and is fed by its ambiguous and menacing abundance in one direction, as well as by the dearth of it in others. The map of our cognisable world has been transformed out of all recognition. To understand this change and its implications is the real problem.

Descartes was right. The re-thinking of our ideas is even more fundamental and important than the transvaluations of values announced two centuries later by Nietzsche. In any case the two tasks must be done jointly. We are bound to reconsider our *morale par provision* and our world *par provision* jointly. We choose our world through a kind of cognitive *morale,* and our ethics through the kind of concepts which make sense in the world we choose.

Descartes was also right on some points of more detailed strategy. He was right in displaying utmost distrust for the bulk of his own ideas, and to seek salvation in some small sub-set of his ideas which were both his *and* had a sounder claim to our assent. His way of identifying this subset ('clear and distinct' ideas) may not have amounted to much, and his way of finding a warranty for their trustworthiness, to even less. In the three succeeding centuries thought has, it seems to me, made some advances towards identifying and characterising this trust-worthy subset. Much of the present argument is an attempt to describe this search and its results.

Of course, one must also note that this epistemic quest was enacted twice: first during the classical period of epistemology in the seventeenth and eighteenth centuries, when it was articulated in reaction against the preceding orthodoxies, and the second time mainly in the twentieth century, in reaction against the re-endorsement efforts of the nineteenth.To follow the old aphorism and characterise the first occasion as tragedy and the re-play as farce, would be too harsh; but there is no doubt that there has been some loss of seriousness, reflecting, in part, a certain recovery of consensus and confidence, however ill-codified. This partial recovery has been misinterpreted by contemporary thinkers when they have concluded that the inherited complex of ideas has no case to answer when subjected to sustained doubt. Their weakness, over and above specific technical error, has been to feel *far* too much at home in the world.

For the question concerning its general nature is not a trivial one and has no obvious answer. We have attempted to explore the way in which philosophic thought has tried to answer it, the various intellectual strategies available, their mutual relationships, consquences and options. It is for this reason that it has been concerned with knowledge.

By giving us inherently plausible models of how we can know the world—models plausible normatively, not genetically—it sets the limits to the world. It tells us what kind of world we can be in, it limits the number of possibilities. Our Cartesian starting-point was precisely that, quite literally, we do not know what kind of world we are in: all the competing faith-systems inwardly validate themselves in a circular argument, each claiming not merely the monopoly of truth but also of the sources or criteria of truth. This simple little device—capture the wells of truth and starve out all rivals—is of course their central feature, as ideologies. A plague on all their houses, but we are still faced with the problem of finding an alternative house to live in. Its identification and justification would seem to raise the insoluble problem of overcoming the regress: who guarantees the guarantors? Formally, the problem is insoluble. As it happens to be a practical and inescapable problem for us—for the traditional norms have lost all authority—we cannot but make do with the best solution available, whether or not it satisfies the strictest formal criteria.

The argument has also highlighted why the solution, at any rate in its general outlines, must be monistic—in the sense of appealing to a limited number of explicit principles, whose inherent plausibility is subjected to scrutiny—rather than to an unbounded and uncircumscribed good sense, built into a supposed tradition, form of life or whatnot.

What is real nonsense, nonsense on stilts, is the claim that when a culture is subjected to Cartesian doubt, there is no case to answer. The classical theory of knowledge of the seventeenth and eighteenth century formulated the case in a most forceful manner; contemporary dismissals of it are simply parasitic on its achievements. The re-play, the second coming of epistemological themes in our century, was significantly different despite the formal repetition of themes, not merely because this time it was academic, but also because there was a different opponent: no longer the dogmatisms of the old faiths, but the new faiths of the nineteenth-century positive re-endorsement philosophies—all those systems which sought to recover confidence by seizing the key to the global, all-embracing developmental story. Fascinating though these new faiths were, they are not academically fashionable in our time and we have not scrutinised them here, or given them the attention which they really deserve. Today, the critical vision needs to be defended against *negative* re-endorsers, whose merit is much smaller, but whose contemporary influence is great.

Thus, the effective role of that preoccupation with knowledge which was central to modern philosophy, was not to provide any successful descriptive or explanatory account of the actual processes or mechanisms of cognition, but to codify and justify a new cognitive ethic. It provided a surrogate angel's viewpoint, a way of opting out of the world in order to evaluate it. Whether feasible or not, we had and have no choice but to attempt it. Our culture is not a solution, it is a problem. We need some way of looking at it without doing so on its own terms.

No doubt there is *hubris* in this. Karl Marx was amongst those who noticed this. In the most interesting of the *Theses on Feuerbach* he observes

The ... doctrine that men are products of circumstances and upbringing and that, therefore, changed men are products of other circumstances and changed upbringing, forgets that circumstances are changed precisely by men and that the educator must himself be educated. Hence this doctrine necessarily arrives at dividing society into two parts, of which one towers above society ...

The coincidence of the changing of circumstances and of human activity can only be conceived and rationally understood as revolutionising practice.

The educator must himself be educated; the criteria which are to guide assessment and change can hardly be drawn from the unregenerate, problematic order. As a formulation of the problem, Mary's aphorism is excellent.

And he is right in suggesting that the typical philosophical response involved a kind of bifurcation, the presumption of attaining a superior, or at any rate external viewpoint. What is less clear is why this should be spurned, and still less clear why he should think that he was in possession of an alternative and better way of solving the problem. Stripped of rhetoric, this alternative merely replaces the old 'kneel and thou shalt believe' by 'indulge in revolutionary practice and thou shalt see'. This of course was of the essence of the old re-endorsement philosophies: the supposition that they knew the secret of the global process and of the cognitive activities which were part of it, and be able to identify sound faith in terms of adopting the right stance within that world . . . If you do not make yourself such a present of a faith in that vision of the world, however, the procedure can be seen to be blatantly circular.

Since the nineteenth century, the great age positive re-endorsement theories, re-endorsement has become negative and shifty, and has altogether declined in quality. Ramshackle reasons are invented for why doubt is unnecessary in the first place. These buttressed bowdlerised faiths are only usable in conditions of no stress.

In more serious areas, where convictions have to endure genuine stress, a halting, partial, uncodified consensus is emerging, partly thanks to the philosophic work of recent centuries. Our time has tempted us to misinterpret this very partial recovery of confidence as some kind of birthright, and give little thanks to those who have helped bring it about.

If we adopt the simile of shipwreck, we might say that Descartes made the mistake of supposing that, when the old ship sank, a really reliable and seaworthy new one could be found. In truth, there is flotsam floating about, and it does not seem that any one piece of it will carry our weight. But some bits are better than others, and some jointly, when lashed together, will make a passable raft. There would seem to be four such planks in our raft—four elements in the emerging consensus.

There is the empiricist insistence that faiths must not fill out the world, but must stand ready to be judged by evidence which is not under their control, which is not pervaded, interpreted by them to the point of being forced to confirm the faith in question. (All systems which do so control their own supply of evidence, their own wells as it were, and use no others, are excluded.) It goes further in identifying these extraneous, unsuborned judges as being something reasonably close to the ordinary notion of 'experience'. There is no merit in the contemporary exaggeration of the valid point that experience is never pure; indeed it is not, but there are very marked and narrow limits to the extent to which it can be corrupted, and hence a reverence for experience makes an enormous and salutary difference.

Secondly, there is the 'mechanistic' insistence on impersonal, structural explanations. We have of course no guarantee that the world must be such as to be amenable to such explanations; we can only show that *we* are constrained to think so. It was Kant's merit to see that this compulsion is in us, not in things. It was Weber's to see that it is historically a specific kind of mind, not human mind as such, which is subject to this compulsion. What it amounts to is in the end simple: if there is to be effective knowledge or explanation *at all*, it must have this form, for any other kind of 'explanation', tied to individuality or idiosyncrasy, is *ipso facto* powerless.

We have become habituated to and dependent on effective knowledge, and hence have bound ourselves to this kind of genuine explanation. It was also Kant's merit to see the inescapable price of this Faustian purchase of real knowledge, and to spurn the cheap and in the end unavailing efforts to evade paying it. 'Reductionism', the view that everything in the world is really something else, and that something else is coldly impersonal, is simply the ineluctable corollary of effective explanation. No doubt explanations can and do assume a wide variety of different forms, and are certainly not bound to any crude, simple model of structures built of heavy stuff—the anti-reductionists' bogey; but whatever form they take, in as far as they remain effective, they will also inevitably have those morally disturbing traits which are, in the end, inherent in public formulation and repeatability.

It is this publicity and symmetrical applicability of explanations which is really central, which is the key to cognitive effectiveness, and which also exacts its inherent moral, 'dehumanising' price. Properly it is to be contrasted not so much with the absence or suspension of causation—if that were the case, we should not be here to note it—as with the sliding-scale, meretricious styles of thought, within which 'explanation' is linked to a socially specific 'normality', and vacillates between serving this normality by ritually restoring order, and offering explanations in a more genuine sense. In traditional 'common sense' anything could count as an 'explanation': for this was merely a kind of restoration of the moral order, within a cosy world in which identities and moral norms were linked in a closed circle of definitions. Thus the price of real knowledge is that our identities, freedom, norms, are no longer underwritten by our vision and comprehension of things. On the contrary we are doomed to suffer from a tension between cognition and identity.

Thirdly, there is ironic cultural nationalism—the acceptance of 'forms of life', from styles of food, handshakes and wallpaper to political rituals or personal relationships—but an acceptance which no longer endows anything with an aura of the absolute, but is ironic, tentative, optional, and above all, discontinuous with serious knowledge and real conviction. In this limited sphere of 'culture', relativism is indeed valid. In the sphere of serious conviction, on the other hand, relativism is not an option open to us *at all*.

Fourthly, there is truncated evolutionism, the concern, not with the 'development of all things', but with the specific development of the industrial civilisation to which we are ineluctably wedded. We tread our way amongst the options that we have, in the light of our understanding of the preconditions, alternatives, implications and limitations inherent in this kind of civilisation. In simpler words, our serious thought cannot dispense with sociology. This is what remains of the grand systems of the nineteenth century.

These are the four usable planks of our raft. If there are any others, they have entirely escaped my attention.

Index